System of Transcendental Idealism (1800)
by F. W. J. Schelling

System of Transcendental Idealism (1800)
by F. W. J. Schelling

Translated by PETER HEATH

with an Introduction by MICHAEL VATER

University Press of Virginia

Charlottesville

THE UNIVERSITY PRESS OF VIRGINIA
Copyright © 1978 by the Rector and Visitors
of the University of Virginia

First published 1978

Library of Congress Cataloging in Publication Data

Schelling, Friedrich Wilhelm Joseph von, 1775-1854.
  System of transcendental idealism (1800)

Translation of System des transcendentalen Idealismus.
  Includes index.
  1. Idealism.   2. Transcendentalism.
I.   Heath, Peter Lauchlan, 1922-   II.   Title.
B2883.E5H4   141'.3   78-6638
ISBN 0-8139-0780-2

Printed in the United States of America

TRANSLATOR'S NOTE

The text of this translation follows that of the
one-volume German edition prepared by Ruth-Eva Schulz, and
issued in 1957 as volume 254 of the Philosophische
Bibliothek by Felix Meiner Verlag of Hamburg. This edition
is itself based on Vol. III of the Sämtliche Werke, published in 1856-61 by K. F. A. Schelling, the author's son,
whose pagings are given (in brackets) for purposes of
reference. The additional bracketed entries in the Table
of Contents, and the page-headings, are not due to the
author, who originally provided no Table of Contents at
all, but have been adapted, for the most part, from the
Meiner text.

Initially undertaken as a companion-piece to my
translation (with John Lachs) of Fichte's Science of
Knowledge (Appleton-Century 1970), the present work has
languished in typescript for some years, owing to the
demise of its intended publisher. I am greatly indebted
to the University Press of Virginia for enabling me to
rescue it from oblivion. I should also like to express
my gratitude to Professor Michael Vater, of Marquette
University, for his admirable Introduction; to Professor
H. S. Harris, of Glendon College, York University, Toronto,
for a number of textual corrections and improvements; to
the University of Virginia, for a grant to help defray
production expenses; and to Miss Bonnie Wood and Mrs.
Joan F. Baxter, for their skill and stamina in typing,
respectively, the original draft and the final version
of the book.

P.L.H.

CONTENTS

Introduction [by Michael Vater]   xi

Glossary   xxxvii

Foreword   1

Introduction
  1. Concept of Transcendental Philosophy   5
  2. Corollaries [on 'I am' and 'there is']   7
  3. Preliminary Division of Transcendental
      Philosophy   10
  4. The Organ of Transcendental Philosophy   13

PART ONE
  On the Principle of Transcendental Idealism
  Section I: On the Necessity and Character of a
               Supreme Principle of Knowledge   15
               [Supreme Principle of Knowledge:
               Self-Consciousness]
               [In the Supreme Principle of Knowledge,
               Content and Form condition each other]
  Section II: Deduction of the Principle Itself   21
               Elucidations   24
               [The Self is one with the Act of
               Self-Thinking]
               [The Self is Intellectual Intuition]
               [The Self is Identity of Being and
               Producing]
  General Observations   31
               [Self and Object; and Individual;
               and Thing-in-Itself]

PART TWO
  General Deduction of Transcendental Idealism
  Introductory   34
      [According to Fichte's Wissenschaftslehre]

PART THREE
  System of Theoretical Philosophy according to the
  Principles of Transcendental Idealism
  Introductory   42
      [On the 'Self for us' and the 'Self itself']
  I   Deduction of the Absolute Synthesis Contained
      in the Act of Self-Consciousness   43
          [Positing and Counter-Positing as Original
          Syntheses]
  II Deduction of the Middle Terms of the
      Absolute Synthesis
  Introductory   47
      [Philosophy as Repetition of the Original
      Series of Acts]
      [Philosophy as History of Self-Consciousness
      in Epochs]

First Epoch: From Original Sensation to
Productive Intuition
A   Problem: To explain how the Self comes to
                intuit itself as limited   51
    Solution   [Self-Intuition in Limitation:
                Sensation]
    Additional Remarks   56
                [On the Possibility and Reality
                of Sensation]
                [All Limitation only through the
                Act of Self-Consciousness]
B   Problem: To explain how the Self intuits itself
                as sensing. Explanation [of Problem]   60
    Solution   I   [Derivation of Producing]   61
               II [Complete Derivation of Produc-
                    tive Intuition]   65
C   Theory of Productive Intuition
    Introductory   72
    I   Deduction [of the Product] of Productive
        Intuition   77
    II Deduction of Matter   83
    Corollaries   [On the Three Moments in the
        Construction of Matter: Magnetism,
        Electricity, Chemical Process]   86
    General Note upon the First Epoch [On Mind
        and Matter]   90

Second Epoch: From Productive Intuition to
Reflection
    Introductory   ¡94
D   Problem: To explain how the Self comes to
    intuit itself as productive
    Solution
    I   [Inner and Outer Intuition]   95
    II   [Inner Sense and the Sensory Object]   100
    III   [Space and Time]   103
          [Substance and Accident]
          [Causality as Succession and Reciprocity]
          [The Universe]
          [The Series of Succession]
    IV   [Deduction of the Organic]   120
    V   [Transition to Free Reflection]   129
General Note upon the Second Epoch   131
          [Reciprocity]
Third Epoch: From Reflection to the Absolute
Act of Will
    I   [Abstraction of Action from the Produced]   134
          [Judgment]
          [Schematism]
    II   [Transcendental Abstraction of the Concept
          from Intuition]   139

III [Transcendental Schematism and the
       Categories]   142
IV   [Absolute Abstraction as Postulate of
       Theoretical Philosophy]   148
General Note upon the Third Epoch   151
       [On the Conclusion of Theoretical
       Philosophy]
       [A Priori and A Posteriori]

PART FOUR
  System of Practical Philosophy According to the
  Principles of Transcendental Idealism
  [First Proposition: Absolute Abstraction = Self-
     Determination of the Intelligence = Willing]   155
  Corollaries [On the Relationship of Theore-
     tical and Practical Philosophy]   156
  [Second Proposition: The Act of Self-Deter-
     mination explicable only by the Action of
     an Intelligence external to it]   161
  Additional Remarks
     1. [Operations of Other Intelligences
          on an Object]   171
     2. [Only through Intelligences outside me
          does the World become Objective for me]   173
  E Problem: To explain how willing again
     becomes objective for the Self
     Solution
     I   [Third Proposition: Willing is
          necessarily directed upon an
          External Object]   175
     A   [Transition from the Ideal to the
          Objective: Time]   177
     B   [Change only of the Contingent Deter-
          minations of Things]   179
          [Acting and Intuiting originally one]
          [The truly Objective: The Activity at
          once Real and Ideal]
     II [Matter as Organ of Free Activity]   185
          [Pure Self-Determining as a Demand: The
          Categorical Imperative]
          [Natural Inclination]
          [The Absolutely Free and the Empirically
          Free Will]
          [Natural Necessity, Absolute Willing,
          Choice]
     Additional Remarks   193
          [Deduction of Law]
          [League of Nations]

III [Deduction of the Concept of History]   199
A   [Individual Consciousness and Universal
     History]   201
B   [Infinite Progress in History: Gradual
     Realization of the Rule of Law]   202
C   [History as Unity of Freedom and
     Necessity]   203
     [History as Act of the Entire Species]
     [The Absolute: Religion within Transcen-
     dental Idealism]
     [Three Periods of Revelation]
F   Problem: To explain how the Self itself can
    become conscious of the Original Harmony
    between Subjective and Objective
    Solution I   [Principle of Teleology]   212

PART FIVE
  Essentials of Teleology according to the
  Principles of Transcendental Idealism
        [Nature]   215
    II [Art]   217

PART SIX
  Deduction of a Universal Organ of Philosophy, or:
  Essentials of the Philosophy of Art according
  to the Principles of Transcendental Idealism
    1. Deduction of the Art-Product as such   219
    2. Character of the Art-Product   225
    3. Corollaries [Relation of Art to
        Philosophy]   229
  General Observation on the Whole System   233
    [Review]

INTRODUCTION

The Odyssey of Consciousness

The System of Transcendental Idealism, written late
in 1799 and published in 1800, is by far the most
polished and complete of the works that Schelling published within his lifetime. In its breadth, clarity and
integrity the work justifies the sudden fame it brought
its young author. Ironically, this work which for the
next decade established Schelling's position at the pin-
nacle of German philosophy and provided him the platform
for elaborating the first system of absolute idealism is
far from the most original of his writings.[1] In the
main, it belongs to the early works, the philosophical
apprenticeship under Fichte. The System, in fact, maintains its continuity with the rest of Schelling's philosophy only in its muted voicing of certain themes which
elsewhere attain their proper development--themes such
as the reality and ultimacy of nature in an idealistic
perspective, nature's function as the ground and antitype of spirit, the self-identity of the Absolute within
dispersed finite being, the conceptual though unconscious element in art, and philosophy's task of constructing a general metaphysics upon the model of human freedom.
It is predominantly a work of consolidation, not of
Schelling's own previous philosophy, but of the tradition
of transcendental idealism, the position suggested in
Kant's three Critiques and elevated into an epistemology
and general methodology in Fichte's Science of Knowledge.
Schelling is clear on the kind of consolidation needed:

> The most general proof of the overall ideality
> of knowledge is therefore that carried out in the
> Science of Knowledge, by immediate inference from
> the proposition I am. There is yet another proof
> of it possible, however, namely, the factual, which
> in a system of transcendental idealism is carried
> out in the very process of actually deducing the
> entire system of knowledge from the principle in
> question. (System, p. 34)

---

[1]Schelling's System became known to the English-speaking world
through Coleridge's Biographia Literaria, which drew heavily upon
it and other early essays of Schelling for a forty-page critique of
perceptual realism. The adaptation took the form both of direct
translation and of paraphrase, with scant acknowledgement of the
exact sources. The critic's laxity later gave rise to charges of
plagiarism. For a comparison of Coleridge's text and its sources
see G. Orsini, Coleridge and German Idealism (Carbondale, Ill.,
1969), pp. 198-221.

Schelling's predecessors had enunciated the principle
that the togetherness of subject and object, of presentation and thing, can be founded only in self-consciousness
or its constitutive activity, imagination. Fichte called
this unitive consciousness the 'self' or the 'I.' What
remains is to prove this theoretical position, to see the
abstract principle of the subjectivity of all known being
verified in a system of idealism. This system would give
flesh and substance to the stance of a perceptual and
cognitive idealism by demonstrating that the objective
world in the totality of its being and its operations is
a process of emergence from the self and its activities,
most basically presentation. The world in its objectivity,
in its sensible singularity and its generality as nature,
and also this objectivity spiritualized as the human
community living under law, subject to time and history--
this whole world is to be constructed from the self's
fundamental quality, freedom or activity. "Freedom is
the one principle on which everything is supported, and
what we behold in the objective world is not anything
present outside us, but merely the inner limitation of
our own free activity" (p. 35). The system Schelling
proposes is to annex to the idealism of this epistemological and metaphysical principle a 'real-philosophy,'
a total and faithful account of the objectivity of the
physical world and of the human structures of experience
and social sharing. Or better, its task is to prove the
identity of transcendental idealism and real-philosophy,
and thus to elevate transcendental philosophy into an
'ideal-realism' (p. 41).

     In his 1827 Munich lectures Towards a History of
Recent Philosophy Schelling reluctantly underscores the
non-originality of his 1800 System, its dependence on
"Fichtean Idealism" and on the principle first enunciated by Fichte that freedom must ground all philosophy.
For it was Fichte who discovered that the Kantian autonomy of self founds not only practical or moral philosophy
but also theoretical philosophy, the account of knowledge
and being (S.W., X, 96).[2] But the one-time disciple and
popularizer of Fichte now maintains that he came to his
own method while working under this "cloak of Fichtean
thought."[3] The essence of this method consists in the
clarification "of that which is utterly independent of
our freedom, the presentation of an objective world which

---

[2]Non-English Schelling references are to the Sämtliche
Werke, ed. K. F. A. Schelling, 1856 f., reproduced in the Munich
Jubilee Edition, ed. M. Schröter, 1927. The first numeral indicates
the volume, the second the page.

[3]Schelling definitively broke from Fichte in 1806, though
the two were in substantial disagreement from 1800 on.

indeed restricts our freedom, through a process in which
the self sees itself develop through a necessary but not
consciously observed act of self-positing" (S.W., X, 97).
This process, unnamed in 1800, is now given the name
dialectic--Schelling insinuates that credit for the discovery of "the dialectic" is popularly misplaced.

In this dialectic or clarificatory process the
positing and self-expanding activity of the self and the
limitation of that activity are seen to be both and
equally the self's activity. The self is primordially
both activity and limitation; inside the process it consciously makes itself to be both, i.e., the self itself
makes itself to be both subject and object, finite and
infinite. The self is doubled in that it appears to
itself; it loses the abstract simplicity of the Fichtean
self-positing (I = I); it ceases to be in-itself and
becomes for-itself. As Schelling explains it in 1827,
inside the dialectical process, which is the system, the
self returns from limitation to its original freedom and
for the first time becomes for itself (or in the System's
language, consciously) what it already was in itself,
namely pure freedom or activity. Schelling further
remarks that this one process makes up the whole mechanism
of the system. What in a preceding moment is posited in
consciousness (i.e., is admitted as real) only for the
philosopher, is in the succeeding moment raised in the
self itself; in the end the objective self (the self
itself, the subject of experience) is raised to the
standpoing of philosophizing consciousness and the two
coincide (S.W., X, 98).

That this was indeed Schelling's method and intent
is evident from a reading of the System, though often the
'method' seems a clumsy didactic device and hardly the
simple mirroring of a process inside consciousness. The
claim that this dialectical procedure is his method
rather than Fichte's is plainly extravagant,[4] although
the System's main advantage over the Science of Knowledge
is the adoption of this one method over the three or four
that Fichte variously employs.[5] It is, at least in

----

[4] For Fichte's statements on science as the dialectic of the
philosophizing and the objective self see Science of Knowledge, tr.
Heath and Lachs (Appleton-Century-Crofts, 1970), pp. 113, 120-21,
198-202. Also see the "Second Introduction to the Science of Knowledge," op. cit., sections 5, 7, and particularly 9 and 11.

[5] In the 1794 Foundations of the Entire Science of Knowledge
the first three sections on the ground-principles employ a deductive approach; the theoretical philosophy adopts an analytic and
metaphysical method of exploring the possible factors inside the
one real synthesis of experience; the cryptic "Deduction of Presentation" (pp. 203-17) a descriptive and (abortively) synthetic
method; and the practical philosophy a method at once synthetic

general form, the same method that Hegel was to take up
and perfect in the Phenomenology of Spirit, and not the
method alone, but the ordering of the strata of experience determined by it. It seems difficult, if not
impossible, to understand the order of experiential
levels in the Phenomenology from Hegel's transitions
alone, without the pattern of materials inherited from
Fichte and Schelling before one's eyes. The pattern of
the System indicates the road that Hegel was to follow,
viz. from theory to praxis, from the individual consciousness to the objective social order, and from a
world-embedded consciousness to a philosophically reflective one. But it shows, too, the Kantian and Fichtean
systems which lie at its origin. Here is the System's
basic structure:

    (1) A general consideration of self-consciousness,
dialectic and the methodology of the system--Parts I and
II, Part III in part; pages 1-47.

    (2) A theoretical philosophy: the deduction of
cognitive phenomena ranging from rudimentary (and properly unconscious) presentation up to the categories
generally necessary to secure objectivity for experience--
Part III, pages 47-154.

    (3) A (sketchily outlined) philosophy of nature,
contained within the theoretical philosophy, in which
cognitive phenomena are seen of necessity to involve a
reflection and validation in an objective intuited
order, viz. nature--Part III, First Epoch (conclusion)
and Second Epoch; pages 83-129.

    (4) A transcendental analysis of cognitive and
judgmental faculties, again contained within the theoretical philosophy. Here the previous stages of the self's
activity, viz. as productive intuition and as matter
organized in nature, are seen to be equally grounded in
free reflection or self-relation, the activity which in
practical philosophy emerges on its own as will--Part
III, pages 129-54.

    (5) A practical philosophy which advances from the
perceptual and volitional solipsism implicit in the
theoretical standpoint to a deduction of the rational
human community as guarantor both of the objectivity of
the world of experience and the ideality (value) of the
moral order--Part IV, pages 155-93.

    (6) A philosophy of history contained within the
practical philosophy and evidencing the objectivity of
will, much as the philosophy of nature does in the

---

and genetic--i.e., once the category of feeling is introduced,
we watch the actual growth of consciousness. Ironically, Fichte
was to criticize the System for a lack of dialectical rigor
(Letter of the Summer of 1801, Fichte-Schelling Briefwechsel,
ed. W. Schulz [Frankfurt a. M., 1968], p. 126).

theoretical philosophy. Here practical philosophy,
having deduced the moral, legal and political orders of
social existence, finds its subject matter (will)
existing as objectified in history and as necessarily
and collectively moving toward the ideal fulfilment of
world polity--Part IV, pages 193-214.

(7) An extra-systematic concluding section, including a (negligently sketched) teleology and a philosophy of art, wherein certain abiding problems of the
system, e.g., the inaccessibility of the Absolutely
Identical or absolute self-consciousness, and the recourse
to a hypothesis of a pre-established harmony of freedom
and determinism, receive a solution of sorts. Aesthetic
intuition is seen to be the counterpart of philosophical
intuition and to provide an access to the hidden identity
which was both the ground and the goal of striving for
the consciousness torn throughout the whole dialectic
between intuition and production--Parts V and VI, pages
215-33.

The final section is extra-systematic since on the
Fichtean model of consciousness--an activity ever-de-
flected from complete reflection into unconscious and
preconscious production--a fully transparent philosophical moment of self-reflection is not possible. The
philosophy of art, then, stands as a philosophical
epilogue to the System of Transcendental Idealism and the
first announcement of Schelling's own system of absolute
philosophy, the System of Identity.

The System is a rich and intricate work, and we
certainly do not exhaust its significance in mentioning
the pivotal place it occupies in speculative idealism's
march from Fichte to Hegel, nor even in pointing to the
place it holds within Schelling's own philosophical
development. Written at the turn of the century, it
belongs to two different epochs. Its origin lies in the
classic calm of the philosophy of consciousness which
dominated European thought from Descartes through Kant;
its impulse is toward the uneasy philosophies of will
which were to dominate the nineteenth century and which
define man, not in terms of the infinite reach of the
concept timelessly attained in theoria, but in terms of
a dialectic of striving, need and finite fulfilment.
Let us look to some of the central philosophical themes
that the System raises, problems and positions that the
20th Century reader can still appreciate despite the
oddness of, and the general philosophical antipathy
towards, the outlook of speculative idealism.

The Primacy of the Practical

Like Fichte, his predecessor and exemplar, Schelling sets out to render the Kantian philosophy clear and cogent. Read with an eye turned back to the Kantian sources, the System seems a compendium of the three Critiques, an attempt to organize Kant's wayward and varying assessments of reason's function in intramundane experience, in moral judgment and in aesthetic/teleological harmonizations of experience, and to gather them under one transcendental deduction.[6] Like other readers and interpreters of Kant, Schelling is at times overwhelmed by the material he is trying to control and seems not so much to systematize Kant as to be setting didactic expositions of the mechanisms of Kant's understanding alongside his own dialectical treatment of consciousness. In other places he is a more successful interpreter: Difficult as it is, the deduction of presentation as a reality-producing intuition (Part III, pp. 51-93) clarifies the mysterious "merely given" character of the Kantian sensible manifold. And in his insistence upon the central role of time in consciousness, upon its being in fact the basic character of that synthesis of the finite and the infinite which is the self, Schelling rescues Kant's schematism from its obscure hiding place in the text of the First Critique and gives it its proper prominence.

To someone philosophizing after Kant it could appear that, over and above the critical results of the examination of reason, and despite all the cautionary notes, a positive Kantian philosophy was indeed possible. Kant had left a legacy of positive doctrine pointing in the direction of a systematic development--for instance, the ideal of a systematic form for all philosophy and of philosophy's function as a metascience, developed in the Critique's "Architectonic"; the revolutionary notion of transcendental questioning as a methodology; and, in texts drawn from theoretical as well as practical philosophy, a fully positive description of pure reason, operating in and for itself, as a function of self-relation.

Following out these hints of Kant, Fichte took the decisive step toward a speculative criticism in his apprehension that cognition and action are fundamentally the same, that an identity, or better, a striving for identity is the ground and motivation of reason both in cognition and action. Reason strives for self-coincidence.

---

[6] On the relation of Fichtean idealism to Kant's texts and to a possible system of Kantianism drawn from them, see "Second Introduction to the Science of Knowledge," op. cit., pp. 42-62. See also Schelling, "On the Possibility of a Form of All Philosophy," tr. F. Marti, Metaphilosophy, VI, 1 (1975).

The unification of sensible experience into a world, and
the further (but for Kant, illicit) unification of
experiential concepts into ideas, are but special cases
of reason's functioning, which is more basically exempli-
fied in practical reason's struggle to establish and maintain autonomy against heteronomy, independence against
external determination. Reason is self-relation and
seeks to maintain identity in the face of otherness--
this is Fichte's great insight: He concludes his quest
to define and clarify the objectivity of the mysterious
not-self by saying,

> The self, as such, is initially in a state of
> reciprocity with itself, and only so does an
> external influence upon it become possible.[7]

And again,

> The ultimate ground of all consciousness is an
> interaction of the self with itself, by way of a
> not-self that has to be regarded from different
> points of view.[8]

Reason as act seeks to find and establish itself in the
other. This is the heart of the Science of Knowledge and
it is this insight which for Fichte, Schelling and Hegel
determines the primacy of the practical over the theoretical, the priority of spirit over nature. It is this
primacy of the practical, the vision that reason is active
rather than passive, that turns transcendental idealism
decisively away from the kind of epistemological and
ontological preoccupations exhibited by even the Kantian
philosophy and toward moral, social and political philosophy, and the philosophy of history. The issue everywhere is freedom, the relative self-sufficiency of a
finite spirit, rooted firmly in worldly being. The post-
Kantian idealists are not concerned to dispute spirit's
anchoring in an objective natural and social world, but
they want to see it interpreted in terms of the suf-
ficiency and the life of spirit. They want to view worldly
being and its objectivity, not as an absolute and established plenum of being, but as a totality relative to
consciousness, as acquiring meaning only in terms of
that relation. It is not mute being but meaning that
is the standard, and not a meaning rooted in brute being
and finding arbitrary expression in language, but a
meaning that stems from activity, from that peculiar
activity of self-consciousness where act and awareness
fully coincide. Thus in Fichte's eyes, and for the
tradition after him, cognition as clarified and explained
by theoretical philosophy is a limited and unsatisfactory
form of self-activity because it is always an activity

---

[7]The Science of Knowledge, p. 244.
[8]Ibid., p. 248.

related to an other--until, that is, it is brought by
philosophy to that state wherein it becomes fully self-
directed and self-conscious, in will or activity proper.
  Both within the System and over the course of his
long speculative career, Schelling is basically in accord
with Fichte in granting priority to praxis rather than to
theory.[9] The philosophical system, he insists, is itself
an act of freedom. It is not a vision of reality passively
received, impressed from without, rather it is a free
recapitulation of the act of selfhood, the primordial
synthesis (p. 49). The philosophical system is primarily
about selfhood and its conditions, and has the basic
character of an act. There is no question, then, of
catching things as they are, of probing the being of things
or of doing any sort of ontology: "Being, in our system,
is merely freedom suspended" (p. 33). Even the self, the
principle of system itself, is not a thing but a postulate;
it is not a piece of objectivity lying ready-to-hand, but
something that must be enacted. "What the self is, is for
that reason no more demonstrable than what the line is; one
can only describe the action whereby it comes about" (p.
29).
  An idealistic philosophy, so Schelling maintains, can
have only a practical basis; it is grounded in the free
act of spirit taking itself as central. As such, an
idealistic system is, strictly speaking, without any
purely theoretical basis; it can call upon no primary
datum and educe no proof other than its own free activity.
It must in fact attempt to reduce or re-interpret the whole
theoretical standpoint in light of free activity: Ultimacy
is not to be accorded to the presentation, or to the presentation's objective factor (Kant's sensible manifold), or
even to some final ground of givenness (Kant's thing-in-
itself). The System, accordingly, undertakes to explain
givenness itself as an interplay of conscious and unconscious activities; it reads the obviously non-conscious
activity of mechanical and organic nature as equivalent
to willing and action (p. 12). To avoid ceding ultimacy
to objectivity, it has recourse to a pre-established harmony
of sorts, which links free activity and non-conscious production without engulfing the one factor in the other
(p. 129). So that spirit shall not be lost in a world of
matter and motion, nature is itself spiritualized. Ultimately the standpoint of cognition itself is abolished,
its distinctness negated: "What is commonly called
theoretical reason is nothing else but imagination in the

---

[9]The one notable departure from his lifelong allegiance to the
practical and spirit-centered orientation of the Fichtean outlook is
the System of Identity of 1801-1806 which is prefigured in the System's
concluding sections on history and art. It seeks a model of being not
in man's activity but in a quantified and formalistic approach to
physical being.

service of freedom" (p. 176).

In the light of the tenuous nature of Schelling's allegiance to Fichteanism at the System's writing, one might be critical of all this emphasis on freedom. He had, after all, been struggling to articulate a philosophy of nature within idealism and had not met with Fichte's approval. Then, too, the System contains many hints of the transition to the realistic metaphysics of the System of Identity, a system patently modelled after Spinoza. Nonetheless, the emphasis upon freedom is genuine, not merely a formal repetition of the Science of Knowledge. From his earliest writings, Schelling was moved by the spirit of Kantian freedom to criticize and methodologically to delimit what then appeared the only consistent meta- physics, Spinozism. (The center of the critical tradition always appeared to be its defense of freedom.) Even in the System of Identity, inaugurated by a work which adopts not only the deductive form of Spinoza's Ethics but a good deal of its naturalistic and deterministic spirit as well,[10] freedom is still of capital importance for Schelling: The existence of quantifiable conceptual shapes (ideas) as sensible particulars is described as a 'fall' from the Absolute, an exercise of 'self-will,' a free act.[11] Being, at least in its particular and existential aspects, if not in its eidetic character, is still conceived as activity and life.

In the 1809 Philosophical Investigations of the Nature of Human Freedom Schelling clearly returned to the pragmatic or spirit-centered standpoint of the System. He now inter- prets all being, in its objective aspects as well as its subjective ones, through categories of willing. He out- lines the construction of a total system of philosophy, ranging from a theory of nature to a philosophy of history, upon the complex interplay of dependence and independence in human freedom and upon the moral, social and historical decisiveness of action. "Primordial being is will," main- tains Schelling,[12] and, in a deliberately anthropomorphic move, he identifies this primal will with the human exer- cise of will. Resorting to the theosophical myth of the Creation's inherence in a cosmic Adam, Schelling para- doxically makes being's articulation in cosmogony, its stabilization in nature, and its eventual fulfilment in history the consequences of the emergence of finite spirit. All being bears the stamp of the decisiveness first

---

[10]The Presentation of My Own System, 1801.

[11]See the dialogue Bruno (1802) and Philosophy and Religion (1804).

[12]Heidegger has called this statement the turning point in modern metaphysics. See What Is Called Thinking? tr. Wieck and Gray (Harper & Row, 1968), pp. 90-91. See also Schellings Abhandlung über das Wesen der menschlichen Freiheit (Tübingen, 1971), pp. 114-20.

attained by human freedom in the creation of value, in the
fashioning of good and evil. A comment in the System
evokes the kernel of the 1809 essay, where Schelling
suggests that the complex finitude of human consciousness--
involving a possible predetermination of the freely determined, the limitation of freedom due to individuality, and
the influence of other intellects--is thinkable only in
terms of an original act of freedom, an act originative of
ontological as well as moral definiteness, determinative
of character as well as individuality.[13]

Nor was Schelling's interest in the sovereignty of
freedom exhausted in the 1809 essay. All of his later
work, from the 1815 Ages of the World to the lectures on
mythology and religion of the 1840s and '50s, show
Schelling in search of a principle of freedom and actuality
not confined to and determined by reality as merely conceived. Freedom must be more than the activity postulated
by philosophical thought behind the world as presented and
experienced. It must be more than a concept in the domain
of the possible, more than the result of thought dia-
lectically playing through all the possible. It must be
the origin, the principle of existence and actuality.
Freedom is the place where thought (as an interplay of concepts) leaves off and reality begins. The complete system
of philosophy, as conceived by the late Schelling, faces
a double task--starting from the conceptual, to attain to
freedom and, within thought, to give birth to the actual
and living subject; then, from the side of existence, to
trace its course empirically through history.

In all the phases of his long career, freedom is one
of Schelling's crucial and operative concepts. It is
prior to all categories, beyond the play of the possible
which is the proper concern of metaphysics or theoretical
philosophy--the one reality beyond concepts, beyond naming,
the touchstone by which to judge the rest of the vision
of the universe that a philosophy projects. We know it,
as Fichte said, because we are it, we do it.[14] The actual
takes precedence over the possible, the practical over the
theoretical--not from any conceptual reason or ground, but
from our existence as spirit.

System and Facticity

The System of Transcendental Idealism is above all a
system, an ordering will toward a comprehensive knowledge.
Its single goal, says Schelling, is to discover a system
in human knowledge, to determine the principle whereby all
individual knowing is determined (p. 18).

Now it was Kant who first brought to light the
systematic character of reason and, within the very

---

[13]See p. 193 below.
[14]"First Introduction to the Science of Knowledge," section 1;
"Second Introduction," sections 3 and 4, op. cit.

discussion of the generally misleading character of reason
as a faculty of ideas, underlined its legitimacy. In
addition to its function of unifying experiential concepts
into pure concepts or ideas, reason pursues an "ideal:"
It elaborates a complete system of all possible predicates,
arranged in antithetical pairs, and attempts the complete
determination of any being which is its object by assigning
one member of every pair to it.[15] Every concrete predica-
tion logically presumes this total field of predicates;
conversely the system of predicates presumes the complete
determinacy of every object. Now Kant thinks such a
systematic elaboration of transcendental logic both a
necessary and a valid procedure. Reason can err only in
hypostatizing this ideal, in using it to form the idea of
an absolutely determined object which embraces the whole
field of predicates, that is to say, God. Later in the
First Critique Kant revises his estimate of the legitimacy
of the notion of system. Rather than perceiving it as
proceeding to an unwarranted hypostatization in the idea
of an absolute object, he sees it as the defining and
guiding ideal of philosophy. Under this ideal philosophy
seeks to combine all systems of knowledge, i.e., all
sciences, into one "system of human thought."[16]
     Fichte and Schelling indeed set out to regularize
and systematize the Kantian philosophy, not merely in the
sense of bringing the multiplicity of texts (and of
philosophical perspectives too) to some unity, but in the
sense of pursuing this ideal of reason. Reason--the self
as autonomous in the practical sphere, if not in the
cognitive--must see itself reflected in the totality of
worldly being, must grasp the sum of its self-determinations
as the comprehensive specification of the natural and
intersubjective worlds' objectivity. It is this total
reflexivity of reason that Fichte stipulates as the heart
of transcendental idealism:

>   So what then, in a couple of words, is the import
>   of the Science of Knowledge? It is this: reason
>   is absolutely independent; it exists only for it-
>   self; but for it, too, it is all that exists. So
>   that everything that it is must be founded in
>   itself and explained solely from itself, and
>   not from anything outside it....[17]

Reason is in essence systematic, an ordering and patterning
will to know, a will to discover itself in the known.[18]

[15] Critique of Pure Reason, A568-583, B596-611.

[16] Critique of Pure Reason, A832-839, B860-867.

[17] "Second Introduction to the Science of Knowledge," op. cit.,
p. 48.

[18] See Martin Heidegger, Schellings Abhandlung über das Wesen
der menschlichen Freiheit, op. cit., pp. 31-41.

Schelling initiated his reflections on the possibility
of a system of philosophy in his first philosophical essay,
written in 1794. Looking into the Kantian notion of
system, he sees that system means not only the reduction of
a multiplicity to a unity--as in Kant's categories of the
understanding, which are all specifications of the one
primary concept, relation--but implies a reciprocity of
form and content as well. A system is an organism, as it
were, in which content and form, subject-matter and methodology, cannot be arbitrarily isolated, but reflect into
one another. This organic reciprocity is the hallmark of
scientific form.
     The notion of system becomes doubly important in the
System of Transcendental Idealism, for the work, unconsciously documenting Schelling's move from Fichtean idealism
to the "ideal-realism" of the Identity System, has two distinct senses of system in play: (1) The obvious one,
inherited from Fichte, of an immanent unification of human
knowledge under its principle or guiding process, viz.,
reflexive self-relation; but (2) system also in the sense
of a comprehensive science, a total philosophy comprehending
all the different possible perspectives upon reality.
System in the second sense comprehends and includes the
first, which, limited as it is to the immanent standpoint,
is only one portion of the total account. This latter (at
least as described, problematically and programmatically,
in the System) parallels the transcendental system with a
co-equal system of natural science, a philosophy of nature,
and contemplates joining the two through a transcendental
logic, a metaphysical theory of identity and difference.[19]
     This duality in working notions of system riddles the
whole work and introduces a degree of internal inconsistency.
Despite its massiveness and its detail, the System counts
as a transitional work in Schelling's own philosophical
development, an entr'acte between the Philosophy of Nature
of 1797-1799 and the Identity System of 1801 and thereafter.
     The Foreword and Introduction of the System essentially
look back to the philosophy of nature. They point out
the necessary but complementary opposition between nature-
philosophy and transcendental idealism, and suggest that
philosophy can complete its one task, the exhibition of
the work of absolute consciousness, only in a double
manner--in paralleling a realism to an idealism, and
demonstrating their identical principle. The system-principle these sections suggest seems to be the polar nature
of absolute consciousness, which attains actualization in
separate real and ideal orders, and thus makes nature and
spirit equally primary. They operate, in short, within

_____
[19]The System recognizes and allows only an intuitive approach
to this transcendental logic of identity/difference, namely through
the philosophy of art.

the second and broader of the definitions of system distinguished above.

The body of the System, comprising the general remarks
on transcendental philosophy and the theoretical and
practical deductions, is solely a system of transcendental
idealism. "My only concern," says Schelling, "is to bring
system into my knowledge itself and to seek within knowledge itself for that by which all individual knowing is
determined" (p. 18). Here the system-principle is "a
universal mediating factor in our knowledge" (p. 15), a
reconciliation of identical (or analytic) and synthetic
modes of thinking (pp. 22-24)--intellectual intuition.
In this context intellectual intuition is not the immediate
intuition. In this context intellectual intuition is not
the immediate ascent to the Absolute which it will be in
the Identity-System, the holistic grasp of the totality.
Here in the System, intellectual intuition is the mode of
being of the self, of the totality of the known and knowing;
the self is said to be intellectual intuition subsistent
(pp. 27-28). But precisely as an intuition, this intellectual intuition is insufficiently self-reflexive to be
both immediate and total, and thus is from the first, and
irrevocably so, sundered into unconscious production and
conscious intuition. It seems a paradoxical play of words
(and perhaps Schelling's language here is careless and
uncommunicative), but intellectual intuition is an unconscious principle of consciousness; our awareness is always
an intuition directed back upon a production, i.e. upon a
production-intuition, an activity become objectified. In
the transcendental system proper, up to the point in the
history of consciousness where practical philosophy dis-
solves into the action of history, no totalization of
intuition is possible. Intellectual intuition cannot be
realized except as process, as the ongoing flux of our
experiencings. Transcendental philosophy cannot ascend
to the Absolute Identity as such. The absolute synthesis,
the reconciliation of freedom and necessity, lies outside
its domain: Schelling can mention it at the conclusion of
the practical philosophy only as a regulative idea, in
the strict Kantian sense of the term. For transcendental
idealism at least, "the opposition between conscious and
unconscious activity is necessarily an unending one"
(p. 210). As in Fichte's Science of Knowledge, an absolute
consciousness, a totalization of intellectual intuition, is
postulated as an origin and principle of system, but is
unreachable as a result. Fichte himself explained the
incongruity of principle and of result, the abiding
difference between pure self-positing and lived synthesis,
in this fashion.

> The form of the system is based on the highest
> synthesis [of self and not-self, of conscious
> and unconscious activity]; that there should be

a system at all, on the absolute thesis [the
self-positing of the self, intellectual intui-
tion].20
The system of transcendental idealism is a system of the
forms of empirical consciousness, whose principle or
transcendental ground of explanation is an absolute consciousness. The latter simply cannot appear as an item
within the system; it stands behind it as a postulate.

Given Schelling's basic agreement, at least in the
body of the System, that absolute consciousness is
ineffable, it is odd, and for his future development,
quite significant, that the work in conclusion moves
beyond the dialectic of empirical consciousness. At
this point Schelling advances a metaphysical appendix
patterned on Kant's Critique of Judgment. Teleological
interpretations of natural phenomena and aesthetic intuition are seen to be immediate and non-discursive approaches
to that Absolute Identity which is the ineffable origin and
unreachable goal of transcendental philosophy properly so
called (viz., the system of human knowing). Schelling
cautiously suggests that philosophy as a systematic totality
and a metascience can be completed, with a philosophy of
art serving as an approach to a pure identity-theory. For
art, as Schelling sees it, is a symbolic and necessarily
asymptotic approach to the Identity underlying all consciousness. The work of art is a concrete intuition of
identity-in-difference, of multiple and inexhaustible
meanings packed into one meaning; thus it accomplishes
symbolically what philosophy attempts to do discursively--
present the totality, exhibit the Absolute. Art thus
becomes the sole concrete analogue of intellectual intuition, the one place where producing and intuiting fully
coincide. In this appendix, then, Schelling returns to
the second and broader of the definitions of system we
distinguished. He makes obvious too his abandonment of
the Fichtean principle that there is no absolute consciousness outside of empirical consciousness and vice
versa,21 and in so doing displays a drift toward an
absolute and objective system of philosophy, a system
again embracing ontology and overstepping the critical-
transcendental cautions which would confine philosophy to
a phenomenology of consciousness.

It is the destiny of Schelling's whole sixty year
long career in philosophy, and in a certain sense its
ruin, to again and again confront this ideal of a systematic and properly scientific philosophy, to put it under
critical scrutiny, but ultimately to set it aside and
reluctantly affirm the factual and discrete character of

------

20 Science of Knowledge, p. 114.
21 See The Science of Knowledge, pp. 108-9, 118.

reality, its irreducible particularity and dispersion.
Nietzsche once suggested that it is characteristic of
modernity that a thinker cannot write the work, but must
undertake an authorship and embrace in perspective and
in series that which defies total and direct statement.
It is the tension between the leading concepts of system
and facticity which inhabits all Schelling's thought and
which makes him such a 'modern,' and from the reader's
point of view, protean and unsettled thinker.

As Schelling begins consciously to approach the
standpoint of an absolute system of reason here in the
System of Transcendental Idealism, we see the problem of
the equivocal nature of the isolated individual entity
arise as well: If everything is most truly in reason (or
in the Absolute), how does it exist outside the totality
of reason? And whence comes the extra-systematic intel-
ligibility of the particular given in sensory experience?

In 1795 the young follower of Fichte had said that
there can be no leap from the absolute and systematic
perspective to that of the individual existent, no deduction of the finite (S.W. I, 314).[22] And yet he sensed
that the whole point of systematic philosophy is to subdue and, as it were, domesticate the otherness that
individuals exhibit in their contingent and mutually
external existence. Fichte before him had pointed out
that philosophy's business is to conceptualize otherness
and bring it within the ambit of the self, but the Science
of Knowledge is ample proof of the elusive and dialectical
character of the undertaking. There Fichte is forced to
admit that the whole project seems contradictory, almost
unthinkable:

> Hence if ever a difference was to enter the self
> there must already have been a difference
> originally in the self as such; and this difer-
> ence, indeed, would have had to be grounded in
> the absolute self as such.[23]

In the System we can already detect Schelling's pre-
occupation with the factual and discrete character of
particulars and see the beginnings of his tortuous, some-
times labored attempts to respect the factual in its
uncanny and pertinacious resistance to reason, and, at
the same time, to reduce the irreducibly singular to the
formula, and, so quantified, to include it within the
structured totality that reason articulates. The dialectical, perhaps antithetical, purposes motivating Schelling's vision of systematic philosophy become more sharply
outlined in the Identity-System, particularly after 1804.

---

[22]Even in the Identity-System he maintains that position, making
the finite particular an ultimate surd. Cf. S.W., VI, 38.

[23]Op. cit., p. 240.

The predominant tone of the System, however, is a differ-
ential respect for the individual, a prizing of the concrete over the general, a cautious realism. Many times
over in the course of the deductions, Schelling gives
prominence to a real factor over an ideal one, adopts
idealism solely as a methodological stance and prefers an
idealistically motivated realism which preserves the
phenomena in all their complexity over any metaphysical
idealism which would reduce and simplify the richness of
experience. For example, in the theoretical philosophy
he stresses the second limitation of the self, individuality,
and its experiential correlate, time, over the more general
limitation to intuiting intelligence and objectivity (pp.
116-17). Further he maintains that everything is at once
a priori and a posteriori; the distinction holds only
within philosophic reflection, and so all our knowledge
is empirical through and through (pp. 151-53). In the
practical philosophy he emphasizes that selfhood can be
raised to consciousness only as individual selfhood or
will; thus the crucial limitation of the self is not its
restriction to intelligence, but the third and individuating
limitation which poses the will as specified prior to its
willing, and posits the self as opposed to and determined
by the willing of other selves (pp. 165-69). It is in this
third restrictedness, individuation, that the theoretical
and practical philosophies find themselves united. For
consciousness, in its full concreteness, becomes possible
only in simultaneously confronting a definite objective
world and interacting with other selves: "Only by the
fact that there are intelligences outside me [and thus
that I am individual] does the world as such become
objective to me" (p. 173). From this focal point the
rest of the System's meditations on the paradoxes of the
concrete existence of spirit unfold, viz., that choice,
conditioned by natural inclination, is the only appearance
of freedom (p. 190); that history evidences the free
performance of an unconscious and involuntary necessity
(pp. 203 f .); that the Absolute itself, or Identity,
must be considered equally as free and as necessitated,
equally as conscious activity and as unconscious (pp.
208-12). Schelling the idealist shows himself everywhere prepared to turn away from consciousness seeking
to grasp itself in the full transparency of thought, and
to recognize and respect instead the hard, resisting,
opaque and experientially locating features of reality.
The strange result: The idealist is forced to accord
primacy to the unconscious.

The Dominance of the Unconscious

The moment really characteristic of Schelling's philosophizing in the System of Transcendental Idealism, the moment most in continuity with the rest of his thought, is his insistence upon the unconscious. The principle of system is self-consciousness--or perhaps we might better say, setting aside the contemporary connotation of reflexive self-awareness, self-activity. The self qua system-principle, and not as the delimited focus of empirical consciousness, is originally mere activity (p. 36). It is infinitely non-objective, non-thing-like, for all things are thoroughly conditioned, while the system-principle (reason demands) is to be unconditioned. The self is thus pure inwardness (p. 26), a process and only derivatively a being or a state of a being. It is a continuing self-enactment which, while indeed it comes to light in self-awareness, is not at all circumscribed by it. It is a performance not exhausted in intuition, a continual energizing. The self--or, equivalently, self-consciousness--is essentially self-constituting. Schelling names this self-enactment intellectual intuition.

Intellectual intuition turns out to be a paradoxical concept. It is not properly a cognitive state and thus bears no similarity to any intuition given in empirical consciousness. It is not merely an activity of, or a faculty in, the subject; it is the subject. The self is intellectual intuition subsistent; it exists by knowing itself in this non-objective manner (p. 28). This 'special knowing,' therefore, is more than a mere knowing. It is, as Kant first defined the term,[24] an archetypal knowing, a knowing which constitutes as well as cognizes. Now an infinite self or a God would transparently 'know' in this manner, but the self which is the principle of the system of human consciousness is (as Fichte had insisted from the first) an absolute consciousness inside human consciousness, and thus finite. Finitude means that intellectual intuition is not unitary, immediate and fully self-reflected, that self-consciousness is not pure self-awareness. The philosopher in his imitation of intellectual intuition discovers a fragmented consciousness which can be gathered back into itself only through mediation-- through experience, reflection, and finally systematic philosophy or its surrogate, aesthetic intuition.

The 'special knowing,' then, which constitutes our consciousness is at one and the same time a sundering of the self's activity into productive and intuitive facets or capacities, the maintenance of this division as, in

[24]See "On the Form of the Sensible and Intelligible Worlds and Their Principles" (1770), paragraph 10.

principle, a polar opposition, and finally, within time, a stepwise relativization of that opposition in the series of presentations. The self's being (or knowing, or activity) is the coming-to-be of a world for it. Self-consciousness is thus (1) a steady, enduring juxtaposition of conscious (intuiting) activities and unconscious (producing) ones, of activities constitutive of subjective awareness and worldly objectivity respectively; and (2) an ongoing translation from unconscious over to conscious and properly intuiting activity. Since this self-constituting and self-bifurcating self which is the postulate behind the system (pp. 28, 33) does not and cannot appear in empirical consciousness, and since it enacts itself as production prior to and beyond the reach of cognitive awareness, it is largely, in fact dominantly, unconscious.

Fichte, of course, set the terms of this comparison in the Science of Knowledge, but he preferred not to stress, as Schelling does, the absolute contrast between activity (almost by definition unconscious) and awareness; instead he sought to interpose terms connoting both affect and effect between the two--terms like striving and feeling-- and thus to effect their mediation. In grounding self-consciousness in an opaque activity which is 'inward' only when internally directed and which, when directed outward, only realizes or produces but does not illuminate, Schelling abandons the old Cartesian ideal of consciousness as complete self-transparency. Fichte had made the same moves, to be sure, but he was reluctant to embrace to the full the consequences of his introduction of finitude into the basic model of consciousness. He transposed the absolute identity of the first ground-principle, excluded from realization in empirical consciousness by the mysterious persistence of the not-self, into a moral ideal. In his hands, the failure of the "is" becomes the justification of the "ought."[25]

Things are quite different with Schelling. There is a frank recognition of the in principle unconscious nature of the activity of self-constitution. It is significant that the ultimate ascent to the Absolute which Schelling proposes in the System is neither cognitive nor moral but aesthetic, that it is not an eidetic intuition of some sort, nor an intimation of transcendent value, but a symbolic and produced totality of subjective and objective elements residing in the unconsciously produced work of art, which fully reveals the nature of self-consciousness. "[Art] ever and again continues to speak to us of what philosophy cannot depict in external form, namely the unconscious element in acting and producing, and its original identity with the conscious" (p. 231). Art,

---

[25] The Science of Knowledge, pp. 229-30.

thinks Schelling, divines the unconscious and active force
behind things and so has priority as a philosophical
instrument over both empirical consciousness and theore-
tical-reflective activity. The idealist of 1799 who
speaks in terms of self-consciousness is really not far
from the chthonic and irrationalist philosopher of 1809
who was to say,
> In the final and highest instance there is no
> other being than Will. Will is primordial
> Being, and all predicates apply to it alone--
> groundlessness, eternity, independence of time,
> self-affirmation. All philosophy strives only
> to find this highest expression.[26]

In the System of Transcendental Idealism the unconscious functions as a kind of absolute principle. It is
the opaque knot of actuality in the self, the productive
or realizing intuition which opposes the limitant activity
(which is the self's) to its properly intuitive activity
of cognition and keeps them thus tied together. But this
productive element remains hidden, unconscious, and its
workings remain forever enigmatic (pp. 78-9). Idealism,
thinks Schelling, is forced to admit such an unconscious
production and actualization in spite of its allegiance
to self-consciousness. For it can in no wise explain the
distinction of inner and outer activity, i.e., of the
experiential self and the experienced 'thing,' except by
analogy to a kind of actualizing intelligence which loses
itself (and self-awareness) in its productions, just as
the inspired artist loses himself in his work (pp. 74-5).
In unconscious producing, real and ideal (i.e., object-
constituting and object-intuiting) activities are somewhow
one; when the cognizing self arrives at awareness of the
product, they will be differentiated, but are as yet
unseparated. Explanation must stop at this point, for
philosophy can only postulate this unconscious producing--
the idealistic counterpart of the Kantian ultimate ground
of appearance, the thing-in-itself--but cannot elucidate
it. It cannot at all illuminate what it must postulate
as the basic fact of consciousness, "the infinite tendency
of the self to become an object for itself," i.e., to
bound its own activity and subsequently to intuit its
boundedness as objective, existing and external to itself.
"It is not the fact that I am determinately limited which
cannot be explained, but the manner of this limitation
itself" (p. 59). The manner of this limitation--the
concretizing of the self's activity as objectivity which
productive intuition effects--is as paradoxical and
inexplicable as the self itself: an identity which is

---

[26]Of Human Freedom, tr. J. Gutmann (Chicago, 1936), p. 24;
S.W., VII, 350.

not an identity but a synthesis; a synthesis which is not
one synthesis but many syntheses packed into one; not a
timeless and immediate resolution of the infinite conflicts
of its opposed modes of activity, but an indefinitely extended and ongoing partial solution (pp. 45-6, 50). The
self, which produces only in order to come to self-identity out of antithetical opposition, can nonetheless produce only as conditioned by this conflict (pp. 113-14).
Like the mysterious and dark Indifference of the Identity-
System (an absolute identity somehow 'already' differentiated) the self-consciousness which is the principle and
subject of the System has a paradoxical and dark side,
a hidden ground which is in fact its antitype. At the
basis of self-consciousness itself is a knot of pure fact,
quite hidden from reason, viz., its origin in and ultimate
dependence upon unconscious activity.

It is this centrality of productive activity, and
its irreducibly unconscious character, that most illu-
minates the fatalism which lies at the heart of Schelling's
practical philosophy. Transcendental Idealism is a philosophy of praxis wherein activity everywhere predominates
over being (or previously determined activity). Yet
within the system, Schelling curiously avows, the philosophy of action can only show itself objectively; praxis
can appear only as history, as an objective order of
world-events, shaped and guided, perhaps, by some teleological impulse toward a universal world-order (p. 4).
The subjective and personal aspect of praxis cannot appear;
the consciously guided aspect of an individual's activity,
the element of personal freedom, cannot appear as act, but
only obliquely, as past deed.[27] The sole efficacious
element in action, the sole objectivity, is an intuiting,
and the intuiting appears not as act, but as an intuited,
an objective something. The causality of my will, so
Schelling maintains, is consumed and exhausted in the
construction/intuition of an objective world; there is no
possibility of this world's alteration. "We act freely
and the world comes to exist independently of us" (p.
182). There is no sense of freedom other than that self-
determination whereby I know (and determine the existence
of) a world; there is no efficacious altering of reality
other than my bringing it forth as a series of presentations
and cognizing it. The self, which is will and act, is
nothing other than an act of knowing: "The self exists
only in that it appears to itself; its knowing is a form
of being" (p. 185). More than that, knowing is its only
conscious form of being; its originative (and central)
activity can be intuited only as past, as the objectivity
of a thoroughly determined world. On the level of

[27]See the lengthy discussion pp. 177-88 below.

conscious awareness, there is such a thorough-going identity of acting and intuiting that freedom itself is manifested only as a natural phenomenon. Absolute freedom
appears objectively only as natural inclination (p. 186).

This is a thoroughly deterministic reading of the human
situation of action, one which excludes the notion of a
personal and voluntary participation in a moral order.
The System's analysis of the ethical situation explains
all ethics away, inasmuch as it makes the moral law a
subjective necessity (the purely personal ideal of total
self-determination) posed over and against the objective
necessity of inclination. The only place, consequently,
where practical activity can appear as action rather than
as response to determination is in the arbitrary choice,
which is said to reconcile the conflicting subjective and
objective demands (p. 190). There is none of the Kantian
exaltation of the moral sphere here, despite the Kantian
language the analysis employs. Schelling's intent is to
move beyond the ethical, toward the global and objective
order of the self's action in history. Only insofar as
the active self or will appears, only insofar as it pertains to the world of phenomena, as it is conditioned in
and by empirical consciousness, can it be said to be free;
"the will itself transcends freedom" (p. 191).

An analysis of history similarly deterministic--
wherein events are patterned by the emergence of a drive
toward world polity, a drive which in part stems from
human cooperation but is in part impelled and necessitated by a higher providential source--moves Schelling
to adopt the notion of a hidden Absolute, an Identity
behind all conscious exercise of will which is the
reconciliation of the highest paradox, the apparent
opposition of freedom and lawfulness. The contradictions
between freedom and determinism, between the self as
intelligence and the self as will, cannot be solved on
the conscious level; an ultimate synthesis is called for,
beyond all consciousness:

> Such a pre-established harmony of the objective
> (or law-governed) and the determinant (or free)
> is conceivable only through some higher thing,
> set over them both, and which is therefore neither
> intelligence nor free, but rather is the common
> source of the intelligent and likewise of the free.
> (P. 208)

Ultimately consciousness is put to one side and made
synonymous with appearance, while the hidden Absolute is
identified with the irreducibly unconscious element in self-
consciousness and with the essential and indissoluble
tension between the conscious and the unconscious. The
unconscious as determinant activity becomes the ground of
consciousness and of freedom, a ground never wholly to be
clarified and translated into the light of consciousness.

A thorough-going determinism pervades the whole realm of
consciousness and freedom becomes mere appearance.[28]
> The opposition between conscious and unconscious
> activity is necessarily an unending one, for were it
> ever to be done away with, the appearance of freedom,
> which rests entirely upon it, would be done away
> with too. (P. 210)

Radical Finitude, Time and History

In the name of freedom or activity as such, freedom
of act is abrogated; on the principle of self-consciousness, individual consciousness is reduced to unconscious
activity--the System either veers into inconsistency and
paradox of an amateurish sort, or, more probably, points
to an essential paradox deep in the heart of its subject-
matter, human consciousness. Fichte had grappled with the
same paradox in a schematic fashion and concluded that it
is at very least odd for consciousness to be sovereignly
independent and yet finite. Schelling, we suggest, undertakes a more detailed analysis of the finitude of consciousness, and, child of the Enlightenment though he is, comes
closer to voicing the radically finite nature of human
consciousness, and the precarious nature of man's career
as finite spirit, than ever his predecessor did.

In Schelling's insistence upon the unconscious nature
of the self's activity lies an essential ambiguity which
he senses, but cannot properly articulate or conceptually
resolve. The realm of unconscious activity is equated
with the transcendent principle, with an Absolute Identity,
which is said to ground all consciousness and selfhood,
but which is nonetheless "divided in the first act of
consciousness" (p. 209). Is not the classical notion of
transcendence relativized in this equation, a notion to
which Schelling seems to adhere, especially in his talk
of system and the system-principle? A principle behind,
perhaps beneath, consciousness is made a principle over
consciousness--in a philosophy that is nothing other than
a system of human knowledge.

Schelling cautions us, indeed, that questions about
this Identity prior to consciousness, prior to the dialectic of conscious and unconscious activity, are ill-formed
and inappropriate, "for it is that which can only reveal
itself through self-consciousness, and cannot anywhere
part company from this act" (p. 234). Nonetheless in the
historical perspective, questions do arise about the
character of its transcendence, the status of its

---

[28]The freedom, then, which is all that supports this system of
human consciousness and is its foundation (p. 35), turns out to be a
purely formal freedom, synonymous with activity-as-such. It nowhere
partakes of the attributes of conscious awareness and decision which,
as Schelling realized in 1809 and thereafter, constitute human freedom.

relative consciousness/unconsciousness: Is it beyond consciousness, like a Platonic form, or beneath consciousness
like Schopenhauer's primal will? Is its ineffability due
to a surpassing character or to a privative one? It is
indeed not clear from the whole of the System whether we
are dealing here with a spiritual transcendence, a principle the classical traditions would name a cause of
knowing and being known, or with a dark and essentially
mute ground of activity or being, a ground only periph-
erally and fleetingly revealed in conscious awareness.[29]
    Schelling seems midway between a classifical philo-
sophy of transcendence as seen in Plotinus or Spinoza,
where ultimate productive agency is indeed unconscious,
but unconscious in the manner of pre-eminent and trans-
finite mentality, and the kind of material transcendence
of Will or Being over its finite forms, voiced by
Schopenhauer, Nietzsche, and in our day Heidegger. His
"unconscious activity" is certainly not the intra-psychic
and individual dynamism of conflict that Nietzsche and
Freud were to describe, the source of repression, guilt
or the life-poisoning "rancor against time." But by the
same token it is not the conflict-free and benign principle of Neoplatonic emanation, nor a placid substance beyond
knowledge, a resting and complete source of being such as
Spinoza describes. It is an activity and a principle of
activity. It is in conflict with itself, at least
potentially, so that its life can be spoken of as the
unfolding of the infinite contradictions implicit within
it. Schelling describes it as an act which is an infinity
of actions, an absolute self-consciousness never realized
definitively and exhaustively in any conscious awareness,
but rather the life and source of the whole system of
finitude (pp. 49-50). It is a will which realizes itself
only in the dialectic of the conscious and the unconscious,
a self-finitizing infinity.
    In the System's notion of self-consciousness, there-
fore, we have a transcendent principle curiously transformed and altered. In its very self or its transcendent
aspect, absolute self-consciousness or Identity is wholly
ineffable. The mechanism explanatory of all other intuitions, the principle of the graduated sequence of intuitions which collectively form the system, remains obscure
and unilluminated. We do not see how the principle of
the system of human knowledge is an act of knowledge--
unless, as Schelling variously suggests, we have a vague
adumbration of it as a genus or a type gathered from the

---

[29] A crucial feature of Schelling's later metaphysics, begun
with Of Human Freedom (1809) and Ages of the World (1815), is the
distinction of two types of causality, the active causality of
freedom or decisive will and the kind of material-temporal priority
of antecedent over consequent which Schelling calls grounding.

total survey of its instances, in nature as well as in
spirit (pp. 2-3), or else fashion some kind of analogy
between this supremely active and creative cognition and
the fashioning cognition of the artist lost in his work
(pp. 75, 230). We can know and recognize some kind of
absolute consciousness only in (or in between) the finite
forms of consciousness and the succession of those forms.
And what we recognize, in fact, is that there must be
something like an absolute consciousness, i.e. we know
it as a postulate.

     Schelling propounds a radically finite model of con-
sciousness and (both in the spirit of Kant and on the
model of the fragmentary system of reason suggested by
the three Critiques) limits philosophical recognition to
the finite modes of knowledge, taken singly and in the
contingency of their succession in the "history of consciousness." Before him, Fichte had searched for an
absolute consciousness inside empirical consciousness
and for some kind of privileged access to it, whereby
the heteronomy both of willing and of knowing would be
abrogated, and consciousness accede to total self-
coincidence; The Science of Knowledge documents the ardor
of his search, and its futility. Hegel was again to take
up the task in the Phenomenology of Spirit, and with
success, for in his stipulation that the principle of
consciousness as such is a self-negating, finitizing
return to self, rather than the Fichtean identity of
self-coincidence (I = I), he marries absolute consciousness and finite consciousness--and provides a principle
for the succession of its forms, a formula for their flow
and transition, a matrix for their generation. It is
this step, the transempirical formulation of a principle
for the finitude of consciousness and for the succession
of its forms, that the System lacks--or that it only
programmatically adumbrates. The System's self-consciousness is a plastic, flowing source of our knowledge and
its indwelling realization, but it escapes formula, and
thus transcends the realm of the intelligible and the
expressible. Lacking the self-negation and self-return
that Hegel finally ascribes to consciousness, Schelling's
self-consciousness remains a principle of activity but
not of knowledge. His self enacts the whole succession
of finite, empirical forms of subjectivity and objectivity without fully returning to itself, without
definitively knowing itself. Spirit--as Schelling was
obliged to conceive it from the basically Fichtean standpoint of 1799--does not return to itself. Indeed, as he
himself says,

     What we speak of as nature is a poem lying pent
     in a mysterious and wonderful script. Yet
     the riddle could reveal itself, were we to
     recognize in it the odyssey of the spirit, which,

marvellously deluded, seeks itself, and in seeking flies from itself. (P. 232)
Yet the spirit remained deluded, locked in the forms of
finitude. In its alienation, in its inexplicable odyssey
of self-objectification (p. 59), it can never find rest
and full return.

The self-consciousness of the System, then, is a
finitized transcendence, a real and basically unspiritual
activity and source of realization such as Schelling was
to later conceive under the names 'ground' and 'unground,'
a restless, irresistible and infra-intelligible energi-
zation such as Schopenhauer and Nietzsche were subsequently
to describe.[30] Its life is essentially succession--pro-
ductivity splayed forth as time or the alteration of matter
in nature, and as social movement and political deed in
history--change whose ultimate rational shape or purpose
is, if admitted at all, said to be merely postulatory.
Unlike the fully self-transparent Reason of the System of
Identity and the Absolute Subject of Hegel's system, both
of which live in a kind of eternity--the eternity of movement completed, reality fully comprehended and rational-
ized--the self-consciousness of the System of Transcendental Idealism is bound to time. The subject of the
Hegelian system can be said to be fully itself while it
is coming to itself, it lives its life as a play in and
among appearances. Schelling's self-consciousness, however, is a principle never fully itself, never being but
only becoming, essentially dependent upon appearances
and the continued succession of appearances. For the
author of the System, the self's life is time, and not a
mathematicized interplay of cidctic shapes within time.
The finite endures and resists inclusion within any
arbitrary totalization. The odyssey of consciousness
ends, not with any grand rationalization of the universe,
nor with the transition to any timeless and final logical
language underpinning all, but with a recognition of the
finite and fragmented textures of empirical reality and
the multiplicity of its partial intelligible schemata.

We are left with a history which equally shows
flashes of senselessness and rationality (world political
organization), whose goal and purpose cannot finally be
decided, and whose paradoxical mixture of voluntary cooperation and external determination even philosophy cannot sort out. We are left with a philosophy insufficiently
aware of its principle to determine its own methodology,
with a philosophy lacking intellectual intuition and
depending instead upon the surrogate of aesthetic intuition. We are left finally, not with a monolithic system
of human knowings, but with a multiplicity of intellectual
approaches, a multiplicity of natural languages.

---

[30]See Of Human Freedom and Ages of the World.

Science, art and philosophy remain sundered, and so the goal of fashioning one comprehensive metascience is not accomplished. But the solution Schelling envisages to this scandal of plurality is not to reduce and simplify. The System has accomplished all that a general and abstractive approach can do. What is needful now, says Schelling, is a turn to the concrete, the fabrication of a "new mythology,"[31] the integration of the particularistic 'knowing' of the arts with the conceptual generality of the sciences--a task not to be accomplished in thought alone, or by the philosopher in isolation, but one to be worked out by a "new race, personifying, as it were, one single poet," an accomplishment of history, not of thought alone (p. 233).[32]

                                                    M.G.V.

[31]A myth or its subject, the god or hero, plays the role of a concrete universal for Schelling. Concepts indicate with empty generality, but symbolic forms with absolute specificity. A myth is its meaning, and all science aspires to that exactitude. See The Philosophy of Art, S.W., V, 407-11.

[32]The remark has political overtones. The 'new mythology' might well be the ideology of the Republican polity. Compare Schiller's Letters on the Aesthetic Education of Man.

GLOSSARY

Anschauen, -d, -ung	Intuit, intuitant, intuition
Aufheben	Annul, cancel, eliminate
Bedingen, -ung	Condition
Bestimmen, -ung	Determine, define, determination
Beziehen, -ung	Relate, relation
Einbilden	Imagine
Einwirken, -ung	Influence, operate on, operation
Empfinden, -ung	Feel, feeling, sensation
Entgegensetzen	Oppose, counterposit
Gegensatz	Opposite, contrary, opposition
Gegenstand	Object
Grenze, Begrenztheit	Limit, boundary, limitation
Handeln, Handlung	Act
Hervorbringen	Bring forth, engender
Ich	Self, I
Intelligenz	Intelligence
Leiden	Passivity
Potenz	Power (mathematical sense)
Produzieren, Produkt	Produce, producing, product
Richtung	Direction
Schranke, Beschränktheit	Restriction, confinement, restrictedness
Schweben	Waver, oscillate
Streben	Strive, striving
Tätigkeit	Activity
Täuschung	Deception, illusion
Trieb	Drive
Unendlichkeit	Infinity
Vermitteln, -ung	Mediate, mediation
Vorstellen, -ung	Present, presentation, idea
Vorurteil	Prejudice
Wechselbestimmung	Interdetermination
Wechselwirkung	Interaction, reciprocity
Willkür	Choice
Zurückgehen	Revert
Zweck, -mässig	Purpose, purposive

System of Transcendental Idealism

by F. W. J. Schelling

FOREWORD

That a system which completely alters and even overthrows
the whole view of things prevailing, not merely in common
life, but also in the greater part of the sciences, should
encounter, despite the rigorous demonstration of its
principles, a continuing opposition even among those in a
position to feel or really to discern the force of its
arguments, is a circumstance that can be due only to an
incapacity for abstracting from the multitude of individual problems, which, on such an altered view, the busy
imagination at once conjures up from the whole wealth of
experience, so that the judgment is in consequence dis-
tracted and disturbed. We cannot deny the strength of
the arguments, nor do we know of anything certain and
assured to put in place of the principles; but we are
afraid of the supposedly monstrous consequences that are
foreseen to follow from them, and despair of resolving
all those difficulties which the principles, in their
application, must inevitably encounter. Nevertheless
one may legitimately demand of anyone who takes any part
whatever in philosophical enquiries, that he be capable
of this abstraction, and know how to grasp the principles
in the highest degree of generality, wherein details
disappear entirely, and wherein, if it be only the
highest, the solution of all possible problems is assuredly
also contained in advance; and it is therefore natural that
in first setting up the system, all enquiries descending
into detail should be set aside, and only the first thing
needful be done, namely to bring the principles into the
open, and to put them beyond all doubt. And by this,
indeed, such a system finds the surest touchstone of its
truth, that it not only provides a ready solution to
problems hitherto insoluble, but actually generates
entirely new problems, never before considered, and by a
general shattering of received opinion gives rise to a new
sort of truth. But this is precisely characteristic of
transcendental idealism, that as soon as it is once
admitted, it puts us under the necessity of generating all
knowledge afresh, as it were, of once more putting to the
test what has long since passed as established truth, and,
assuming that it stands the test, of at least compelling
it to emerge therefrom in a wholly novel shape and form.

   Now the purpose of the present work is simply this,
to enlarge transcendental idealism into what it really
should be, namely a system of all knowledge. The aim,
then, is to provide proof of the system, not merely in
general, but in actual fact, that is, through the real
extension of its principles to all possible problems in
regard to the main objects of knowledge, whether these

have already been raised earlier, but not resolved, or
have only now been rendered possible and have newly come
into existence through the system itself. It follows
accordingly that this work must treat of topics and
questions that have simply never been agitated or artic-
ulated among a great many of those who now presume nonetheless to have an opinion in philosophical matters;
inasmuch as they still halt at the first rudiments of
the system, and cannot get beyond them, either because
of an initial incapacity even to understand what the
first principles of all knowledge require, or because
of prejudice, or for whatever other reason. Now although
the enquiry does of course revert to elementary first
principles, the above class of persons has little to
hope for from the present work, since in regard to basic
enquiries nothing can be found herein that has not already
been said long since, either in the writings of the orig-
inator of the Science of Knowledge, or in those of the
present author; save that in the present treatment, the
exposition in regard to certain points may perhaps have
achieved a greater clarity than it previously possessed--
though even this can never, at any rate, make up for a
fundamental want of understanding. The means, furthermore,
whereby the author has sought to achieve his aim of setting
forth idealism in its full extent, consist in presenting
every part of philosophy in a single continuum, and the
whole of philosophy as what in fact it is, namely a
progressive history of self-consciousness, for which
what is laid down in experience serves merely, so to
speak, as a memorial and a document. In order to trace
this history with precision and completeness, it was
chiefly a matter, not only of separating exactly the
individual stages thereof, and within these again the
individual moments, but also of presenting them in a
sequence, whereby one can be certain, thanks to the very
method employed in its discovery, that no necessary intervening step has been omitted; the result being to confer
upon the whole an internal coherence which time cannot
touch, and which in all subsequent development remains,
as it were, the unalterable framework, to which everything must be related. The author's chief motive for
devoting particular care to the depiction of this
coherence, which is really a graduated sequence of
intuitions, whereby the self raises itself to the highest
power of consciousness, was the parallelism of nature
with intelligence; to this he has long since been led,
and to depict it completely, neither transcendental
philosophy nor the philosophy of nature is adequate by
itself; both sciences together are alone able to do it,
though on that very account the two must forever be
opposed to one another, and can never merge into one.
The conclusive proof of the perfectly equal reality of

the two sciences from a theoretical standpoint, which the
author has hitherto merely asserted, is thus to be sought
in transcendental philosophy, and especially in that
presentation of it which is contained in the present
work; and the latter must therefore be considered as a
necessary counterpart to his writings on the philosophy
of nature. For in this work it will become apparent,
that the same powers of intuition which reside in the self
can also be exhibited up to a certain point in nature; and,
since the boundary in question is itself that of theoretical and practical philosophy, that it is therefore indifferent, from a purely theoretical standpoint, whether
objective or subjective be made primary, since this is a
matter that practical philosophy (though it has no voice
at all in this connection) is alone able to decide;
whence it will also appear that even idealism has no
purely theoretical basis, and to that extent, if theoretical evidence alone be accepted, can never have the eviden-
tial cogency of which natural science is capable, whose
basis and proof alike are theoretical through and through.
Readers acquainted with the philosophy of nature will,
indeed, conclude from these observations, that there is
a reason, lying pretty deep in the subject itself, why
the author has opposed this science to transcendental
philosophy and completely separated it therefrom, whereas,
to be sure, if our whole enterprise were merely that of
explaining nature, we should never have been driven into
idealism.

But now as to the deductions which are effected in
the present work from the primary objects of nature,
from matter as such and its general functions, from the
organism, etc., there are certainly idealistic, though
not on that account teleological derivations (albeit
many regard them as equivalent), which are as little
capable of giving satisfaction in idealism as in any
other system. For supposing I prove, for example, that
it is necessary for the sake of freedom, or for practical
purposes, that there should be matter having such and
such properties, or that the intellect intuit its deal-
ings with the external world as mediated through an
organism, this demonstration continues to leave unanswered
for me the question as to how and by what mechanism the
intellect actually intuits precisely that which is necessary for this purpose. On the contrary, all proofs that
the idealist offers for the existence of determinate
external things must be derived from the primordial
mechanism of intuition itself, that is, by a genuine
construction of objects. Since the proofs are idealistic,
the merely teleological application of them would not in
fact advance true knowledge a single step, since notori-
ously the teleological explanation of an object can teach

me nothing whatever as to its real origin.

In a system of transcendental idealism as such, the truths of _practical_ philosophy can themselves emerge only as intervening links, and that part of practical philosophy actually pertaining to the system consists only of what is objective therein, and this, in its broadest generality, is history; a topic that, in a system of idealism, requires to be deduced transcendentally no less than does the objective of first order, namely nature. This deduction of history leads directly to the proof that what we have to regard as the ultimate ground of harmony between the subjective and the objective in action must in fact be conceived as an absolute identity; though to think of this latter as a substantial or personal entity would in no way be better than to posit it in a pure abstraction--an opinion that could be imputed to idealism only through the grossest of misunderstandings.

So far as concerns the basic principles of _teleology_, the reader will doubtless recognize for himself that they point to the only way of explaining the coexistence of mechanism with purposiveness in nature in an intelligible manner. --And finally, with reference to the precepts concerning the _philosophy of art_, whereby the whole is concluded, the author begs those who may have some special interest in this subject to remember that the whole enquiry, which considered in itself is an infinite one, is here instituted merely in regard to the system of philosophy, whereby a multitude of aspects of this immense topic has had to be excluded from consideration in advance.

The author observes in conclusion that one of his subsidiary aims has been to provide an account of transcendental idealism that shall be, so far as possible, generally readable and intelligible; and that the possibility of some success in this, in virtue of the very method that he has chosen, is something of which he is already convinced by a twofold experience in publicly presenting the system.

This brief foreword will be sufficient, nonetheless, to arouse some interest in the book among those who share the author's standpoint and seek with him a solution of the same problems, and to attract those who wish for information and instruction; while those who are neither acquainted with the one, nor genuinely desirous of the other, will be scared away from it at the outset; and all its objects will be thereby achieved.

Jena, End of March, 1800

INTRODUCTION

§ 1

Concept of Transcendental Philosophy

1. All knowledge is founded upon the coincidence of an objective with a subjective. --For we <u>know</u> only what is true; but truth is generally taken to consist in the coincidence of presentations with their objects.

2. The intrinsic notion of everything merely <u>objective</u> in our knowledge, we may speak of as <u>nature</u>. The notion of everything <u>subjective</u> is called, on the contrary, the <u>self</u>, or the <u>intelligence</u>. The two concepts are mutually opposed. The intelligence is initially conceived of as the purely presentative, nature purely as what can be presented; the one as the conscious, the other as the nonconscious. But now in every <u>knowing</u> a reciprocal concurrence of the two (the conscious and the intrinsically nonconscious) is necessary; the problem is to explain this concurrence.

3. In knowing as such--<u>in the fact that</u> my knowing--objective and subjective are so united that one cannot say which of the two has priority. Here there is no first and second; both are simultaneous and one. --Insofar as I <u>wish to explain</u> this identity, I must already have <u>done away with</u> it. To explain it, inasmuch as nothing else is given me (as explanatory principle) beyond these two factors of knowledge, I must necessarily <u>give priority</u> to one over the other, <u>set out</u> from the one, in order thence to arrive at the other; from <u>which</u> of the two I start, the problem does not specify.

4. Hence there are only two possibilities.

A. <u>Either the objective is made primary, and the question is: how a subjective is annexed thereto, which coincides with it?</u>

The concept of the subjective is not <u>contained</u> in that of the objective; on the contrary, <u>they exclude</u> one another. The subjective must therefore <u>be annexed</u> to the objective. --The concept <u>of nature</u> <u>does not entail</u> that there should also be an <u>intelligence</u> that is aware of it. Nature, it seems, would exist, even if there were nothing that was aware of it. Hence the problem can also be formulated <u>thus</u>: how does intelligence come to be added to nature, or how does nature come to be presented?

The problem assumes nature or the <u>objective</u> to be <u>primary</u>. Hence the problem is undoubtedly that of <u>natural science</u>, which does just this. --That natural science in fact--and without knowing it--at least <u>comes</u> <u>close</u> to the solution of this problem can be shown only briefly here.

If all <u>knowing</u> has, as it were, two poles, which
mutually presuppose and demand one another, they must seek
each other in all the sciences; hence there must necessarily
be <u>two</u> basic sciences, and it must be impossible to set out
from the one pole without being driven toward the other.
The necessary tendency of all <u>natural science</u> is thus to
move from nature to intelligence. This and nothing else is
at the bottom of the urge to bring <u>theory</u> into the phenomena
of nature. --The highest consummation of natural science
would be the complete spiritualizing of all natural laws
into laws of intuition and thought. The phenomena (the
matter) must wholly disappear, and only the laws (the form)
remain. Hence it is, that the more lawfulness emerges in
nature itself, the more the husk disappears, the phenomena
themselves become more mental, and at length vanish entirely.
The phenomena of optics are nothing but a geometry whose
lines are drawn by light, and this light itself is already
of doubtful materiality. In the phenomena of magnetism
all material traces are already disappearing, and in those
of gravitation, which even scientists have thought it possible to conceive of merely as an immediate spiritual
influence, nothing remains but its law, whose large-scale
execution is the mechanism of the heavenly motions. --The
completed theory of nature would be that whereby the whole
of nature was resolved into an intelligence. --The dead and
unconscious products of nature are merely abortive attempts
that she makes to reflect herself; inanimate nature so-
called is actually as such an immature intelligence, so that
in her phenomena the still unwitting character of intelligence is already peeping through. --Nature's highest goal,
to become wholly an object to herself, is achieved only
through the last and highest order of reflection, which is
none other than man; or, more generally, it is what we
call reason, whereby nature first completely returns into
herself, and by which it becomes apparent that nature is
identical from the first with what we recognize in ourselves
as the intelligent and the conscious.

This may be sufficient to show that natural science has
a necessary tendency to render nature intelligent; through
this very tendency it becomes <u>nature-philosophy</u>, which is
one of the necessary basic sciences of philosophy.[1]

B. Alternatively, <u>the subjective is made primary, and
the problem is: how an objective supervenes, which coincides with it?</u>

If all knowledge rests upon the coincidence of these
two (1), then the problem of explaining this coincidence
_____
[1]The further elaboration of the concept of a nature-philosophy,
and its necessary tendency, is to be found in the author's <u>Sketch for
a System of Nature-Philosophy</u>, coupled with the <u>Introduction</u> to this
sketch and the elucidations that are to appear in the first number of
the <u>Journal for Speculative Physics</u>.

is undoubtedly the supreme problem for all knowledge; and
if, as is generally admitted, philosophy is the highest and
foremost of all sciences, we have here undoubtedly the main
problem of philosophy.

However, the problem only requires an explanation of
the concurrence as such, and leaves it completely open as
to where explanation starts from, as to which it should make
primary and which secondary. --Yet since the two opposites
are mutually necessary to each other, the result of the operation is bound to be the same, whichever point we set out from.

To make the objective primary, and to derive the subjective from that, is, as has just been shown, the problem
of nature-philosophy.

If, then, there is a transcendental philosophy, there
remains to it only the opposite direction, that of proceeding from the subjective, as primary and absolute, and
having the objective arise from this. Thus nature-philosophy and transcendental philosophy have divided into the
two directions possible to philosophy, and if all philosophy must go about either to make an intelligence out of
nature, or a nature out of intelligence, then transcendental philosophy, which has the latter task, is thus the
other necessary basic science of philosophy.

§ 2

Corollaries

In the course of the foregoing, we have not only deduced the
concept of transcendental philosophy, but have also furnished the reader with a glimpse into the entire system of
philosophy; this, as we see, is constituted of two basic
sciences which, though opposed to each other in principle
and direction, mutually seek and supplement one another.
Here we shall not set forth the entire system of philosophy,
but only one of the basic sciences, and the derived concept
thereof will thus first receive a more exact characterization.[1]

1. If the subjective--the first and only ground of all
reality--is for transcendental philosophy the sole principle of explanation for everything else (§1), then it
necessarily begins with a general doubt as to the reality
of the objective.

Just as the nature-philosopher, directed solely
upon the objective, has nothing he more dearly wishes to
prevent than an admixture of the subjective into
knowledge, so the transcendental philosopher, by contrast,
wishes nothing more dearly than to avoid an admixture

[1]Only on completion of the system of transcendental philosophy
will one come to recognize the necessity of a nature-philosophy, as a
complementary science, and thereupon desist from making demands upon
the former, which only a nature-philosophy can satisfy.

of the objective into the purely subjective principle
of knowledge. The means of separation lie in absolute
scepticism--not the half-scepticism which merely contends
against the common prejudices of mankind, while never
looking to fundamentals, but rather that thoroughgoing
scepticism which is directed, not against individual
prejudices, but against the basic preconception, whose
rejection leads automatically to the collapse of everything else. For in addition to the artificial prejudices implanted in mankind, there are others far more
fundamental, laid down in us not by art or education,
but by nature herself; prejudices which, for everyone
but philosophers, serve as the principles of all knowledge, and for the merely self-made thinker rank even
as the touchstone of all truth.

The one basic prejudice, to which all others reduce,
is no other than this: that there are things outside us.
This is a conviction that rests neither on grounds nor
on inferences (since there is not a single reputable
proof of it) and yet cannot be extirpated by any argument
to the contrary (naturam furca expellas, tamen usque
redibit); it makes claim to immediate certainty, since
it assuredly relates to something entirely different
from us, and even opposed to us, of which we understand
not at all how it enters into immediate consciousness;
and hence it can be regarded as nothing more than a
prejudice--innate and primary, to be sure--but no less
a prejudice on that account.

The contradiction, that a principle which by nature
cannot be immediately certain is yet accepted as blindly
and groundlessly as one that is so, is incapable of
resolution by the transcendental philosopher, save on
the presupposition that this principle is not just
covertly and as yet uncomprehendingly connected with,
but is identical with, one and the same with, an immediate
certainty, and to demonstrate this identity will in fact
be the concern of transcendental philosophy.

2. But now even for the common use of reason,
nothing is immediately certain save the proposition I
exist; which, since it actually loses its meaning outside
immediate consciousness, is the most individual of all
truths, and the absolute preconception, which must first
be accepted, if anything else is to be certain. --The
proposition There are things outside us will therefore
only be certain for the transcendental philosopher in
virtue of its identity with the proposition I exist,
and its certainty will likewise only be equal to the
certainty of the proposition from which it borrows its
own.

Transcendental cognition would thus differ from
ordinary cognition on two counts.

First, that the certainty that external things exist
is for it a mere prejudice, which it goes beyond, in order
to discover the grounds thereof. (It can never be the
transcendental philosopher's business to demonstrate the
existence of things-in-themselves, but merely that it is
a natural and necessary prejudice to assume that external
objects are real.)

Second, that it separates the two propositions, I
exist, and There are things outside me, which in ordinary
consciousness are fused together; setting the one before
the other, precisely in order to prove their identity,
and so that it can really exhibit the immediate connection
which is otherwise merely felt. By this very act of
separation, if complete, it shifts into the transcendental
mode of apprehension, which is in no way natural, but
artificial.

3. If only the subjective has initial reality for
the transcendental philosopher, he will also make only
the subjective the immediate object of his cognition:
the objective will become an object for him indirectly
only, and whereas in ordinary cognition the knowing
itself (the act of knowing) vanishes into the object,
in transcendental cognition, on the contrary, the object
as such vanishes into the act of knowing. Transcendental
cognition is thus a knowing of knowing, insofar as it is
purely subjective.

Thus in intuition, for example, only the objective
element attains to ordinary consciousness, the intuiting
itself being lost in the object; whereas the transcendental mode of apprehension merely glimpses the intuited
through the act of intuiting. --Again, ordinary thinking
is a mechanism governed by concepts, though they are not
distinguished as concepts; whereas transcendental thinking suspends this mechanism, and in becoming aware of
the concept as an act, attains to the concept of a concept. --In ordinary action, the acting itself is lost
sight of in the object of action; philosophizing is
likewise an action, yet not only an action but also at
the same time a continuous scrutiny of the self so
engaged.

The nature of the transcendental mode of apprehension must therefore consist essentially in this, that
even that which in all other thinking, knowing, or
acting escapes consciousness and is absolutely nonobjective, is therein brought to consciousness and becomes
objective; it consists, in short, of a constant objec-
tifying-to-itself of the subjective.

The transcendental artifice will thus consist in the
ability to maintain oneself constantly in this duality
of acting and thinking.

3

Preliminary Division of Transcendental Philosophy

This division is <u>preliminary</u>, because the principles of
division can only be first derived in the science itself.
    We revert to the concept of the science.
    Transcendental philosophy has to explain how know-
ledge as such is possible, it being presupposed that the
subjective element therein is to be taken as dominant
or primary.
    It therefore takes as its object, not an individual
portion, nor a special object of knowledge, but <u>knowledge
itself</u> and <u>knowledge as such</u>.
    But now all knowledge reduces to certain primordial
convictions or primordial prejudices; transcendental
philosophy must trace these individual convictions back
to one fundamental conviction; this one, from which all
others are derived, is formulated in the <u>first principle
of this philosophy</u>, and the task of finding such a principle is nothing other than that of finding the absolute
certainty whereby all other certainty is mediated.
    The division of transcendental philosophy itself is
determined by those original convictions whose validity
it vindicates. These convictions must first be sought in
the common understanding. --And if we thus transport
ourselves back to the standpoint of the common outlook,
we find the following convictions deeply rooted in the
human understanding.
    A. That there not only exists a world of things
outside and independent of us, but also that our presentations are so far coincident with it that there is
<u>nothing else</u> in things save what we attribute to them.
This explains the constraint in our objective presentations, that things should be unalterably determined,
and that our own presentations should also be mediately
determined by this determinacy of things. This first
and most fundamental conviction suffices to determine
the first task of philosophy: to explain how our presentations can absolutely coincide with objects existing
wholly independent of them. --The assumption that things
are just what we take them to be, so that we are
acquainted with them as they are <u>in themselves</u>, underlies the possibility of all experience (for what would
experience be, and to what aberrations would physics,
for example, be subject, without this presupposition
of absolute identity between appearance and reality?).
Hence, the solution of this problem is identical with
<u>theoretical</u> philosophy, whose task is to investigate
the possibility of experience.
    B. The second and no less basic conviction is this,

that presentations, arising <u>freely and without necessity</u>
in us, pass over from the world of thought into the
real world, and can attain objective reality.

This conviction is in opposition to the first. The
first assumes that objects are <u>unalterably determined</u>,
and thereby also our own presentations; the second assumes
that objects are <u>alterable</u>, and are so, in fact, through
the causality of presentations in us. On the first view
there is a passage from the real world into the world of
presentation, or a determining of presentation by an
objective; on the second, there is a passage from the
world of presentation into the real world, or a determining of the objective by a presentation (freely
generated) in ourselves.

This second conviction serves to determine a second
problem, namely how an objective can be altered by a mere
thought, so that it perfectly coincides therewith.

Upon this conviction the possibility of all free
action depends, so that the solution of this problem is
identical with <u>practical philosophy</u>.

C. But with these two problems we find ourselves
involved in a contradiction. --<u>B</u> calls for a dominance
of thought (the ideal) over the world of sense; but
how is this conceivable if (by <u>A</u>) the presentation is in
origin already the mere slave of the objective? --Con-
versely, if the real world is a thing wholly independent
of us, to which (as <u>A</u> tells us) our presentation must
conform (as to its archetype), it is inconceivable how
the real world, on the contrary, could (as <u>B</u> says) conform itself to presentations in us. --In a word, for
certainty in theory we lose it in practice, and for
certainty in practice we lose it in theory; it is impossible both that our knowledge should contain truth and
our volition reality.

If there is to be any philosophy at all, this contradiction must be resolved--and the solution of this
problem, or answer to the question: <u>how can we think</u>
<u>both of presentations as conforming to objects, and</u>
<u>objects as conforming to presentations?</u> is, not the
first, but the <u>highest</u> task of transcendental philosophy.

It is easy to see that this problem can be solved
neither in theoretical nor in practical philosophy, but
only in a higher discipline, which is the link that
combines them, and neither theoretical nor practical,
but <u>both</u> at once.

How both the objective world accommodates to presentations in us, and presentations in us to the objective world, is unintelligible unless between the two
worlds, the ideal and the real, there exists a <u>pre-</u>
<u>determined harmony</u>. But this latter is itself <u>unthink-</u>
<u>able</u> unless the activity, whereby the objective world

is produced, is at bottom identical with that which
expresses itself in volition, and vice versa.

Now it is certainly a productive activity that finds
expression in willing; all free action is productive,
albeit consciously productive. If we now suppose, since
the two activities have only to be one in principle,
that the same activity which is consciously productive in
free action, is productive without consciousness in
bringing about the world, then our predetermined harmony
is real, and the contradiction resolved.

Supposing that all this is really the case, then this
fundamental identity, of the activity concerned in producing the world with that which finds expression in
willing, will display itself in the former's products,
and these will have to appear as products of an activity
at once conscious and nonconscious.

Nature, both as a whole, and in its individual
products, will have to appear as a work both consciously
engendered, and yet simultaneously a product of the
blindest mechanism; nature is purposive, without being
purposively explicable. --The philosophy of natural
purposes, or teleology, is thus our point of union
between theoretical and practical philosophy.

D.   All that has so far been postulated is simply
an identity of the nonconscious activity that has brought
forth nature, and the conscious activity expressed in
willing, without it being decided where the principle
of this activity belongs, whether in nature or in
ourselves.

But now the system of knowledge can only be regarded
as complete if it reverts back into its own principle.
--Thus the transcendental philosophy would be completed
only if it could demonstrate this identity--the highest
solution of its whole problem--in its own principle
(namely the self).

It is therefore postulated that this simultaneously
conscious and nonconscious activity will be exhibited
in the subjective, in consciousness itself.

There is but one such activity, namely the aesthetic,
and every work of art can be conceived only as a product
of such activity. The ideal world of art and the real
world of objects are therefore products of one and the
same activity; the concurrence of the two (the conscious
and the nonconscious) without consciousness yields the
real, and with consciousness the aesthetic world.

The objective world is simply the original, as yet
unconscious, poetry of the spirit; the universal organon
of philosophy--and the keystone of its entire arch--
is the philosophy of art.

4

The Organ of Transcendental Philosophy

1. The sole immediate object of transcendental concern is the subjective (§2); the sole organ of this mode of philosophizing is therefore inner sense, and its object is such that it cannot even become, as can that of mathematics, an object of outer intuition. --The mathematical object is admittedly no more located outside the knowing-process than that of philosophy. The whole existence of mathematics depends upon intuition, and so it also exists only in intuition, but this intuition itself is an external one. The mathematician, furthermore, is never concerned directly with intuition (the act of construction) itself, but only with the construct, which can certainly be presented externally, whereas the philosopher looks solely to the act of construction itself, which is an absolutely internal thing.

2. Moreover, the objects of the transcendental philosopher exist not at all, save insofar as they are freely produced. --One cannot be compelled to such production, as one can, say, by the external depiction of a mathematical figure, be compelled to intuit this internally. Hence, just as the existence of a mathematical figure depends on outer sense, so the entire reality of a philosophical concept depends solely on inner sense. The whole object of this philosophy is nothing else but the action of the intellect according to determinate laws. This action can be grasped only through immediate inner intuition on one's own part, and this too is possible only through production. But that is not all. In philosophizing, one is not simply the object of contemplation, but always at the same time the subject. Two conditions are therefore required for the understanding of philosophy, first that one be engaged in a constant inner activity, a constant producing of these original acts of the intellect; and second, that one be constantly reflecting upon this production; in a word, that one always remain at the same time both the intuited (the producer) and the intuitant.

3. Through this constant double activity of producing and intuiting, something is to become an object, which is not otherwise reflected by anything. --We cannot here demonstrate, though we shall in the sequel, that this coming-to-be-reflected of the absolutely nonconscious and nonobjective is possible only through an aesthetic act of the imagination. This much, however, is apparent from what we have already shown, namely that all philosophy is productive. Thus philosophy depends

as much as art does on the productive capacity, and the
difference between them rests merely on the different
direction taken by the productive force. For whereas
in art the production is directed outwards, so as to
reflect the unknown by means of products, philosophical
production is directed immediately inwards, so as to
reflect it in intellectual intuition. The proper sense
by which this type of philosophy must be apprehended is
thus the aesthetic sense, and that is why the philosophy
of art is the true organon of philosophy (§3).

From ordinary reality there are only two ways out--
poetry, which transports us into an ideal world, and
philosophy, which makes the real world vanish before
our eyes. --It is not apparent why the gift for philosophy should be any more widely spread than that for
poetry, especially among that class of persons in whom,
either through memory-work (than which nothing is more
immediately fatal to productivity), or through dead
speculation, destructive of all imagination, the aesthetic
organ has been totally lost.

4. It is needless to linger over the commonplaces
about a native sense of truth, since we are wholly
indifferent to its conclusions, though one might ask
what other conviction could still be sacred to one who
takes for granted the most certain of all (that there
are things outside us). --Let us rather take one more
look at the so-called claims of the common understanding.

In matters of philosophy the common understanding
has no claims whatever, save that to which every object
of enquiry is entitled, namely to be completely accounted
for.

Thus it is no concern of ours to prove the truth of
what it takes to be true; we merely have to lay bare the
inevitability of its delusions. --It is agreed that the
objective world belongs only to the necessary limitations
which make self-consciousness (the I am) possible; for
the common understanding it is sufficient if from this
opinion itself the necessity of its own view is again
derived.

For this purpose it is necessary, not only that the
inner workings of our mental activity be thrown open,
the mechanism of necessary presentation unveiled, but
also that it be shown by what peculiarity of our nature
it is ordained, that what has reality merely in our
intuition is reflected to us as something present
outside us.

Just as natural science brings forth idealism out
of realism, in that it spiritualizes natural laws into
laws of mind, or appends the formal to the material
(§1), so transcendental philosophy brings forth realism
out of idealism, in that it materializes the laws of
mind into laws of nature, or annexes the material to the
formal.

PART ONE

On the Principle of Transcendental Idealism

SECTION ONE

On the Necessity and Character of a Supreme Principle of
Knowledge

1. It will be assumed meantime as a hypothesis, that
there is indeed <u>reality</u> in our knowledge, and we shall
ask what the <u>conditions</u> of this reality may be. --Whether
there is <u>actually</u> reality in our knowledge will depend
on whether <u>these</u> initially inferred conditions can be
actually exhibited later on.
     If all knowledge rests upon the coincidence of an
objective and a subjective (<u>Introd</u>. §1), the whole of our
knowledge consists of propositions which are not <u>immediately</u>
true, which derive their reality from something else.
     The mere putting-together of a subjective with a sub-
jective gives no basis for knowledge proper. And conversely,
knowledge proper presupposes a concurrence of opposites,
whose concurrence can only be a <u>mediated</u> one.
     <u>Hence there must be some universally mediating factor
in our knowledge, which is the sole ground thereof.</u>
2. It will be assumed as a hypothesis, that there is
a <u>system</u> in our knowledge, that is, that it is a whole
<u>which is</u> self-supporting and internally consistent with
itself. --The sceptic denies this presupposition, like
the first, and like the first it can be demonstrated
only through the fact itself. --For what would it be like,
if even our knowledge, and indeed the whole of nature (for
us) were internally self-contradictory? --Let us then
<u>assume</u> merely, that our knowledge is a primordial whole,
<u>of which</u> the system of philosophy is to be the outline,
and renew our preliminary enquiry as to the conditions of
such a whole.
     Now every true system (such as that of the cosmos,
for example) must contain the ground of its subsistence
within <u>itself</u>; and hence, if there be a system of knowledge, <u>its</u> principle must <u>lie within knowledge itself</u>.
3. <u>There can only be one such principle</u>. For all truth
is <u>absolutely on a par</u>. There may certainly be degrees
of probability, but there are no degrees of truth; one
truth is as true as another. But that the truth of all
propositions of knowledge is absolutely equal is impossible, if they derive their truth from different principles (or mediating factors); so there can only be one
(mediating) principle in all knowledge.
4. This principle is the mediating or indirect principle in every science, but the immediate and direct

principle only of <u>the science of all knowledge</u>, or
transcendental <u>philosophy</u>.

The task of establishing a science of <u>knowledge</u>,
a science which puts the subjective first and foremost,
immediately compels one towards a highest principle of
all knowledge.

All objections against such an <u>absolutely</u> highest
principle of knowledge are already precluded by the very
concept of transcental philosophy. They arise merely
from this, that the limited nature of the first task of
this science is overlooked; it is a science which abstracts
at the very outset from everything objective, and takes
only the subjective into account.

There is no question at all of an absolute principle
of <u>being</u>, for against any such these objections are all
valid; what we seek is an absolute principle of <u>knowledge</u>.

But now it is obvious that if there were not an
absolute limit to knowledge--<u>something</u> that, even without
our being aware of it, absolutely fetters and binds us
in knowledge, and that, <u>in the course of our knowing</u> never
once becomes an object, precisely because it is the principle of all knowledge--then we could simply never arrive
at knowledge, even of one solitary thing.

The transcendental philosopher does not ask what
ultimate ground of our knowledge may lie <u>outside</u> the
same. His question is, what is the ultimate <u>in our</u>
<u>knowledge itself</u>, beyond which we cannot go? He seeks
the principle of knowledge <u>within knowledge</u>; (thus it
is itself something that can be known).

The claim that there is a highest principle of
knowledge is not a <u>positive</u> claim, like that on behalf
of an absolute principle of being, but <u>a negative</u>,
<u>limiting</u> one, amounting merely to this: There is an
ultimate of some sort, from which all knowledge begins,
and beyond which there is no <u>knowledge</u>.

Since the transcendental philosopher (Introd. §1)
invariably takes only the subjective as his object, he
likewise maintains that it is only subjectively, that is,
<u>for us</u>, that there is a <u>primary knowledge</u> of some kind;
whether, in abstraction from us, there is anything else
whatever beyond this <u>primary</u> knowledge, he does not
initially care at all, and the sequel must decide it.

Now undoubtedly this <u>primary knowledge</u> is for us
the knowledge of ourselves, or self-consciousness. If
the idealist makes this knowledge into the principle of
his philosophy, this is in accordance with the limited
nature of his whole task, which has nothing for its
object beyond the subjective element in knowledge.
--That self-consciousness is the fixed point, to which
everything is attached <u>for us</u>, is something that requires
no proof. --But that <u>this</u> self-consciousness might merely

be the modification of a higher being--(perhaps of a
higher consciousness, and this of a higher one still,
and so ad infinitum)--in a word, that even self-consciousness might still be something explicable as such,
explicable by something of which we can know nothing,
because the whole synthesis of our knowledge is first
made precisely through self-consciousness--this is something that is of no concern to us as transcendental
philosophers; for self-consciousness is not a kind of
being for us, but a kind of knowing, and in fact the
highest and most ultimate that there can ever be for us.
      To proceed further, it needs in fact to be proved,
and has already been partly proved above (Introd. §1),
that even when the objective is arbitrarily posited as
primary, we still never get beyond self-consciousness.
We are then either driven back endlessly in our explanations, from the grounded to the ground, or we must
arbitrarily break the sequence, by positing an absolute
that is both cause and effect--both subject and object--
of itself, and since this is initially possible only
through self-consciousness, by again positing a self-
consciousness as primary; this occurs in natural science,
for which being is no more fundamental than it is for
transcendental philosophy (see my Sketch of a System of
Nature-Philosophy, p. 5 [Sämtliche Werke, ed. K. F. A.
Schelling (1856-64), 3, 1-268]), and which posits its
sole reality in an absolute that is both cause and
effect of itself--in the absolute identity of the subjective and the objective, which we call nature, and
which in its highest potentiality is again nothing else
but self-consciousness.
      Dogmatism, for which being is fundamental, can
explain things no otherwise than by an infinite regress;
for the series of causes and effects, by which its
explanation proceeds, could be closed only by something
that is at once cause and effect of itself; but by that
very fact it would be transformed into a science of
nature, which itself again reverts on completion into
the principle of transcendental idealism. (A consistent
dogmatism is to be found only in Spinozism; but as a real
system Spinozism again can endure only as a science of
nature, whose last outcome is once more the principle
of transcendental philosophy).
      It is evident from all this that self-consciousness
circumscribes the entire horizon of our knowing even
when extended into infinity, and that it remains in
every direction the highest principle. Yet for present
purposes we have no need of so commanding a thought,
but only of reflection on the meaning of our first
task. --The following argument will surely be found
intelligible and plain to everyone.

My only concern at the outset is to bring system into my knowledge itself, and to seek within knowledge itself for that by which all individual knowing is determined. --But now undoubtedly that which determines everything in my knowledge is the knowledge of myself. --Since I seek to ground my knowledge only in itself, I ask myself further as to the ultimate ground of this primary knowledge (self-consciousness), which, if it exists, must necessarily lie outside knowledge. Self-consciousness is the lamp of the whole system of knowledge, but it casts its light ahead only, not behind. --Even admitting that this self-consciousness were merely the modification of a being independent of it, a thing that no philosophy, to be sure, can render intelligible, it is no kind of being for me at present, but rather a kind of knowledge, and only in this capacity do I consider it here. Owing to the limitations of my task, which endlessly pens me back into the circle of knowledge, it becomes for me an autonomous and absolute principle--not of all being, but of all knowledge, since all knowledge (and not only my own) must start from it. --That knowledge as such, and in particular this primary knowledge, is dependent on something existing independently thereof, has yet to be proved by any dogmatist. Till now it remains just as possible, that all existence is merely the modification of a cognition, as that all cognition is merely the modification of an existent. --But yet disregarding entirely, and quite apart from the question whether it is existence that is necessary as such, and knowledge merely the accident thereof--for our science knowledge is for this reason autonomous, that we have regard to it solely as it is grounded in itself, that is, insofar as it is purely subjective.

Whether it is absolutely autonomous can be left undecided, until such time as the science itself has determined whether anything whatever can be thought, which is not to be derived from this knowledge itself.

Against the task itself, or rather against the definition thereof, the dogmatist can offer no objection, if only because I quite freely restrict my concern, and am only unable freely to extend it to something which, as will be evident in advance, can never fall within the sphere of my knowledge, such as an ultimate ground of knowledge beyond all knowledge. --The only possible objection to our procedure is that the task so defined is not a philosophical task, and its outcome not philosophy.

But what philosophy may be, is precisely the question that has not so far been agreed upon, and whose resolution can only be the outcome of philosophy itself.

That the accomplishment of this task is philosophy,
can be decided only by the fact itself, in that by
achieving this task we simultaneously solve all the
problems whose solution has hitherto been sought in
philosophy.

We thus maintain, with no less right than the dogmatist in maintaining the opposite, that what has
hitherto been regarded as philosophy is possible only
as a science of knowledge, and has knowledge, not being,
as its object; and that its principle, likewise, can be
no principle of being, but only a principle of knowledge.
--Whether we shall have more success in getting from
knowledge to being, in deriving everything objective
from a knowledge previously assumed as autonomous only
for purposes of our science, and in thereby raising it
to absolute independence--whether we shall do better in
this than the dogmatist does in the opposite endeavor,
of bringing forth knowledge from a being assumed as
independent--the sequel must decide.

5. The first task of our science is to discover
whether a passage can be found from knowledge as such
(so far as it is an act) to the objective element therein (which is no act, but a being or subsistent); this
task already postulates the autonomy of knowledge, and
prior to the attempt there can be no objection lodged
against it.

The task itself therefore postulates at the same
time that knowledge has an absolute principle within
itself, and this principle lying within knowledge
itself is likewise to be the principle of transcendental
philosophy as a science.

But now every science is a body of propositions
under a determinate form. So if the entire system of
science is to be based on this principle, it must not
only determine the content, but also the form of this
science.

It is generally assumed that philosophy possesses
a characteristic form, which we call the systematic
form. To presuppose this form without deducing it is
acceptable in other sciences, which already presuppose
the science of sciences, but is not so in that science
itself, which has as its object the very possibility of
form as such.

What is scientific form as such, and what is its
origin? The science of knowledge must answer this
question for all other sciences. --But this science of
knowledge is itself already a science, and would thus
require a science of knowledge concerning itself; but
this too would be a science, and so ad infinitum. The
question is how we are to account for this circle, since
it obviously cannot be resolved.

This circle unavoidable to science can have no
explanation unless its original source lies in knowledge
itself (the object of the science), in the following
fashion: that the original content of knowledge presupposes the original form, and conversely, the original
form of knowledge presupposes its original content, and
both are mutually conditioned by each other. --For this
purpose we should require to discover in the intellect
itself a point at which, by one and the same indivisible
act of primordial cognition, both content and form are
generated. The task of finding such a point would be
identical with that of discovering the principle of all
knowledge.

The principle of philosophy must thus be one in
which content is conditioned by form, and form in turn
by content--not the one presupposing the other, but
each in reciprocity.--Among other arguments against a
first principle of philosophy, the following is also
employed. The principle of philosophy must admit of
being expressed in a fundamental proposition: this
must assuredly be not just a formal, but a material
proposition. But now every proposition, whatever its
content, falls under the laws of logic. Hence every
material principle, merely by being such, presupposes
higher principles, namely those of logic. --Nothing is
wanting to this argument, save that it also be reversed.
Let us consider any formal proposition, say, $A = A$, as
the highest; the logical element in this proposition is
merely the form of identity between A and A; but where,
then, do I get A itself from? If A exists, it is equal
to itself; but where does it come from? This question
can assuredly be answered, not from the proposition
itself, but only from a higher one. The analysis $A = A$
presupposes the synthesis A. So it is evident that no
formal principle can be thought without presupposing
a material principle, or a material without presupposing
a formal one.

From this circle, that every form presupposes a
content, every content a form, there is no escape
whatever, unless some proposition can be found in which
form is reciprocally conditioned and made possible by
content, and content by form.

The first mistaken assumption of the above argument
consists, therefore, in taking the principles of logic to
be unconditioned, that is, derivative from no higher
propositions. --But now the principles of logic arise
for us in this way only, that we turn what in other
propositions is merely form into the actual content
of the principles in question; thus logic can only
arise as such by abstraction from determinate propositions. If it arises in a scientific manner, it can do

so only by abstraction from the <u>highest</u> principles of
knowledge, and since these, as <u>principles</u>, <u>themselves</u>
on the other hand <u>already</u> presuppose the logical form,
they must be such <u>that in them both</u> factors, the form
and the content, reciprovally <u>condition</u> and involve
each other.

But now this abstraction cannot take place until
such time as these highest principles of knowledge are
established, and the science of knowledge is itself
brought into existence. This new circle, that the
science of knowledge is at once the foundation of logic,
and yet has to be brought about in accordance with logical
laws, is to be accounted for on the same lines as that
exhibited earlier. Since, in the highest principles of
knowledge, form and content are conditioned by each
other, the science of knowledge must be at once the law
and the most perfect embodiment of scientific form, and
be absolutely autonomous in both form and content alike.

SECTION TWO

Deduction of the Principle Itself

We are speaking of a deduction of the highest principle.
It cannot be a question of deriving it from one still
<u>higher</u>, and certainly not of a proof of its <u>content</u>.
The proof can proceed only upon the <u>dignity</u> <u>of this</u>
principle, or upon proving that it <u>is the highest</u>, and
possesses all those characteristics which appertain
thereto.

This deduction can be carried out in many different
ways. We adopt that which, being the easiest, allows
us at the same time to perceive most immediately the
true meaning of the principle.

1. That knowledge as such is possible--not of this
or that particular thing, but of anything, be it only
the knowledge that we know nothing, is admitted even
by the sceptic. If we know anything at all, then this
knowledge is either conditioned or unconditioned. --Con-
ditioned?--we know a thing thus, only because it is
connected with something unconditioned. So we arrive
in any case at an unconditioned knowledge. (That there
must be something in our knowledge, which we do not in
turn know from some higher thing, has already been
shown in the preceding section).

The question is thus simply, what it is that we
unconditionally know.

2. I know unconditionally only that of which the
knowledge is conditioned solely by the subjective, not
by anything objective. --Now it is claimed that only a

knowledge expressed in _identical_ propositions is conditioned by the subjective alone. For in the judgement
A = A there is a total abstraction from the content of
the subject, A. Whether A as such has reality or not is
a matter of entire indifference for this knowledge. And
so, if complete abstraction is made from the _reality_
of the subject, A is considered simply insofar as it
is posited in us, _presented_ by us; whether this presentation corresponds to anything outside us is simply not
asked. The proposition is evident and certain, quite
regardless of whether A is something really existing,
or merely imagined, or even impossible. For it says no
more than this: in thinking A, I think nothing else
but A. The knowledge in this proposition is thus conditioned purely by my thinking (the subjective), that
is, as explained above, it is unconditioned.

3. But in all knowledge an _objective_ is thought of
as coinciding with the subjective. In the proposition
A = A, however, no such coincidence occurs. Thus all
fundamental knowledge advances beyond the _identity_ of
thinking, and the proposition A = A must itself presuppose such knowledge. --Having thought A, I admittedly
think of it as A; but how, then, do I come to think A
in the first place? If it is a concept freely engendered, it begets no knowledge; if it is one that arises
with the feeling of necessity, it must have objective
reality.

Now all propositions in which subject and predicate
are linked, not by the mere identity of thinking, but by
something alien to the thought and distinct from it, are
called _synthetic_; and if so, the whole of our knowledge
consists of nothing but synthetic propositions, and only
therein do we find true knowledge, that is, a knowing
that has its _object_ outside itself.

4. But now synthetic propositions are not _uncon-
ditioned_, self-evidently certain, for this is the case
only with identical or analytic propositions (cf. 2
above). So if there is to be certainty in synthetic
propositions--and thereby in all our knowledge--they
must be traced back to an unconditional certainty,
that is, to the identity of thinking as such, which is,
however, a contradiction.

5. This contradiction would be soluble only if
some point could be found in which the identical and the
synthetic are one, or some proposition which, in being
identical, is at once synthetic, and in being synthetic,
is at once identical.

In every synthetic judgement, A = B, a wholly alien
objective coincides with a subjective; the predicate,
the concept, always stands here for the subjective, and
the subject term for the objective; and how we can

attain to certainty in regard to such propositions is
unintelligible,
      a) unless something, as such, is <u>absolutely true</u>.
For if our knowledge involved an endless regress from
principle to principle, then in order to arrive at that
feeling of compulsion (the certainty of the proposition),
we should have, unconsciously at least, to run through
that unending series backwards, which is obviously
absured. If the series is genuinely without end, there
can be no way of running through it. If it is not,
then there is something absolutely true. --If there is
such, then our whole knowledge, and every single truth
in what we know, must be involved with that absolute
certainty; <u>the covert feeling</u> of this connection is
responsible for that sense of compulsion we have in
taking any proposition to be true. --It is the task of
philosophy to resolve this covert feeling into overt
concepts, by exhibiting the connection in question, and
the major linkages therein.
      b) This absolute truth can only be an <u>identical</u>
piece of knowledge; but now since all true <u>knowing</u>
is synthetic, the absolute truth, for all it is an
identical cognition, must necessarily also be at the
same time a synthetic one; so if there is such a truth,
there must also exist a point at which the synthetic
springs directly from the identical cognition, and the
identical from the synthetic.
      6.   In order to solve the problem of finding such
a point, we must undoubtedly enter more deeply into the
contrast between identical and synthetic propositions.
      In every proposition two concepts are compared
together, that is, they are either set equal or
unequal to each other. Now in identical propositions
<u>the thought</u> is compared merely <u>with itself</u>. --The
synthetic proposition, on the other hand, goes beyond
the <u>mere</u> thought; in thinking the subject of the proposition, I do not also think the predicate; the latter
is <u>annexed</u> to the subject. Thus the object here is not
<u>merely</u> determined by the thought of it; it is regarded
as <u>real</u>, since anything is real that cannot be brought
about <u>merely</u> by thought.
      Now if an identical proposition is one in which
concept is compared only with concept, while a synthetic
proposition is one in which the concept is compared with
an object distinct from itself, the task of finding
a point at which identical knowledge is at the same time
synthetic amounts to this: <u>to find a point at which</u>
<u>the object and its concept, the thing and its presenta-</u>
<u>tion, are originally, absolutely and immediately</u> one.
      That this task is identical with that of finding a
principle of all knowledge, can be still more briefly

shown as follows. --There is absolutely no explaining
how presentation and object can coincide, unless in
knowledge itself there exists a point at which both
are originally one--or at which being and presentation
are in the most perfect identity.

7. Now since presentation is the subjective, while
being is the objective, the task, in a nutshell, consists of finding the point at which subject and object
are immediately one.

8. By this even more exact delimitation of the
problem, it is now as good as solved. This unmediated
identity of subject and object can exist only where the
presented is at the same time that which presents, where
the intuited is also the intuitant. --But this identity
of presenter and presented occurs only in self-consciousness; it is here, therefore, that the desired
point has been found.

Elucidations

a) If we now look back at the principle of identity,
$A = A$, we find that we could immediately derive from
it our own principle. --In every identical proposition,
so we claimed, a thought is compared with itself, which
assuredly takes place by an act of thinking. The proposition $A = A$ therefore presupposes a thinking which
immediately becomes its own object; but an act of thinking that thus becomes an object to itself occurs only
in self-consciousness. There is admittedly no seeing
how one could pluck something real out of a proposition
of logic purely as such; but it is possible to see how,
by reflection on the act of thinking in this proposition, one might discover something real, for instance
categories, from the logical functions of judgement,
and thus the act of self-consciousness, from every
identical proposition.

b) The fact that, in self-consciousness, the subject
and object of thinking are one, can only become clear
to anyone through the act of self-consciousness itself.
What is involved here, is that one should simultaneously
undertake this act, and in so doing should again reflect
upon oneself. --Self-consciousness is the act whereby
the thinker immediately becomes an object to himself,
and conversely, this act and no other is self-consciousness. --This act is an exercise of absolute freedom,
to which one can certainly be directed, but not compelled.
--The ability to intuit oneself therein, to discriminate
oneself as thinker and as thought, and in so discrimina-
ting, again to acknowledge oneself as identical, will
be constantly presupposed in what follows.

c) Self-consciousness is an act, yet by every act something is brought about in us. --Every thinking is an act,

and every determinate thinking a determinate act; yet
by every such act there originates for us also a determinate concept. The concept is nothing else but the act
of thinking itself, and abstracted from this it is
nothing. The act of self-consciousness must likewise
give rise to a concept for us, and this is nothing other
than that of the self. In becoming an object of myself
through self-consciousness, there arises for me the concept of the self, and conversely, the concept of the self
is merely the concept of becoming-an-object-to-oneself.
d)   The concept of the self arises through the act of
self-consciousness, and thus apart from this act the self
is nothing; its whole reality depends solely on this act,
and it is itself nothing other than this act. Thus the
self can only be presented qua act as such, and is otherwise nothing.
     Whether the external object may be nothing distinct
from its concept, whether here too concept and object
are one, is a question that has first to be decided; but
that the concept of the self, i.e., the act whereby
thinking as such becomes its own object, and the self
itself (the object) are absolutely one, is in no need
of proof, since apart from this act the self is obviously
nothing, and exists as such only in this act.
     Thus we have here that original identity of thought
and object, appearance and reality, for which we were
searching, and which is nowhere else to be found. The
self simply has no existence, prior to that act whereby
thinking becomes its own object, and is thus itself
nothing other than thinking becoming its object, and
hence absolutely nothing apart from the thought. --That
this identity between being-thought and coming-to-be,
in the case of the self, remains hidden from so many, is
due solely to the fact that they neither perform the act
of self-consciousness in freedom, nor are able to reflect
in so doing upon what arises therein. --As to the first,
it should be noted that we assuredly distinguish self-
consciousness, qua act, from merely empirical consciousness; what we commonly term consciousness is something
that merely continues along with presentations of objects,
and maintains identity in the flux of presentations; it
is thus of a purely empirical kind, in that I am thereby
aware of myself, certainly, but only as a subject of
presentations. --But the act here under discussion is
one whereby I am aware of myself, not with this determination or that, but originally, and this consciousness,
in contrast to the other, is called pure consciousness
or self-consciousness.
     The genesis of these two types of consciousness can
be further elucidated as follows. On abandoning oneself
entirely to the involuntary succession of presentations,
these latter, however manifold and diverse they may be,

will still appear as belonging to a single identical
subject. If I reflect upon this identity of the subject
among its presentations, there arises for me the proposition 'I think'. It is this 'I think' which accompanies
all presentations and preserves the continuity of consciousness between them. --But if we free ourselves from
all presentation, so as to achieve an original self-awareness, there arises--not the proposition I think, but the
proposition 'I am', which is beyond doubt a higher proposition. The words 'I think' already give expression
to a determination or affection of the self; the proposition 'I am', on the contrary, is an infinite proposition,
since it is one that has no actual predicate, though for
that very reason it is the locus of an infinity of
possible predicates.
e) The self is nothing distinct from its thinking; the
thinking of the self and the self as such are absolutely
one; thus the self is nothing whatever beyond the thinking, and hence is not a thing or affair, but rather the
unendingly nonobjective. This must be understood as
follows. The self is indeed an object, but only for
itself, and is thus not originally in the world of
objects; it first becomes an object by making itself
into an object, and does not become one for anything
external, but always only for itself. --
     Everything else, that is not self, is originally an
object, but for that very reason is so, not for itself,
but for an intuitant outside it. The originally objective
is always merely a known, never a knower. The self becomes a known only through its knowing of itself. --Matter
is said to be without self, precisely because it has no
inwardness, and is apprehended only in the intuition of
another.
f) If the self is not a thing or affair, it is likewise
in vain to enquire about any predicate thereof, for it
has none, save only this, that it is not a thing. The
character of the self consists in this very fact, that
it has no other predicate than that of self-consciousness.
     The same result can now be derived from other angles
as well.
     That which is the highest principle of knowledge
cannot have the ground of its cognition in something
higher still. Hence, for us too, its principium essendi
and principium cognoscendi must be one, and coincide in
a unity.
     For that very reason, this unconditioned cannot be
sought in any kind of thing; for whatever is an object
is also an original object of knowledge, whereas that
which is the principle of all knowledge can in no way
become an object of knowledge originally, or in itself,
but only through a specific act of freedom.

Hence the unconditioned cannot possibly be sought
in the world of objects (whence it follows that even
for natural science the purely objective, namely matter,
is nothing fundamental, being no less an appearance
than it is for transcendental philosophy).

We call unconditioned, that which absolutely cannot
become a thing or matter of fact. Hence the first problem
of philosophy can also be formulated as that of finding
something which absolutely cannot be thought of as a
thing. But the only candidate here is the self, and conversely, the self is that which is intrinsically nonobjective.

g) Now if the self is absolutely not an object, or
thing, it seems hard to explain how any kind of knowledge
of it is possible, or what sort of knowledge we have of
it.

The self is pure act, a pure doing, which simply
has to be nonobjective in knowledge, precisely because
it is the principle of all knowledge. So if it is to
become an object of knowledge, this must come about
through a type of knowing utterly different from ordinary
knowledge. This knowing must be

aa)   absolutely free, if only because all other knowledge
is not free; a knowing, therefore, that is not arrived
at by way of proofs, or inferences, or any sort of aid
from concepts, and is thus essentially an intuition;

bb)   a knowing whose object is not independent thereof,
and thus a knowing that is simultaneously a producing
of its object--an intuition freely productive in itself, and
in which producer and product are one and the same.

In contrast to sensory intuition, which does not
appear as a producing of its object, and where the
intuiting itself is therefore distinct from the intuited,
an intuition of the above type will be called intellectual
intuition.

The self is such an intuition, since it is through
the self's own knowledge of itself that that very self
(the object) first comes into being. For since the self
(as object) is nothing else but the very knowledge of
itself, it arises simply out of the fact that it knows of
itself; the self itself is thus a knowing that simultaneously produces itself (as object).

Intellectual intuition is the organ of all transcendental thinking. For the latter sets out to objectify
to itself through freedom, what is otherwise not an
object; it presupposes a capacity, simultaneously to
produce certain acts of mind, and so to intuit that the
producing of the object and the intuiting itself are
absolutely one; but this very capacity is that of
intellectual intuition.

Transcendental philosophizing must thus be constantly

accompanied by intellectual intuition: all the alleged
noncomprehension of this philosophizing is due, not to
its own unintelligibility, but to a want of the organ
required to comprehend it. Without this intuition the
philosophizing itself has no substrate to carry and
support its thinking; it is this intuition which in
transcendental thinking replaces the objective world,
and sustains, as it were, the speculative flight. The
self itself is an object that exists by knowing of
itself, that is, it is a permanent intellectual intuition;
since this self-producing object is the sole object of
transcendental philosophy, intellectual intuition is for
the latter precisely what space is for geometry. Just as
geometry would be absolutely unintelligible without
spatial intuition, since all its constructions are simply
different ways and means of delimiting that intuition,
so all philosophy would be unintelligible without
intellectual intuition, since all its concepts are simply
different delimitations of a producing having itself as
object, that is, of intellectual intuition. (Cf. Fichte's
'Introduction to the Science of Knowledge' in the
Philosophical Journal.)[1]
    Why this intuition should have been taken to be
something mysterious--a special sense that only a few
pretend to--is explicable only on the assumption that
many people actually lack it; though this is undoubtedly
no more curious than their lack of numerous other senses,
whose reality is equally beyond dispute.
h) The self is nothing else but a producing that becomes
an object to itself, that is, an intellectual intuition.
But now this latter is itself an absolutely free action,
and so cannot be demonstrated, but only demanded; so if
the self is itself this intuition merely, it too, as
principle of philosophy, is itself merely something that
is postulated.--
    Ever since Reinhold made it his aim to put philosophy
on a scientific basis, there has been much talk of a
first principle that philosophy must start from; and
by this has commonly been understood a theorem in which
the whole of philosophy was to be comprised. Yet it is
easy to see that transcendental philosophy cannot proceed from any theorem, if only because it sets out from
the subjective, i.e., from that which can only become
objective through a special act of freedom. A theorem is
a proposition that proceeds from an existent. Transcendental philosophy, however, proceeds from no existent,
but from a free act, and such an act can only be
postulated. Every science that is not empirical must
already exclude all empiricism by its first principle,
that is, it should not presuppose its object as already
present, but must bring it forth. That, for example,

    [1][Cf. J. G. Fichte: Science of Knowledge, tr. P. Heath and
J. Lachs (1970), 2d Introduction, pp. 38 ff. - Tr.]

is how geometry proceeds, in that it sets out, not from
theorems, but from postulates. In that the most primary
construction therein is postulated, and the pupil himself
left to bring it forth, it is dependent from the start
upon self-construction. --So too with transcendental
philosophy. Unless the transcendental mode of thinking
is already brought with us, we are bound to find it
unintelligible. It is therefore necessary to transfer
oneself freely from the outset into that way of thinking, and this comes about by means of the free act
whereby the principle originates. If transcendental
philosophy presupposes its objects not at all, it can
least of all presuppose its _primary_ object, the _princi-_
ple; this it can only postulate as something to be
freely constructed, and just as the principle is a construction of its own, so too are all its other concepts,
and the whole science is concerned only with its own
free construction.

If the principle of philosophy is a postulate, the
object of this postulate will be the most primary construction for _inner sense_, _i.e._, for the _self_, not
insofar as it is determined in this particular fashion
or that, but _qua_ _self_ as such, as the producing of
itself. Now in and through this original construction,
something determinate does indeed come about, just as
it does through every determinate act of mind. But the
product is in no sense _external_ to the construction,
it _exists_ at all only in being constructed, and has no
more existence in abstraction from the construction than
does the geometer's line. --And this line also is
nothing existent, for the line on the blackboard is by
no means the line itself, and is only recognized as
linear by relating it to the original intuition of the
line itself.

What the self _is_, is for that reason no more demonstrable than what the line is; one can only describe the
action whereby it comes about. --If the line could be
demonstrated, it would not need to be postulated. And
so it is with that transcendental line, the act of producing, which in transcendental philosophy must initially
be intuited, and from which all other constructions of
the science first come into being.

What the self is, we experience only by bringing it
forth, for nowhere but in the self is the identity of
being and producing fundamental. (_Cf._ my general review
of philosophical literature in the new _Philosophical_
Journal, No. 10).[1]
i) That which arises for us through the original act of
intellectual intuition can be formulated in a basic
proposition, which may be termed the first basic proposition of philosophy. Now by intellectual intuition

[1]Abhandlungen zur Erläuterung des Idealismus der Wissenschafts-
lehre, _SW_, I, p. 401

there arises for us the self, insofar as it is its
own product, at once producing and produced. This
identity between the self as producing and the self as
produced is expressed in the proposition, self =
self; since it equates opposites to itself, this is by
no means an identical proposition, but a synthetic one.
    Thus the proposition self = self converts the
proposition A = A into a synthetic proposition, and we
have found the point at which identical knowledge
springs immediately from synthetic, and synthetic from
identical. But this point also contains (Section 1)
the principle of all knowledge. Hence that principle
must be expressed in the proposition self = self,
since this very proposition is the only one there can
be that is simultaneously both identical and synthetic.
    Mere reflection upon the proposition A = A could
have led us to the same point. --To be sure, A = A
appears identical, but it might very well also have
synthetic meaning, if the one A, say, were opposed to
the other. One would thus have to substitute in place
of A a concept expressing a fundamental duality within
the identity and vice versa.
    A concept of this sort, is that of an object that
is at once opposed to, and the same as, itself. But
the only such object is one that is at once cause and
effect of itself, producer and product, subject and
object. --The concept of an original identity in duality,
and vice versa, is thus to be found only in the concept
of a subject-object, and only in self-consciousness
does such a concept originally manifest itself.--
    Natural science proceeds arbitrarily from nature,
as the simultaneously productive and produced, in order
to derive from that concept the particular. The identity
in question is an immediate object of knowledge only in
immediate self-consciousness; in that highest power of
self-objectification, to which the transcendental
philosopher raises himself at the outset--not arbitrarily, but through freedom; and the fundamental
duality in nature is itself ultimately explicable only
inasmuch as nature is taken to be an intelligence.
k) The proposition self = self fulfills at the same
time the second requirement imposed upon the principle
of knowledge, that it should simultaneously ground both
the form and the content of knowledge. For the supreme
formal principle, A = A, is indeed only possible through
the act expressed in the proposition self = self--
through the act of thinking that becomes an object to
itself and is identical with itself. Thus, so far from
the self = self falling under the principle of identity,
it is rather the latter that is conditioned by the former.
For did not self = self, then nor could A = A, since

the equivalence posited in the latter proposition expresses, after all, no more than an equivalence between
the judging subject and that in which A is posited as
object, that is, an equivalence between the self as
subject and as object.

General Observations

1. The contradiction resolved in the foregoing deduction was as follows: The science of knowledge cannot
proceed from anything objective, since it actually begins
with a general doubt about the reality of the objective.
The unconditionally certain can therefore lie for it
only in the absolutely nonobjective, which also proves
the nonobjectivity of identical propositions (as the
only ones unconditionally known). But now how an objective emerges from the original nonobjective would be
beyond understanding, if this nonobjective were not a
self, that is, a principle that becomes an object to
itself. --Only what is not originally an object can
make itself into an object and thereby become one.
From this original duality in itself there unfolds for
the self everything objective that enters its consciousness; and it is only that original identity in the duality which brings unification and connection into all
synthetic knowledge.
2. A few remarks may be needed concerning the terminol-
ogy employed in this philosophy.
    Kant, in his Anthropology, finds it remarkable that
as soon as a child begins to speak of itself by the
word 'I', a new world appears to open up for it. In
fact this is very natural; it is the intellectual world
that opens to the child, for whoever can say 'I' to
himself uplifts himself, by that very act, above the
objective world, and steps out of the intuition of
others into his own. --Philosophy must undoubtedly
set out from that concept which contains all intellec-
tuality within it, and from which philosophy itself
evolves.
    From this alone it is evident that something higher
is contained in the concept of the self than the mere
expression of individuality; that it is the act of
self-consciousness as such, with which, admittedly,
the consciousness of individuality must enter at the
same time, but which does not itself contain anything
individual. --It is only of the self as act of self-
consciousness as such that we have so far been speaking,
and all individuality must first be derived therefrom.
    If, under the self as principle, we do not think
the individual, we equally do not think of the empirical

self--as it appears in empirical consciousness. Pure
consciousness, determined and delimited in various ways,
yields empirical consciousness, and the two are thus
distinguished merely by their limitations: take away
the limits of the empirical, and you have the absolute
self that we are presently talking about. --Pure self-
consciousness is an act lying outside time, and by which
all time is first constituted; empirical consciousness
is that which arises merely in time and the succession
of presentations.

The question whether the self is a thing-in-itself
or an appearance is itself intrinsically absurd. It is
not a thing at all, neither thing-in-itself nor appearance.

The dilemma proposed in answer to this, that everything must be either something or nothing, etc., is based
on an ambiguity in the concept 'something'. If 'something'
is without exception to mean something real, in contrast
to the merely imaginary, then the self must certainly
be something real, since it is the principle of all
reality. But it is equally clear that, just because
it is the principle of all reality, it cannot be real
in the same sense as that which enjoys a merely derivative reality. The reality taken by our critics to be
the only true one, that of things, is simply borrowed,
and merely a reflection of the higher reality in question. --Seen in its true light, the dilemma thus
amounts to this: everything is either a thing or nothing;
which can straightway be seen to be false, since there
is assuredly a higher concept than that of a thing,
namely the concept of doing, or activity.

This concept must certainly be higher than that
of a thing, since things themselves are to be understood merely as modifications of an activity limited in
various ways. --The being of things assuredly does not
consist in mere rest or inactivity. For even all
occupancy of space is merely a degree of activity, and
every thing merely a specific degree of activity with
which space is filled.

Since the self actually possesses none of the
predicates that attach to things, we have an explanation
of the paradox that one cannot say of the self that it
exists. For one cannot say of the self that it exists,
precisely because it is being-itself. The eternal,
timeless act of self-consciousness which we call self,
is that which gives all things existence, and so itself
needs no other being to support it; bearing and
supporting itself, rather, it appears objectively
as eternal becoming, and subjectively as a producing
without limit.
3. Before moving on to establish the system itself, it

will be worthwhile to show how the principle could
simultaneously form the basis of both theoretical and
practical philosophy, this being self-evidently a
necessary feature of the principle.

There is no possibility of our principle forming
the basis of both theoretical and practical philosophy
if it be not itself at once theoretical and practical.
Now since a theoretical principle is a <u>theorem</u>, while a
practical one is a <u>command</u>, there must <u>lie</u> something
in the middle between the two--and this is the <u>postulate</u>,
which borders on <u>practical</u> philosophy, since it <u>is</u> simply
a <u>demand</u>, and on <u>theoretical</u>, since its demand is for a
<u>purely theoretical construction</u>. Where the postulate
gets its coercive power from, is at once explained by
the fact that it is used for practical demands. Intellectual intuition is something that one <u>can</u> demand and
expect; anyone who lacks the capacity for such an intuition <u>ought</u> at least to possess it.
4.   Anyone who has followed us attentively thus far
will perceive for himself that the beginning and end of
this philosophy is <u>freedom</u>, the absolute indemonstrable,
authenticated only through itself. --That which in all
other systems threatens the downfall of freedom is
here derived from freedom itself. --Being, in our system,
is merely <u>freedom suspended</u>. In a system that treats
being as primary and supreme, not only must knowledge
be reduced to the mere copy of a fundamental being, but
all freedom likewise becomes merely a necessary deception, since there is no knowledge of the principle, whose
stirrings the seeming manifestations of freedom are.

PART TWO

General Deduction of Transcendental Idealism

Introductory

1. Idealism has already been formulated in our first
principle. For since the self, in being thought, immediately also _exists_ (seeing that it is nothing else but the
thinking of _itself_), the proposition _self_ = _self_ is equivalent to the proposition I am, whereas the proposition
A = A says only: _if_ A is posited, it is posited equal to
itself. The question, _is_ it then posited? simply cannot
be asked of the self. Now if the proposition 'I am' is
the principle of all philosophy, there cannot indeed be
any reality save what is equivalent to the reality of this
proposition. But the latter does not say that I exist for
anything outside me, but only that I am _for myself_. Hence
everything that exists at all will be able to do so only
for the self, and there will be no other reality whatsoever.
2. The most general proof of the overall ideality of
knowledge is therefore that carried out in the _Science of_
Knowledge, by immediate inference from the proposition
_I am_. There is yet another proof of it possible, however,
namely the factual, which in a _system of transcendental_
idealism is carried out in the very process of actually
deducing the entire system of knowledge from the principle
in question. Now since our concern here is not with a
science of knowledge, but with the system of knowledge
itself, according to the principles of transcendental
idealism, we can therefore merely state the general result
of the science of knowledge, so that, starting from the
point thus specified, we may begin our deduction of the
aforementioned system of knowledge.
3. We should proceed forthwith to the establishment of
theoretical and practical philosophy as such, were it not
that this division itself requires prior deduction by the
science of knowledge, which is by nature neither theoretical nor practical, but both of these at once. So we shall
first have to demonstrate the necessary opposition between
theoretical and practical philosophy--the proof, as given
in the science of knowledge, that they each presuppose
one another, and that neither is possible without the
other, in order that we may then erect upon these general
principles the system covering both. --

The proof _that_ all knowledge must be derived from the
self, and that _there_ is no other ground for the reality of
knowledge, continues to leave unanswered the question:
how, then, is the entire system of knowledge (e.g., the
objective world with all its determinations, history,
etc.) posited through the self? It can be demonstrated,

indeed, to the most obstinate dogmatist, that the world consists only in presentations; but full conviction only comes
upon a complete exhibition of the mechanism of its emergence
from the inner principle of mental activity. For nobody,
surely, who has once seen how the objective world, with all
its determinations, develops out of pure self-consciousness
without any affection from outside, will still find need for
another world independent of this; which is approximately the
view taken in misinterpretations of the Leibnizian theory of
preestablished harmony.[1] But before this mechanism is itself
derived, the question arises, how we come to assume such a
mechanism in any case. In deriving it, we consider the self
as an utterly blind activity. We know that the self is originally mere activity; but how do we come to posit it as
blind activity? This determination must first be appended to
the concept of activity. One might make appeal here to the
feeling of compulsion in our theoretical knowledge, and then
argue as follows: since the self is originally mere activity,
the compulsion in question is to be construed merely as blind
(mechanical) activity; but this, as an appeal to fact, is not
permitted in a science such as our own. On the contrary, the
existence of this compulsion must first be deduced from the
nature of the self as such. Moreover, the question as to
the ground of this compulsion presupposes an original free
activity, united with the tied activity in question. And so
in fact it is. Freedom is the one principle on which everything is supported, and what we behold in the objective
world is not anything present outside us, but merely the
inner limitation of our own free activity. Being as such is
merely the expression of an impeded freedom. It is our free
activity, therefore, that is fettered in knowledge. But then
again we should have no conception of an activity restricted,
if there were not at the same time an unrestricted activity
within us. This necessary coexistence of a free but limited,
and an illimitable activity in one and the same identical
subject must, if it exists at all, be necessary, and the
deduction of this necessity appertains to that higher philosophy which is both theoretical and practical at once.

   If, therefore, the system of philosophy itself divides
into theoretical and practical, there must be a general
proof that already in its origin, and in virtue of its
concept, the self cannot be a restricted (albeit free)
activity without being at the same time an unrestricted one,
and vice versa. This proof must itself precede both
theoretical and practical philosophy.

   That this proof, of the simultaneous necessary
coexistence of both activities in the self, is a general
proof of transcendental idealism as such, will become

---

[1] According to such a view, each single monad does indeed produce
the world from out of itself, yet the world still exists concurrently,
independent of the presentations; whereas on Leibniz's own view the world,
insofar as it is real, itself again consists merely of monads, so that in
the last resort all reality rests solely on powers of presentation after
all.

clear from the proof itself.

The general proof of transcendental idealism will be made out solely from the proposition derived in the foregoing: <u>Through the act of self-consciousness, the self becomes an object to itself</u>.

In this proposition, two others can at once be discerned
1. The self is intrinsically an object only <u>for itself</u>, and hence for nothing external. If we suppose an <u>influence</u> upon the self from without, it would have to be an <u>object</u> for some external thing. But for everything external the self is nothing. So nothing external can operate upon the self <u>qua</u> self.
2. The self <u>becomes</u> an object; hence it <u>is</u> not originally an object. We pause at this proposition, in order to draw further conclusions from it.

a) If the self is not originally an object, it is the opposite of an object. But now everything objective is a fixed and static thing which can do nothing itself, but is merely the object of doing. Hence the self is originally <u>mere</u> activity. --The concept of an object, moreover, includes the concept of something limited or restricted. In becoming an object, everything objective <u>ipso facto</u> becomes finite. The self, therefore, is originally (beyond the objectivity posited in it through self-consciousness) infinite--<u>and so is infinite activity</u>.

b) If the self is originally infinite activity, it is therefore also the ground--and inner principle, of all reality. For if a ground of reality were to lie outside it, its infinite activity would be initially restricted.

c) That this originally infinite activity (the inner principle of all reality) should become an object for itself, and so finite and limited, is the condition of self-consciousness. The question is, how this condition can be thought? The self is originally a <u>pure producing</u> out towards infinity, and in virtue of this alone it could never come to be a product. Hence, in order to arise for itself (to be not merely the producing, but also at the same the produced, as in self-consciousness), the self must set limits to its producing.

d) <u>But the self cannot limit its producing without opposing something to itself</u>.

<u>Proof</u>. In that the self limits itself as producing, it becomes something to itself, that is, it posits itself. But all positing is a determinate positing. Yet all determining presupposes an absolute indeterminate (for example, every geometrical figure presupposes infinite space), and so every determination is a blotting-out of absolute reality, that is, negation.

However, negation of a positive cannot be done by mere privation, but only through <u>real opposition</u> (for example, $1 + 0 = 1$, $1 - 1 = 0$).

Hence, in the concept of positing we also necessarily
think the concept of a counterpositing, and thus in the
action of self-positing we likewise have a positing of
something opposed to the self; and only for this reason
is the act of self-positing at once both identical and
synthetic.

But this original something posited counter to the
self arises only through the action of self-positing, and
in abstraction from this act it is absolutely nothing.

The self is a completely self-enclosed world, a monad,
which cannot issue forth from itself, though nor can anything enter it either, from without. So nothing counter-
posited (or objective) would ever come into it, unless
this too were posited simultaneously through the original
action of self-positing.

This counterposit (the not-self) cannot, therefore,
again be the ground for explaining that action whereby the
self becomes finite for itself. The dogmatist explains the
finitude of the self as an immediate consequence of its
restriction by an objective; the idealist, in virtue of
his principle, must turn the explanation round. The
dogmatist's explanation does not perform what it promises.
If, as he supposes, the self and the objective had originally parceled out reality between them, as it were, the
self would not have originally been infinite, as it is,
since it only becomes finite through the act of self-
consciousness. Since self-consciousness is conceivable
only as an act, it cannot be explained by reference to
something that makes conceivable only a passivity.
Regardless of the fact that the objective first arises
for me through my becoming finite, that the self first
opens itself to objectivity through the act of self-
consciousness, that self and object are opposed like
positive and negative quantities, and that only so much
reality can therefore attach to the object as is canceled
out in the self, the dogmatist simply explains the limitation of
the self as one would that of an object, that is, he
explains limitation in and for itself, but not, however,
the knowledge of that fact. But the self as self is
limited only in that it intuits itself as such, for a
self is simply and solely what it is for itself. The
dogmatist's explanation suffices to account for the
fact of limitation, but not for that of the self-intuition therein. The self is to be restricted without ceasing to be a self, not for an intuitant outside it, that
is, but for itself. But now what is that self, for
which the other is to be restricted? Undoubtedly, an
unrestricted self; thus the self is to be limited without
ceasing to be unlimited. The question is, how can one
think this?

That the self should be not only limited, but should

also intuit itself as such, or that in becoming limited
it should simultaneously be unlimited, is possible only
in that it posits _itself_ as limited, itself gives rise to
the limitation. For the self to bring about its own
limitation is equivalent to saying that it abolishes itself
as absolute activity, that is, it abolishes itself altogether. But this is a contradiction that must be resolved
if philosophy is not to contradict itself in its first
principles.

    e) That the originally infinite activity of the self
should limit itself, _i.e._, turn into a finite activity (in
self-consciousness), is intelligible only if it can be
shown _that the self qua self can be unlimited only insofar_
as it is limited, and conversely, that it is limited as a
self only insofar as it is unlimited.

    f) In this proposition two others are contained.

    A. _The self is unlimited as a self only in that_
it is limited.

    The question is, how such a thing can be conceived
of.

    aa). The self is everything that it is, only for
itself. That it is infinite means, therefore, that it is
so for itself. If we posit for a moment that the self _is_
infinite, but without being so for itself, there would
indeed be an infinite, but it would not be a self. (Picture this remark by means of the image of infinite space,
which is an infinite without being a self, and which represents, as it were, the self _dispersed_, the self without
reflection.)

    bb). That the self is infinite for itself means
that it is so for its self-intuition. But _in_ intuiting
itself, the self becomes finite. This contradiction is
soluble only if the self in this finitude _becomes_ infinite
to itself, _i.e._, if it intuits itself as an _infinite_
becoming.

    cc). But a _becoming_ is unthinkable save under a
condition of limitation. If we fancy an infinitely producing activity as expanding without resistance, it will
produce with infinite speed; its product is a being, not
a becoming. So the condition of all becoming is limitation
or restraint.

    dd). However, the self is to be not only a
becoming, but an _infinite_ becoming. To be a _becoming_ it
must be restricted. To be an _infinite_ becoming its
boundary must be abolished. [If the producing activity
does not push on beyond its product (its boundary),
the product is not productive, that is, it is no _becoming_.
But if the production is completed at any specific point,
and the boundary thus abolished (for it operates only as
a counter to the activity that pushes on beyond it), then
the producing activity was not infinite.] Thus the boundary

is to be abolished and at the same time not abolished.
Abolished, so that the becoming shall be an infinite
one; not abolished, so that it shall never cease to be a
becoming.
            ee). This contradiction can be resolved only
through the intermediary concept of an infinite extension
of the boundary. The boundary is abolished for every
specific point, yet it is not abolished absolutely, but
merely thrust out into infinity.
       Boundedness (extended to infinity) is thus the con-
dition under which alone the self as self can be infinite.
       The boundedness of this infinite is thus immediately
posited through its selfhood, i.e., through the fact that
it is not merely an infinite, but at the same time a
self, that is, an infinite for itself.
            B. The self is limited only through the fact that
it is unlimited.
       Suppose a limit assigned to the self, without its
concurrence, and let this limit fall at any desired point
C. If the self's activity does not reach this point, or
only just reaches it, it constitutes no limit for the self.
But one cannot assume the self's activity to reach only
just up to point C, unless that self be originally active
into the indeterminate, that is, to infinity. Thus point C
only exists for the self as such inasmuch as the latter
pushes out beyond it; but beyond this point lies infinity,
for between the self and infinity lies nothing except this
point. Hence the infinite striving of the self is itself
the condition under which it is limited, that is, its
unboundedness is the condition of its being bounded.
       g) From the two propositions A and B we draw further
conclusions, as follows:
aa). We could deduce the bounded character of the self
only as a condition of its unboundedness. But now the
boundary is a condition of unboundedness only inasmuch as
it is extended into infinity. But the self cannot extend
the boundary without acting upon it, and cannot act upon
it unless the boundary exists independently of this action.
Hence the boundary becomes real, only through the assault
of the self against it. If the self did not direct its
activity against this boundary, it would be no boundary
for the self, that is (since it can only be posited
negatively, in relation to the self), it would be nothing
at all.
       The activity directed against the boundary is, by
the proof of B, no other than the original, infinitely
extending, activity of the self, that is, that very
activity which alone attaches to the self beyond self-
consciousness.
bb). But now although this original infinite activity
explains how the boundary may become real, it does not

explain how it may also become <u>ideal</u>, that is, it certainly explains the fact that <u>the self</u> is limited as such, but not its knowledge of that limitation, or its being limited for itself.

cc). <u>But now the boundary must be at once real and ideal</u>. <u>Real</u>, that is, independent of the self, since otherwise the latter is not genuinely bounded; <u>ideal</u>, dependent on the self, since otherwise the self does not posit or intuit itself as limited. Both claims, that the boundary is real, and also that it is merely ideal, are to be deduced from self-consciousness. Self-consciousness says that the self is limited for itself; in order that it be limited, the boundary must be independent of the activity so confined; in order that it be limited for itself, the boundary must depend on the self. The conflict between these claims is therefore soluble only through an opposition obtaining in self-consciousness itself. That the boundary is dependent on the self means that the latter contains another activity besides the one limited, which the boundary must be independent of. So besides that infinitely outreaching activity which we wish to call real, since it alone is really limitable, there must be another in the self, which we may term the ideal activity. The boundary is real for the infinitely outreaching, or--since this very activity is to be limited in self-consciousness--for the <u>objective</u> activity of the self, and ideal, therefore, for an opposing, nonobjective, intrinsically illimitable activity, which must now be more exactly described.

dd). Apart from these two activities, one of which we simply postulate from the outset as necessary to explain the boundedness of the self, no other factors of self-consciousness are given. The second, ideal or nonobjective, activity must therefore be such that through it are given simultaneously the grounds both of the limitation of the objective activity, and of the <u>knowledge</u> that it is so limited. Now since the ideal activity is originally posited merely as the <u>intuitant</u> (subjective) of the other, so as to explain thereby the limitation of the self <u>as</u> self, <u>to be intuited</u> and <u>to be limited</u> must, for the latter, objective, activity, be one and the same. This must find its explanation in the basic character of the self. The latter activity, if it is to be activity of a <u>self</u>, must simultaneously be <u>limited</u> and intuited <u>as limited</u>, for <u>in this very identity of</u> being intuited and of being lies the nature of the <u>self</u>. In that the real activity is limited, it must also be intuited, and in that it is intuited, it must also be limited; and both must be absolutely one.

ee). <u>Both activities</u>, the real and the ideal, <u>mutually</u>

presuppose each other. The real, originally striving
into infinity, but to be limited for the sake of self-
consciousness, is nothing without the ideal, for which,
in its limitation, it is infinite (by dd). Conversely,
the ideal activity is nothing without the to-be-intuited,
the limitable, and, on that very account, the real.

From this reciprocal presupposition of the two
activities, for the sake of self-consciousness, the
entire mechanism of the self will have to be derived.
ff). Just as the two activities reciprocally presuppose
each other, so also do idealism and realism. If I
reflect merely upon the ideal activity, there arises
for me idealism, or the claim that the boundary is
posited solely by the self. If I reflect merely upon
the real activity, there arises for me realism, or the
claim that the boundary is independent of the self.
If I reflect upon the two together, a third view arises
from both, which may be termed ideal-realism, or what
we have hitherto designated by the name of transcendental idealism.
gg). In theoretical philosophy we explain the ideality
of the boundary (or how the limitation, originally
existing only for free action, becomes limitation for
knowledge); practical philosophy has to explain the
reality of the boundary (or how the limitation, which
is initially a purely subjective one, becomes objective).
Theoretical philosophy is therefore idealism, practical
philosophy realism, and only the two together constitute
the complete system of transcendental idealism.

Just as idealism and realism mutually presuppose
each other, so also do theoretical and practical
philosophy; and in the self as such there is initial
union and combination of what we must hereafter
separate, for the sake of the system now to be
established.

PART THREE

System of Theoretical Philosophy according to the Principles of Transcendental Idealism

Introductory

1. The self-consciousness we start from is an absolute act, and by this one act is posited, not only the self itself, with all its determinations, but also, as is sufficiently evident from the preceding part, everything else as well that is posited at all for the self. Our first concern in theoretical philosophy will therefore be the deduction of this absolute act.

But in order to discover the full content of this act we are obliged to take it apart and split it up, as it were, into a number of individual acts. These latter will be mediating elements in that one absolute synthesis.

From these individual acts, taken all together, we can, as it were, have successively presented to our eyes what is posited simultaneously and at once in the one absolute synthesis in which they are all incorporated.

The procedure of this deduction is as follows:

The act of self-consciousness is ideal and real, simultaneously and throughout. By means of it, what is posited as real is also immediately posited as ideal, and what is posited as ideal is likewise posited as real. This thoroughgoing identity of ideal and real positedness in the act of self-consciousness can only be presented in philosophy as arising in succession. This takes place in the following manner.

The concept we start from is that of the self, that is, of the subject-object, to which we elevate ourselves through absolute freedom. Through this act there is now, for us who philosophize, something posited in the self qua object, but hence not yet posited therein qua subject (for the self as such, what is posited as real is in one and the same act also posited as ideal); our enquiry will therefore have to go on until what is posited for us in the self qua object is also posited for us in the self qua subject, that is, until for us the consciousness of our object coincides with our own consciousness, and thus until the self itself has for us arrived at the point from which we started.

This procedure is necessarily carried out by means of our object, and by our endeavor, since subject and object--which are absolutely united in the absolute act of self-consciousness--must be constantly kept distinct for purposes of philosophizing, that is, in order to allow this unification to take place before our eyes.

2. In accordance with the foregoing, the enquiry will divide into two parts. First we shall derive the absolute synthesis contained in the act of self-consciousness, and afterwards must seek out the mediating elements of the synthesis in question.

I

Deduction of the Absolute Synthesis Contained in the Act of Self-consciousness

1. We start from the proposition proved earlier, that the boundary must be both ideal and real at once. If this is so, then, since an original union of ideal and real is thinkable only in an absolute act, the boundary must be posited by an _act_, and this act' itself must be ideal and real at once.
2. But such an act is to be found only in self-consciousness, and so all limitation, even, must first be posited through self-consciousness, and given along with it.
     a) The original act of self-consciousness is at once ideal and real. Self-consciousness is in principle purely ideal, but through it the self arises for us as purely real. Through the act of self-intuition the self also immediately becomes limited; to be intuited and to be are one and the same.
     b) The boundary is posited through self-consciousness alone, and thus has no other reality than what it obtains through self-consciousness. This act is the higher, and the fact of limitation derives from it. For the dogmatist, boundedness comes first, and self-consciousness second. This is unthinkable, for self-consciousness is an _act_, and the boundary, to be a boundary of the _self_, must be simultaneously dependent on, and independent of, the self. This is conceivable (Sec. II) only _if the self is equivalent to an action in which there are two opposite activities_, one which _undergoes limitation_, and of which the boundary is therefore independent, and one which _limits_, and is for that very reason illimitable.
3. This action is, of course, self-consciousness. Beyond self-consciousness the self is _pure_ objectivity. This pure objective (nonobjective originally, precisely because an objective without a subjective is impossible) is the one and only _in-itself_ there is. Only through self-consciousness is subjectivity first added thereto. To this original, _purely_ objective activity, that is limited in consciousness, there stands opposed the limiting activity, which cannot, on that very account, itself become an object. --To come to consciousness, and

to be limited, are one and the same. Only that which is
limited me-ward, so to speak, comes to consciousness:
the limiting activity falls outside all consciousness,
just because it is the cause of all limitation. The fact
of limitation must appear as independent of me, since I
can discern only my own limitedness, never the activity
whereby it is posited.
4.   This distinction between limiting and delimited
activity being accepted, neither of the two, the limiting
or the limited activity, is what we call the self. For
the self exists only in self-consciousness, but through
neither of these two, taken in isolation, does the self
of self-consciousness arise for us.

    a)   The limiting activity does not come to con-
sciousness, or become an object, and is therefore the
activity of the pure subject. But the self of self-
consciousness is not the pure subject, but subject and
object together.

    b)   The limited activity is merely that which becomes
an object, the purely objective element in self-consciousness. But the self of self-consciousness is neither
pure subject nor pure object, but both of these at once.

    Thus neither through the limiting nor the limited
activities, by themselves, do we arrive at self-consciousness. There is, accordingly, a third activity, compounded
of these two, whereby the self of self-consciousness is
engendered.
5.   It is this third activity, oscillating between the
limited and the limiting, whereby the self is first engendered; and, since the producing and the being of the self
are one, it is nothing other than the self of self-consciousness itself.

    The self is thus itself a compound activity, and
self-consciousness itself a synthetic act.
6.   To define this third, synthetic activity more closely,
we must first do the same for the conflict of opposing
activities from which it is born.

    a)   This conflict is a conflict of activities
originally opposed, not so much in subject as in direction, for both are activities of one and the same self.
The origin of these two directions is this. --The self
has an urge to produce the infinite, and this tendency
must be thought of as directed outwards (as centrifugal),
but it is not distinguishable as such without an activity
regressively directed inwards to the self as center. The
outgoing, by nature infinite activity is the objective in
the self; the self-reverting activity is nothing else
but the striving to intuit oneself in that infinitude.
Through this action as such, the inner and the outer
are divided within the self, and with their separation
is posited a conflict in the self that only the necessity
of self-consciousness can explain. Why the self should

have originally to become aware of itself, is not further
explicable, for it is nothing else but self-consciousness.
But within that self-consciousness a clash of opposing
directions is necessary.

The self of self-consciousness is that which pursues
these opposing directions. It consists merely in this
conflict, or rather, it is itself the clash of opposing
directions. As surely as the self is aware of itself,
this conflict must arise and be maintained. The question
is, how is it maintained.

Two opposing directions cancel out and destroy one
another; their conflict, it would seem therefore, cannot
persist. The result would be absolute inactivity, for
since the self is nothing but the striving to be self-
identical, the one ground that determines it to activity
is a persistent contradiction within itself. But now
every contradiction is self-destructive, in and for
itself. No contradiction can survive, unless it be that
through the very effort to maintain or entertain it, by
this third factor itself, there comes about a sort of
identity, a mutual interrelation of the two opposing
elements therein.

The original contradiction in the self's own nature
can neither be abolished, without abolition of the self
itself, nor can it endure in and for itself. It will
persist only through the necessity of doing so, that is,
through the striving that results therefrom, to maintain
it, and thereby bring identity into it.

(It can already be concluded from the foregoing that
the identity expressed in self-consciousness is not an
original identity but a created and mediated one. What
is original is the conflict of opposing directions in the
self; the identity is the resultant of this. Originally,
indeed, we are conscious only of identity, but enquiry
into the conditions of self-consciousness has served
to show that such identity can only be a mediated,
synthetic one).

The highest of which we are conscious is the identity of subject and object, yet this is in itself impossible, and can be such only through a third, mediating
factor. Since self-consciousness is a duality of
directions, the mediating factor must be an activity that
wavers between opposing directions.

b) So far we have been considering the two activities
only in regard to their opposing directions, and it is
still undecided whether both are alike in being infinite,
or not. But since in advance of self-consciousness there
is no ground for positing either one or the other as
finite, the conflict between the two (for that they do
indeed exist, has just been demonstrated) will also be
an infinite one. So the conflict will likewise be
capable of unification, not in a single action, but only

in an infinite series of actions. Now since we conceive
the identity of self-consciousness (the uniting of this
conflict) in the one action of self-consciousness,
there must be an infinity of actions contained in this
one action; it must, that is, be an absolute synthesis,
and if everything is posited for the self only through
its own acting, a synthesis whereby everything is posited
that is posited at all for the self.

How the self is driven to this absolute action, or
how it is possible for an infinity of actions to be
condensed into a single absolute one, is intelligible
only as follows.

The self contains fundamental opposites, namely
subject and object; they cancel one another out, and yet
neither is possible without the other. The subject
asserts itself only in opposition to the object, and the
object only in opposition to the subject; neither, that
is, can become real without destroying the other, but
the point of destruction of one by the other can never
be reached, precisely because each is what it is only
in opposition to the other. Both have therefore to be
united, for neither can destroy the other, and yet nor
can they subsist together. The conflict, therefore, is
not so much a conflict between the two factors, as
between the inability, on the one hand, to unite the
infinite opposites, and the necessity of doing so, on
the other, if the identity of self-consciousness is not
to be blotted out. This very fact, that subject and
object are absolute opposites, puts the self under the
necessity of condensing an infinity of actions into a
single absolute one. If there were no opposition in the
self, it would contain no movement at all, no production,
and hence no product either. If the opposition were
not absolute, the unifying activity would likewise not
be absolute, would not be a necessary and involuntary
one.

7. The progression, so far deduced, from an absolute
antithesis to an absolute synthesis, can now be presented
also in an entirely formal fashion. If we conceive the
objective self (the thesis) as absolute reality, its
opposite will have to be absolute negation. But absolute
reality, just because it is absolute, is no reality, and
both opposites are thus in their opposition merely
ideal. If the self is to be real, that is, to become
an object to itself, reality must be blotted out in it,
that is, it must cease to be absolute reality. But by
the same token, if the opposite is to become real, it
must cease to be absolute negation. If both are to
become real, they must, as it were, share out reality
between them. But this division of reality between the
two, the subjective and the objective, is possible no
otherwise than through a third activity of the self,

that wavers between them, and this third activity is
again not possible unless both opposites are themselves
activities of the self.

This advance from thesis to antithesis, and from
thence to synthesis, is therefore originally founded in
the mechanism of the mind, and so far as it is purely
formal (as in scientific method, for example), is abstracted
from this original, material sequence established in
transcendental philosophy.

II

Deduction of the Middle Terms of the Absolute Synthesis

Introductory

For purposes of this deduction, the following data are
given to us through what has gone before.

1. Self-consciousness is the absolute act, through
which everything is posited for the self.

Under this act we do not include, say, the free
creations postulated by the philosopher, which represent
a higher order of the original activity; we refer, rather,
to that original activity which, since it is the condition
of all limitation and consciousness, does not itself
come to consciousness. The first question to arise is,
what sort of act this may be, and whether it be voluntary
or involuntary? Neither description can in fact be
given to this act; for these concepts only apply within
the sphere of what is explicable as such; an action that
is voluntary or involuntary already presupposes limitation (or consciousness). The action that is cause of all
limitation, and can no longer be explained by any other,
must be absolutely free. But absolute freedom is
identical with absolute necessity. If we could imagine
an action in God, for example, it would have to be
absolutely free, but this absolute freedom would simultaneously be absolute necessity, since in God we can
think of no law or action that does not spring from the
inner necessity of His nature. Such an act is the original act of self-consciousness; absolutely free, since
it is determined by nothing outside the self; absolutely
necessary, since it proceeds from the inner necessity of
the nature of the self.

But the question now arises as to how the philosopher
assures himself of this original act, or knows about it.
He obviously does not do so immediately, but only by
inference. I discover, that is, through philosophy, that
only through such an act am I generated for myself at
every instant, and conclude, therefore, that only
through such an act can I likewise have come into being

in the first place. I find that the consciousness of
an objective world is implied in every moment of my
consciousness, and conclude, therefore, that something
objective must already enter from the beginning into the
synthesis of self-consciousness, and must again issue
from the latter in its developed form.

But now given that the philosopher assures himself
of this act qua act, how does he ascertain its specific
content? Undoubtedly by the free imitation of this act,
with which all philosophy begins. But then how does he
know this secondary, arbitrary act to be identical with
the original and absolutely free one? For if it is
through self-consciousness that all limitation originates,
and thus all time as well, this original act cannot itself
occur in time; hence, of the rational being as such,
one can no more say that it has begun to exist, than that
it has existed for all time; the self as self is absolutely
eternal, that is, outside time altogether. But now our
secondary act necessarily occurs at a particular moment
in time, and so how does the philosopher know this act,
occurring in the middle of the time-series, to be coincident with that wholly extratemporal act whereby all
time is first constituted? --The self, once transposed
into time, consists in a steady passage from one presentation to the next; yet it remains, after all, within its
power to interrupt this series by reflection. The
absolute interruption of the succession is the beginning
of all philosophizing, and from now on what was previously
an involuntary succession becomes a voluntary one. But
how does the philosopher know that this act which has
entered by irruption into the series of his presentations is the same with that original act whereby the
entire series begins?

Anyone who perceives at all that the self arises
only through its own acting, will also perceive that,
through the arbitrary action in midst of the time-series
whereby alone the self arises, nothing else can arise
for me save what comes about for me originally and
beyond all time. And besides that, indeed, this original act of self-consciousness continues all along, for
the whole series of my presentations consists in nothing
else but the evolution of that one synthesis. Hence
it is that at every moment I can come to be for myself,
exactly as I come originally to be for myself. What
I am, I am only through my acting (for I am absolutely
free); but through this specific act it is always just
the self that arises for me, and thus I must conclude
that it also comes about originally through the same
act. --

A general reflection, connected with the foregoing,
may find its place here. If philosophy's first construction is the imitation of an original, all its

constructions will likewise be merely such imitations.
So long as the self is apprehended in its original evolution of the absolute synthesis, there is only one series
of acts, that of the original and necessary acts of the
self; as soon as I interrupt this evolution, and freely
project myself back to its startingpoint, there arises
for me a new series, in which what was necessary in the
first series is now free. The former is the original,
the latter the copy or imitation. If the second series
contains no more and no less than the first, the imitation is perfect, and a true and complete philosophy is
engendered. In the opposite case, the result is a
false and incomplete one.

Philosophy as such is therefore nothing else but
the free imitation, the free recapitulation of the original series of acts into which the one act of self-consciousness evolves. In relation to the second, the
first series is real, while the second is ideal in
regard to the first. It seems unavoidable that an
element of choice should enter into the second series,
for it is freely begun and continued, but the choice
should be merely formal, and not determine the content
of the act.

Philosophy, since its object is the original genesis
of consciousness, is the sole science in which this twofold series occurs. In every other science there is
but one series. Now philosophical talent does not in
fact consist merely in the capacity for freely repeating
the series of original acts; it lies chiefly in again
becoming aware, in the course of this free repetition,
of the original necessity of those acts.

2. Self-consciousness (the self) is a conflict of
absolutely opposed activities. The one that originally
reaches out into infinity we shall call the real, objective, limitable activity; the other, the tendency to
intuit oneself in that infinity, is called the ideal,
subjective, illimitable activity.

3. Both activities are originally posited as
equally infinite. Through the ideal activity (which
reflects the first) we already have a ground for positing the limitable activity as finite. So how the ideal
activity can be limited is therefore the first thing to
be derived. The act of self-consciousness, from which
we start, at first tells us only how the objective
activity is limited, not the subjective; and since the
latter is posited as the ground of all limitation of
the objective, it is for that very reason posited,
not as originally unlimited (and so limitable like the
other) but as absolutely illimitable. If the activity
posited as originally unlimited, but therefore limitable,
is free as to matter but restricted as to form, so
this one, originally posited as illimitable, will for

that very reason, if limited, be unfree as to matter
and free only as to form. This illimitability of the
ideal activity is the basis of all construction in
theoretical philosophy; in practical philosophy the
relationship may well be reversed.

4. Since, therefore (by 2 and 3), there is an
infinite conflict in self-consciousness, the one absolute
act we start from contains--united and condensed--an
infinity of actions whose total enumeration forms the
content of an infinite task; (if it were ever to be
completely accomplished, the whole structure of the
objective world, and every determination of nature down
to the infinitely small, would have to be revealed to
us). So philosophy can enumerate only those actions
which constitute epochs, as it were, in the history of
self-consciousness, and establish them in their inter-
relations with one another. (Thus sensation, for
example, is an action of the self which, if all its
intermediate elements could be set forth, would be
bound to lead us to a deduction of all the qualities in
nature, which is impossible.)

Philosophy is thus a history of self-consciousness,
having various epochs, and by means of it that one
absolute synthesis is successively put together.

5. The progressive principle in this history is
the ideal activity, presupposed as illimitable. The
task of theoretical philosophy, to explain the
ideality of the boundary, is equivalent to that of
explaining how even the ideal activity, hitherto assumed
to be illimitable, can in fact be limited.

From Original Sensation to Productive Intuition

A

Problem

To explain how the self comes to intuit itself as limited

Solution

1. Inasmuch as the opposing activities of self-consciousness merge in a third, there arises a common product of
them both.
      The question is, what character will this common pro-
duct have? Since it is the outcome of opposing infinite
activities, it will necessarily be finite. It is not the
conflict of these activities conceived of as in motion;
it is a static conflict. It unites opposing tendencies,
but a union of such opposites is equivalent to rest.
Yet it has to be something real, for the opposites, which
prior to synthesis are merely ideal, are to become real
by means of it. It has therefore to be thought of, not
as an annihilation of the two activities by each other,
but rather as an equilibrium to which they reduce one
another, and whose continuance is conditioned by the
persistent rivalry between the two.
      [The product could thus be characterized either as
really inactive, or as inactively real. That which is
real without being active is mere stuff, a mere product
of imagination, which never exists without form, and
emerges even here as no more than a middle term of the
enquiry. --The unintelligibility of the gestation (creation) of matter, even as stuff, is already dissipated
by the explanation given here. All stuff is simply
the expression of an equilibrium between opposing
activities, which mutually reduce themselves to a mere
substrate of activity. (Compare the lever, for example;
the two weights merely act upon the fulcrum, which is
thus the common substrate of their activity.) --This
substrate, moreover, does not arise voluntarily, as it
were, through free production but completely involuntarily, by means of a third activity, which is no less
necessary than the identity of self-consciousness.]
      This third common factor, if it persisted, would in
fact be a construction of the self as such, not in its
capacity as a mere object, but as subject and object
at once. [In the original act of self-consciousness
the self strives to become just a sheer object to
itself, but this it cannot do without (for the observer)
becoming, in that very process, a duality. This

opposition must resolve itself into a common construction
out of both, the subject and the object. Now if the
self intuited itself in this construction, it would
become an object for itself, no longer merely qua object,
but qua subject and object together (as a complete
self).]
2.   But this common factor does not endure.
        a)   Since the ideal activity is itself a party to
this conflict, it must also be limited along with it. The
two activities cannot be related to each other, nor merge
in a common product, without being mutually restricted
each by the other. For the ideal activity not only
denies (or is privative) of the other, but is its real
opposite or negation. It is (so far as we see at present) positive like the other, but in the opposite sense,
and so no less capable than the other of restriction,
too.
        b)   But the ideal activity has been posited as
absolutely illimitable, and so cannot in fact be genuinely
limited, and since the persistence of the common product
is governed by the rivalry of the two activities (1.),
the common product cannot endure either.
        [If the self halted at this first construction, or
if the common product were really able to endure, the
self would be inanimate nature, without sensation or
intuition. That nature rears itself up from dead matter
to sensibility is explicable in natural science (for
which the self is merely nature creating itself anew)
only by the very fact that even there the product of
the first cancellation of the two opposites is unable
to endure.]
3.   We said above (1.), that if the self were to intuit
itself in this common product, it would have a complete
intuition of itself (as subject and object); but this
intuition is impossible, if only because the intuiting
activity is itself included in the construction. But
since the self is an infinite tendency to self-intuition,
it is easy to see that the intuiting activity cannot remain implicated in the construction. From this merger
of the two activities, it is only the real, therefore,
that will remain behind as limited, whereas the ideal
will continue as absolutely unlimited.
4.   Thus the real activity is limited by the mechanism
adduced, though without yet being so for the self as such.
The method of theoretical philosophy requires that what
is posited (for the observer) in the real self shall
also be deduced for the ideal self; and the whole enquiry
accordingly turns to the question, how the real self
can also be limited for the ideal self. At this point
the problem is to explain how the self comes to intuit
itself as limited.
        a)   The real and now limited activity is to be

posited as an activity of the self, that is, a <u>ground</u>
<u>of identity</u> must be pointed out between it and the
<u>self.</u> Since this activity has to be attributed to the
self, and thus at the same time distinguished therefrom,
it must also be possible to point out a <u>ground of dis-</u>
<u>tinction</u> between the two.

What we speak of here as the self is merely the
ideal activity. The grounds of relation and distinction
must therefore be sought in one of the two activities.
Such grounds, however, always lie in the relatum; but
here the ideal activity is at the same time that which
relates, so it is in the real activity that they must
be sought.

The distinguishing ground of the two activities is
the limit posited in the real activity, for the ideal
is the absolutely illimitable, while the real is now the
limited. The relating ground of both must likewise be
sought in the real, i.e., there must actually be something ideal contained therein. The question is how we
can think this. The two are distinguishable only by
means of the limit, for even their opposing directions
are distinguishable only in this way. If the limit be
unposited, the self contains pure identity, in which
nothing can be distinguished. If the limit be posited,
it contains two activities, the limiting and the limited,
the subjective and the objective. The two have therefore one thing at least in common, that originally <u>both</u>
are absolutely nonobjective, that is, since we are as
yet acquainted with no other characteristic of the
ideal, both are equally ideal.

b) Taking this to be so, we may conclude further,
as follows.

The ideal activity, till now unlimited, is the
infinite tendency of the self to become an object to
itself in the real activity. By means of what is ideal
in the real activity (what it turns into an activity of
the <u>self</u>), it can be related to the ideal, and the self
can intuit itself therein (the first time the self comes
to be an object for itself).

But the self cannot intuit the real activity as
identical with itself, without at once finding the
<u>negative element</u> therein, which makes it nonideal, as
something alien to itself. The positive factor, which
makes both into activities of the self, they possess
in common, but the negative belongs to the real alone;
insofar as the intuiting self perceives in the objective the positive factor, intuitant and intuited are
one; insofar as it finds there the negative, finder
and found are no longer one. The finder is the absolutely
illimitable and unlimited; it is the limited that is
found.

The limit itself appears to be something abstracted

from what can and cannot be posited; it seems contingent.
The positive element in the real activity appears as
that from which one cannot abstract. The limit, for
that very reason, can appear only as something found,
i.e., foreign to the self and opposed to its nature.

The self is the absolute ground of all positing.
For something to be opposed to the self means, therefore,
that something is posited which is not posited through
the self. The intuitant must therefore find in the
intuited something (the limitation) which is not posited
through the self as intuitant.

(Here for the first time we may perceive very
clearly the difference between the philosopher's standpoint and that of his object. We, who philosophize,
know that the limitation of the objective has its sole
ground in the intuitant or subjective. The intuiting
self as such does not and cannot know this, as now
becomes clear. Intuiting and limiting are originally
one. But the self cannot simultaneously intuit and
intuit itself as intuiting, and so cannot intuit itself
as limiting either. It is therefore necessary that the
intuitant, which seeks only itself in the objective,
should find the negative element therein to be something
not posited by itself. If the philosopher likewise
maintains this to be the case ((as in dogmatism)), this
is because he continually coalesces with his object
and shares with it the same point of view.)

The negative element is encountered as not posited
by the self, and is for this very reason that which can
in principle only be found (and which is subsequently
transformed into the merely empirical).

That the self finds its limitation to be something
not of its own positing, amounts to saying that the
self finds it posited by something opposed to itself,
namely, the not-self. Thus the self cannot intuit
itself as limited, without intuiting this limitation as
an affection on the part of a not-self.

The philosopher who remains fixed at this standpoint can offer no other explanation for sensation (for
it is self-evident that self-intuition in limitation, as
so far derived, is none other than what in ordinary parlance is called sensation), save that it comes about
through affection by a thing-in-itself. Since sensation gives rise only to the determinacy among presentations, he will also be explaining just this as due to
the said affection. For that in presentation the self
merely takes in, and is pure receptivity, he cannot
maintain, owing to the spontaneity involved therein,
and indeed because even in the things themselves (as
presented), there emerges the unmistakable trace of an
activity of the self. The influence in question will
therefore originate, not from things as we present them

to ourselves, but from things as they are independently
of the presentations. So what is spontaneous in presentation will be regarded as belonging to the self, and
what is receptive will be attributed to things-in-themselves. By the same token, what is positive in objects
will be viewed as a product of the self, and what is
negative (the accidental) as a product of the not-self.

That <u>the self should find itself</u> restricted by something opposed to it, has been derived from the mechanism
of sensation itself. It is a consequence of this, however,
that everything accidental (everything pertaining to
limitation) must appear to us as the inconstructible,
incapable of explanation in terms of the self, whereas
the positive in things can be understood as a construction on the part of the self. However, the proposition
that the <u>self</u> (our object) finds itself limited by an
opposite <u>is</u> restricted by the fact that after all the
self finds this opposite only <u>in itself</u>.

The claim is not that there <u>is</u> in the self something
absolutely opposed to it, but that the <u>self finds</u> something in itself to be absolutely opposed to it. That
the opposite <u>is</u> in the self, means that it is absolutely
opposed to the self; that the self <u>finds</u> something to
be opposed to it, means that it is opposed to the self
only with respect to its finding, and the manner thereof;
and so indeed it is.

The finder is the infinite tendency to self-intuition, wherein the self is purely ideal and absolutely
illimitable. That <u>in which</u> finding takes place is not
the pure but the <u>affected</u> self. Finder and finding-
place are thus themselves opposed. What is found there
is for the finder, but only so far as it is the finder,
something foreign to it.

To put the matter more plainly. The self as
infinite tendency to self-intuition finds in itself
as the intuited, or, what comes to the same thing (since
intuited and intuitant are not distinguished in this
act), finds in itself something alien to it. But what,
then, is found (or felt) in this finding? The felt,
or sensed, is in fact again only the self itself.
Everything sensed is immediately present and absolutely
unmediated, as is already implicit in the concept of
sensation. The self indeed finds something opposed,
but this latter, after all, is only in itself. But
the self contains nothing but activity; so nothing can
be opposed to the self save the negation of activity.
For the self to find something opposed within it means,
therefore, that it finds in itself a suspension of
activity. --When sensing, we never sense the object;
no sensation gives us a concept of an object--it is the
absolute opposite of conception (of action), and thus
a negation of activity. The inference from this negation

to an object as its cause is a much later step, whose grounds can again be shown to lie in the self itself.

Now if the self always senses only its own suspended activity, the sensed is nothing distinct from the self; the latter is merely sensing itself, a fact to which ordinary philosophical parlance has already given expression, in that it speaks of the sensed as something purely subjective.

Additional Remarks

1.   The possibility of sensation rests, according to this deduction,

a) On the upset equilibrium of the two activities. --Thus even in sensation the self cannot intuit itself already as a subject-object, but only as a simple limited object, so that sensation is merely this intuition of self in a state of limitation;

b) On the infinite tendency of the ideal self to intuit itself in the real. This is not possible, save by way of what the ideal activity (the self is nothing else at present) and the real have in common with each other, i.e., the positive element in the latter; the opposite will thus take place by means of the negative element therein. So the self, too, will be able only to find, that is, sense, this negative element in itself.

2.   The reality of sensation depends on the fact that the self does not intuit the sensed as having been posited by itself. It is sensed only insofar as the self intuits it as not posited by the self. So although we can certainly see that the negative is posited by the self, our object, the self, cannot see it, for the very natural reason that to be intuited and to be limited by the self are one and the same. The self is (objectively) limited in that it (subjectively) intuits itself; but now the self cannot simultaneously intuit itself objectively and intuit itself as intuiting, and hence cannot intuit itself as limiting. Upon this impossibility, in the original act of self-consciousness, of at once becoming an object to oneself and of intuiting oneself as becoming such an object, the reality of all sensation depends.

The delusive impression of the limitation as something absolutely foreign to the self, to be explained only through affection on the part of a not-self, therefore arises purely from this, that the act whereby the self becomes limited is a different act from that whereby it intuits itself as limited; not in time, to be sure, since everything that we apprehend successively is simultaneous in the self, but certainly different in nature.

The act <u>by which the self limits itself</u> is none
other than that of self-consciousness, and to this we
must confine ourselves, as the basis for explanation of
all limitation, if only because it is utterly inconceivable how any affection from without can transform itself
into a presentation or into knowledge. Supposing, even,
that an object were to act upon the self as if upon an
object, such an affection could still only bring forth
something homogeneous in every case, <u>i.e.</u>, again an
objective determinacy merely. For the law of causality
holds only between things of the same sort (things of
the same world), and does not extend from one world
to the other. So how a primordial being can transform
itself into knowledge, would be conceivable only if it
could be shown that even presentation was itself a kind
of being; and in fact this is the explanation offered by
materialism, a system that would have to be congenial
to the philosopher if only it actually performed what
it promises. However, as materialism stands so far, it
is altogether unintelligible, and as rendered intelligible,
it no longer differs, in fact, from transcendental
idealism. --To explain thinking as a material phenomenon
is possible only by turning matter itself into a phantom,
the mere modification of an intelligence, whose common
functions are thought and matter. Materialism itself
thereby reverts to the intelligent as that which is
primary. To be sure, it is no less out of the question to explain being from knowing by treating the
former as the effect of the latter; between the two there
can be no <u>causal</u> relation whatsoever, and the twain can
never meet, unless they are originally one, as they are
in the self. Being (matter), regarded as productive,
is a knowing, and knowing regarded as a product is a
being. If knowing is productive as such, it must be
productive through and through, not in part merely;
nothing can enter into knowing from without, for everything that exists is identical with knowing and there is
nothing outside it. If one factor in presentation resides
in the self, the other must do likewise, for in the
object both are inseparable. Supposing, for example,
that only stuff pertains to things, then before it
reaches the self this stuff must be without form, at
least in the transition from thing to presentation,
which is assuredly inconceivable.
     But now if the original limitation is posited through
the self as such, how does the latter come to sense it,
that is, envisage it as something opposed to itself?
Everything real about cognition attaches to sensation,
and a philosophy that cannot explain sensation is already,
on that very account, an abortive one. For the truth
of all cognition undoubtedly rests on the feeling of
compulsion which accompanies it. Being (objectivity)

is always merely an expression of a limitation of the
intuiting or producing activity. There is a cube in
this portion of space, means nothing else but that in
this part of space my intuition can be active only in
the form of a cube. The ground of all reality in cognition is thus the ground of limitation independent of
intuition. A system that abolishes this ground would be
a dogmatic transcendent idealism. Transcendental idealism
is in part contested upon grounds which are valid only
against that form of it in which there is simply no
seeing how it could require refutation, or can ever have
entered a human head. If it be a dogmatic idealism to
maintain that sensation is not explicable by impressions
from without, that presentation contains nothing, even
of an accidental kind, pertaining to a thing-in-itself,
and that one cannot ın fact even think in rational terms
of any such impression upon the self, then this, at
all events, is the idealism we profess. The reality of
knowledge would, however, only demolish an idealism
which sought to bring forth the original limitation
freely and with consciousness, whereas the transcendental version leaves us as little freedom in that regard
as even the realist could ever desire. It claims only
that the self never senses the thing itself (for nothing
of the kind yet exists at this stage), nor even anything
passing from the thing into the self; what it senses
immediately is only itself, its own suspended activity.
Nor does our idealism omit to explain why the self is
necessarily unaware of this, in that we intuit this
restriction, posited only through the ideal activity,
as something wholly alien to the self.

      This explanation is furnished in the proposition
that the act whereby the self is objectively limited is
a different act from that whereby it is limited for
itself. The act of self-consciousness explains only
how the objective activity comes to be limited. But
the self, insofar as it is ideal, consists in a boundless reproduction of itself (vis sui reproductiva in
infinitum); the ideal activity knows of no limitation,
in lighting upon the original boundary; through it,
therefore, the self merely finds itself to be limited.
The reason why the self finds itself limited in this
action cannot lie in the present action, but rather in
one that is past. So the self in its present action is
limited without its consent, but that it finds itself
so limited is also the whole of what is contained in
sensation, and is the condition of all objectivity in
knowledge. So in order that the limitation shall appear
to us as a thing independent of ourselves, provision is
made for this purpose, through the mechanism of sensation, that the act whereby all limitation is posited,
as the condition of all consciousness, does not itself
come to consciousness.

3. <u>All limitation arises for us only through the act
of self-consciousness</u>. It is necessary to dwell some-
what further on this proposition, since it is undoubtedly
this which gives most trouble in what we have to say.

The original necessity of becoming conscious of
oneself, of reverting upon oneself, is already limitation,
but it is limitation total and complete.

We do not have a new limitation arising for every
individual presentation; with the synthesis contained
in self-consciousness, limitation is posited once and
for all, and it is this one original limitation within
which the self constantly remains, from which it never
emerges, and which merely develops, in individual
presentations, in one way or another.

The difficulties encountered in this thesis are
grounded, for the most part, on a failure to distinguish
between original and derived limitation.

The original limitation, which we have in common
with all rational beings, consists in the fact of our
intrinsic finitude. In virtue of this we are distinguished, not from other rational beings, but from the
infinite. But all limitation is necessarily <u>determinate</u>
in nature; it is unthinkable that a limitation should
arise at all, without the simultaneous occurrence of a
determinacy thereof; the determinate must therefore arise
as such through one and the same act as that of limitation as such. The act of self-consciousness is an
absolute synthesis; all conditions of consciousness
arise at once through this one act, and so too does the
determinate limitation, which is no less a condition of
consciousness than limitation as such.

That I am limited as such follows directly from the
self's unending tendency to become an object to itself;
limitation as such is therefore explicable, but it leaves
the determinacy entirely free, even though both arise
through one and the same act. Both taken together, that
the determinate limitation cannot be determined through
limitation as such, and yet that it arises along with
the latter, <u>simultaneously</u> and through one act, means
that it is one thing that <u>philosophy can neither conceive
nor explain</u>. As surely, indeed, as I am limited as
such, I must be so determinately, and this determinacy
must reach into the infinite, for this infinitely outreaching determinacy constitutes my entire individuality;
it is not, therefore the fact that I <u>am</u> determinately
limited which cannot be explained, but rather the <u>manner</u>
of this limitation itself. For example, it can certainly
be deduced in general that I belong to a determinate
order of intelligences, but not that I belong to precisely
this order; that I occupy a determinate position in
this order, but not that it is precisely this one. It
can thus be deduced as necessary that there is in

general a system of our presentations, but not that we
are restricted to this particular sphere of presentations. To be sure, if we already presuppose the determinate limitation, the limitation of individual presentations can be derived from this; the determinate limitation is then merely that wherein we comprehend the
limitation of all individual presentations, and so can
derive it again from them; for example, if we once presuppose that this particular part of the universe, and
this particular planet therein, are the immediate
sphere of our outer intuition, then it can certainly be
inferred that within this determinate limitation these
particular intuitions are necessary. For if we could
make comparison of our entire planetary system, we should
undoubtedly be able to deduce why our earth is composed
of precisely these materials and no others, why it
displays precisely these phenomena and no others, and
why, therefore, once this sphere of intuition is presupposed, it is just these intuitions and no others
that occur in the series thereof. Having once been
projected into this sphere through the entire synthesis
of our consciousness, nothing will be able to occur
therein which might contradict it, or be other than
necessary. This follows from the primordial consistency
of our mind, which is so great that every appearance
now actually presented to us, once this determinate
limitation is presupposed, is necessary to such a
degree that, if it did not occur, the entire system
of our presentations would be internally self-contradictory.

B

Problem:

To explain how the self intuits itself as sensing

Explanation

The self has sensation, in that it intuits itself as
originally limited. This intuition is an activity, but
the self cannot at once both intuit, and intuit itself
as intuiting. In this act, therefore, it is not aware
of any activity at all; so in sensation the concept of
an action is nowhere entertained, but only that of a
passivity. In the present moment, the self is <u>for</u>
<u>itself</u> merely the <u>sensed</u>. For the only thing sensed
as such is its real, restricted activity, which does
indeed become an object to the self. It is also that
which senses, but only for us who philosophize, not for
itself. The opposition simultaneously posited along

with sensation (that between self and thing-in-itself)
is for this reason again posited, not for the self
itself, but only for us in the self.

This phase of self-consciousness will hereafter be
called that of original sensation. It is that wherein the
self intuits itself in the original limitation, without
being aware of this intuition, or the latter itself again
becoming an object for the self. In this phase the
self is entirely rooted upon the sensed, and, as it were,
lost therein.

More precisely, then, the problem is this: how
does the self, which was hitherto purely sensed, become
both sensing and sensed at once?

From the original act of self-consciousness, only
the fact of limitation could be deduced. Were the self
to be limited for itself, it would have to intuit
itself as such; this intuition, which reconciles the
unlimited self with the limited, was the act of sensation, though for reasons given, all that remains of this
in consciousness is the mere vestige of a passivity.
This act of sensing must therefore itself in turn be
made into an object, and it has to be shown how this,
too, enters consciousness. It is easy to foresee that
we shall be able to solve this problem only through a
new act.

This is fully in accordance with the progress of
the synthetic method. --Two opposites a and b (subject
and object) are united by the act x, but x contains a
new opposition, c and d (sensing and sensed), and so the
act x itself again becomes an object; it is itself
explicable only through a new act = z, which perhaps
again contains an opposition, and so on.

Solution

I

The self senses when it finds in itself something opposed
to it, namely, since the self is mere activity, a real
negation of activity, or state of being affected. But
to be that which senses, for itself, the (ideal) self
must posit in itself that passivity which till now has
been present only in the real; and this can undoubtedly
occur only through activity.

We are here at the very point around which empiricism
has constantly circulated without being able to explain
it. For the external impression explains to me only the
passivity of sensation; at most it explains a return
action upon the impinging object, as it might be after
the fashion of an elastic body repelling another that
strikes it, or a mirror reflecting the light that falls

upon it; but it does not explain the return action, the
reversion of the self upon itself, or how the latter
relates the external impression to itself as self, or
intuitant. The object never reverts into itself, and
relates no impression to itself; for that very reason
it is without sensation.

Thus the self cannot possess sensation, for itself,
without being intrinsically active. Now the self that is
active here cannot be the limited self, but only the
illimitable. But this ideal self is unlimited only in
contrast to the objective, now limited, activity, and
thus only insofar as it overleaps the boundary. If
we reflect upon what happens in every sensation, we
shall find that in each there must be something that
knows about the impression, but is yet independent
thereof and goes out beyond it; for even the judgment
that the impression proceeds from an object presupposes
an activity which does not attach to the impression, but
is directed, rather, to something beyond the impression.
The self does not sense, therefore, unless it contains
an activity that goes out beyond the limit. It is by
means of this that the self, to have sensation for itself,
has to take up the alien element into itself (qua ideal);
but this alien element is itself again within the self,
for it is the latter's suspended activity. For the sake
of what follows, the relationship of these two activities must now be more exactly determined. The unlimited
activity is originally ideal, like every activity of
the self, including therefore the real as well, but is
in opposition to the real only insofar as it overleaps
the boundary. The limited activity is real insofar as
there is reflection upon the fact that it is limited,
but ideal insofar as we reflect that it is in principle
the same as the ideal; it is real or ideal, depending on
how it is regarded. It is evident, moreover, that the
ideal is distinguishable as intrinsically ideal only
in contrast to the real, and vice versa, as can be
confirmed by the simplest experiment; the way, for
example, that a fictitious object is distinguishable as
such only in contrast to the real, and conversely, that
every real object is distinguishable as such only in
contrast to a fictitious one imported into the judgment.
Taking this for granted, the following conclusions can
be drawn.

1. That the self should have sensation for itself,
means that it should actively take up the opposite into
itself. But this opposite is nothing else but the limit
or checkingpoint, and the latter resides only in the real
activity, which is distinguishable from the ideal only
by the limit. That the self should appropriate the
opposite to itself means, therefore, that it should
take this up into its ideal activity. Now this is not

possible, <u>unless the limit falls within the ideal
activity</u>, and this, too, would have to come about by
way of an activity of the self itself. (As now becomes
increasingly clear, the whole of theoretical philosophy
has this problem only to solve, namely how the restriction becomes ideal, or how the ideal (intuitant)
activity also comes to be limited. It was evident in
advance, that the disturbed equilibrium (above, A.2)
between ideal and real activity would have to be restored,
as surely as the self is a self. <u>How</u> it is to be restored
is our sole remaining problem.) --But the limit falls
only upon the line of the <u>real</u> activity, and conversely,
just that activity of the <u>self</u> is the real one, on which
the limit falls. Apart from the limit, moreover, the
ideal and real activities are originally indistinguishable,
for it is only the limit which marks the point of separation between them. Thus the activity is only ideal,
<u>i.e.</u>, only to be distinguished as ideal, beyond the
boundary, or insofar as it oversteps the limit.

That the limit shall fall within the ideal activity
therefore means that the limit is to fall beyond the
limit, which is a manifest contradiction. This contradiction must be resolved.

2.   The ideal self could go about to <u>abolish</u> the
limit, and in that it did so, the limit would also
necessarily fall upon the line of the ideal activity;
but the limit is not to be done away with; it is to be
taken up <u>qua</u> limit, that is, unabolished, into the
ideal activity.

Alternatively, the ideal self could limit itself,
and thus <u>engender</u> a limit. --But this, too, would provide
no explanation of what has to be explained. For in that
case the limit posited in the ideal self would not be
identical with that posited in the real, which it is
supposed to be. Even if we were willing to assume that
the hitherto purely ideal self should become an object
to itself, and thereby limited, we should still have
failed to advance a single step thereby, and would
indeed have been thrown back to the first stage of
our enquiry, where the hitherto purely ideal self first
separates and, as it were, decomposes itself into a
subjective and an objective.

There is therefore nothing for it but to find a mean
between abolishing and engendering. Such a mean is
<u>determining</u>. That which I am to determine must be
present independently of myself. But in that I determine it, it again becomes, through that very determination, a thing dependent on myself. Moreover, in that
I determine an indeterminate, I abolish it as indeterminate and engender it as determinate.

So the ideal activity will have to <u>determine</u> the
limit.

Two questions immediately arise at this point:

a) What does it then <u>mean</u> to say that the limit is determined through ideal <u>activity</u>?

Nothing is now left of the limit in consciousness, save the vestige of a passivity. Since the self in sensation does not become conscious of the <u>act</u>, only the result remains behind. This passivity has remained till now completely indeterminate. But passivity <u>as such</u> is no more thinkable than limitation as such. All passivity is <u>determinate</u>, as surely as it is possible only through a negation of activity. The limit would thus be determined if the passivity were so.

This sheer passivity is the raw stuff of sensation, that which is purely sensed. The passivity would be determined if the self were to accord it a determinate sphere--a particular field of operation (if this inappropriate expression may be allowed here). The self would accordingly be passive only within this sphere, and active outside it.

The act of determining would thus be a producing, and the stuff of this producing the original passivity.

But the second question now arises:

b) How would it be possible to think of this producing itself?

The self cannot produce the sphere without being active, but it can equally little produce it as a sphere of limitation without itself being limited by that very act. --In that the self is the limitant, it is active, but insofar as it is the limitant of limitation, it itself becomes something limited.

This act of producing is thus the most absolute union of activity and passivity. The self is passive in such an act, for it cannot determine the limitation without already presupposing it. But conversely also, the (ideal) self is limited here only insofar as it goes about to determine the limitation. The act therefore contains an activity that presupposes a passivity, and conversely, a passivity that presupposes activity.

Before ourselves reflecting further upon this union of passivity and activity in a single act, we may look to see what we should actually have gained by such an act, were it really capable of being exhibited in the self.

In the preceding state of consciousness, the self was merely <u>something sensed for itself</u>, not something that senses. In the present act it becomes for itself <u>something that senses</u>. It becomes an object as such to itself, since it is limited. But it becomes such an object as active (as sensing), since it is limited only in its own limiting.

The (ideal) self thus becomes an object to itself, <u>qua limited in its activity</u>.

The self is only limited here, insofar as it is
active. Empiricism has no trouble in explaining impressions, since it completely overlooks the fact that
the self, in order to become limited as self (i.e., to
achieve sensation), must already be active. --But again
the self is only active here insofar as it is already
limited, and just such a mutual restrictedness of
activity and passivity is envisaged in sensation, so
far as it is conjoined with consciousness.

But precisely because the self here comes for itself
to be sensing, it perhaps ceases to be something sensed,
just as in the preceding act, because it was sensed, it
could not be a sensing for itself. The self as sensed
would in that case be expelled from consciousness, and
something else opposed to it would take it place.

And so it turns out. The act derived is a producing.
Now in this producing the ideal self is completely free.
Hence the reason why it becomes limited, in the producing
of this sphere, cannot lie in itself, but must be
located outside it. The sphere is a production of the
self, but the limit of the sphere is not a production of
the self in its capacity as producer; and since, in the
present stage of consciousness, the latter does nothing
but produce, the limit is no product of the self at all.
It is thus a mere boundary between the self and that
which is opposed thereto, the thing-in-itself; so it is
now neither in nor out of the self, but is merely the
common point of contact between the self and its opposite.

Thus if only this act were itself intelligible, in
respect of its possibility, we should also, by means of
it, have deduced that opposition between self and thing-
in-itself--the whole, in short, of what was previously
posited only for the philosopher--and deduced it even
for the self itself.

                          II

We see now, indeed, from this whole discussion, that the
proposed solution to the problem is assuredly the right
one; but this solution itself is not yet comprehensible,
and we may doubtless still be in want of certain middle
terms thereof.

The solution discloses, at all events, that the
ideal self cannot be passive without already being
previously active, and hence that a mere impression upon
the ideal (intuitant) self can in no case account for
sensation; but it also appears that the ideal self in
turn cannot be active, in the manner defined, without
already being passive; it appears, in a word, that
activity and passivity mutually presuppose one another
within this act.

Now it may indeed be that the final act, whereby
sensation is posited completely in the self, is of this
sort. But between it and the original sensation there
must still lie intermediate terms, since with this act
we already see ourselves plunged into that irresolvable
circle which has ever bemused philosophers, and which we
ourselves, if we wish to remain true to our previous
course, must first conjure up before our eyes, in order
to gain a complete grasp of it. That we must fall into
this circle, has assuredly emerged from the foregoing;
but not how. And to that extent our whole problem is
really not yet solved. The problem was to explain how
the original limit passes over into the ideal self. But
it is plain that such a primary transition has not been
made intelligible by what has gone before. We explained
this transition by a limiting of limitation, which we
attributed to the ideal self. --But how does the self
as such even manage to limit a passivity? --We ourselves
admitted that this activity already presupposed a
passivity in the ideal self, just as, conversely, to be
sure, this passivity also presupposes that activity.
We must plumb the origins of this circle to the bottom,
and only so can we hope for a complete solution to our
problem.

We return to the contradiction first established.
The self is everything that it is, solely for itself.
It is thus also ideal only for itself, ideal only insofar
as it posits or recognizes itself to be such. If by
ideal activity we mean only the activity of the self
as such, so far as it simply proceeds therefrom and is
grounded solely therein, the self is originally nothing
but ideal activity. If the boundary falls within the
self, it falls assuredly within the ideal activity
thereof. But this ideal activity, which is limited, and
insofar as it is limited, is not recognized as ideal,
precisely because it is limited. We recognize as ideal
that activity only which goes, and insofar as it goes,
beyond the boundary. This bound-breaking activity
has therefore to be bounded, a contradiction already
implicit in the requirement that the self as sensing
(i.e., as subject) shall become an object; and there is
no resolving this contradiction unless it be that bound-
breaking and becoming bounded are one and the same for
the ideal self, or unless the self become real,
precisely through its being ideal.

Suppose this were so; suppose that the self were to
be limited by its mere overstepping of the limit, it
would in thus overstepping, still be ideal, and hence
qua ideal, or in its ideality, be real and limited.

The question is, how anything of the sort is conceivable.

This problem also we shall be able to resolve only
through our having posited the tendency to self-intuition
as an infinite one. --Of the original sensation, nothing
remains in the self save the limit, purely as such. The
self is not ideal for us save insofar as it oversteps the
limit, in the very act of sensing. But it cannot recognize itself as ideal (i.e., as sensing), without opposing
its activity which has exceeded the limit to that which
is confined therein, namely the real activity. The two
are distinguishable only in their reciprocal opposition
and relation to one another. But this in turn is possible only through a third activity, which is both inside
and outside the boundary at once.

This third activity, at once both ideal and real,
is undoubtedly the producing activity inferred in section
I, wherein activity and passivity were to be reciprocally
conditioned by each other.

Thus we are now able to establish the intermediate
terms in that producing activity, and to derive the
latter in full. --They are as follows:

1. The self, qua infinite tendency to intuit itself,
was already sensing at the previous stage, that is intuiting itself as limited. But a limit lies only
between two opposites, so the self could not intuit
itself as limited without necessarily reaching out to
something beyond the boundary, i.e., overstepping the
limit. Such a limit-exceeding activity was already
posited for us along with sensation, but it also has to
be posited for the self itself, and only to that extent
will the self become an object to itself as sensing.

2. Not only must the hitherto objective element
in the self become an object, but also the subjective
as well. This occurs in that the limit-exceeding activity
becomes an object to the self. But the self cannot intuit
an activity as exceeding the limit without opposing and
relating it to another which does not. This self-intuition in both its ideal and real activities, the one
limit-passing and sensing, the other limit-restricted
and sensed, is possible only through a third activity,
at once confined within the limit and extending beyond
it, at once real and ideal, and it is in this activity
that the self becomes an object to itself as having
sensation. Insofar as the self senses, it is ideal;
insofar as it is an object, real; that activity,
therefore, whereby, as sensing, it becomes an object,
must be simultaneously both ideal and real.

The problem of explaining how the self intuits
itself as sensing, could thus also be formulated as one
of explaining how, in one and the same activity, the self
becomes both ideal and real. This simultaneously ideal
and real activity is that producing activity we postulated, wherein activeness and passiveness are reciprocally

conditioned by each other. The genesis of this third
activity thus explains for us, at the same time, the
origin of that circle, which we saw ourselves to have
fallen into with the self (I.).

The genesis of this activity is, however, as follows.
In the first act (that of self-consciousness), the self
is intuited-as-such, and in being intuited is thereby
limited. In the second act it is intuited, not as such,
but determinately, as limited; yet it cannot be intuited
as limited, unless the ideal activity oversteps the
boundary. Hence there arises in the self an opposition
between two activities which, as activities of one and
the same self, are automatically united in a third, in
which there has necessarily to be a mutual conditioning
of affectedness and activity, or in which the self is
ideal only insofar as it is simultaneously real, and
vice versa; and by this, then, the self as sensing
becomes an object to itself.

3. In this third activity the self is vacillating
between the activity that has passed the limit and that
which is still confined. Through this vacillation of the
self, they acquire a reciprocal relation to each other,
and become fixated as opposites.

It may be asked:

a) what the ideal activity becomes fixated as? So
far as it is fixated at all, it ceases to be pure
activity. It becomes in the same action opposed to
the activity confined within the limit, and is thus
apprehended as an activity fixated but set in opposition to the real self. So far as it is apprehended as
fixated, it acquires an ideal substrate; so far as it
is apprehended as an activity opposed to the real self,
it itself becomes--but only in this opposition--a real
activity; it becomes the activity of something really
opposed to the real self. But this real opponent to
the real self is nothing other than the thing-in-itself.

Thus the ideal activity, having passed the limit
and now become an object, at this point disappears as
such from consciousness and is transformed into the
thing-in-itself.

The following observation is easily made. The sole
ground of the original limitation is, by the foregoing,
the self's intuitant or ideal activity; but this latter
is here reflected, as ground of limitation, to the self
itself, though not indeed as an activity thereof, for
the self is now simply real; rather, as something opposed
to the self. The thing-in-itself is therefore nothing
else but the shadow of the ideal activity, now over the
boundary, which is thrown back to the self by intuition,
and is to that extent itself a product of the self. The
dogmatist, who regards the thing-in-itself as real, is
in the same position as that now currently occupied

by the self. The thing-in-itself arises for it through
an action; the outcome remains behind, but not the action
that gave rise to it. Thus the self is originally
ignorant of the fact that this opposite is its own
product, and must remain in the same ignorance so long
as it stays enclosed in the magic circle which self-
consciousness describes about the self; only the
philosopher, in breaking out of the circle, can penetrate behind the illusion.

The deduction has now progressed to the point at
which something outside the self is for the first time
present to the self as such. In the current action the
self is directed for the first time to something beyond
the limit, and this latter is now nothing but the common
point of contact between the self and its opposite. In
the original sensation, only the limit was disclosed;
here, something beyond the limit, whereby the self
explains the limit to itself. It is to be expected
that the limit also will thereby acquire an altered
significance, as will soon appear. The original sensation, in which the self was merely the sensed, is
transformed into an intuition, in which the self for
the first time becomes for itself that which senses,
but for that very reason ceases to be the sensed. For
the self that intuits itself as sensing, the sensed is
the (previously sensing) ideal activity which has crossed
the boundary, but is now no longer intuited as an
activity of the self. The original limitant of the real
is the self itself, but it cannot enter consciousness
as a limiting factor without transforming itself into
the thing-in-itself. The third activity, here deduced,
is that in which the limited and the limitant are
simultaneously separated and gathered together.

It still remains to enquire
b) what becomes in this action of the real or
restricted activity?

The ideal activity has transformed itself into the
thing-in-itself, and so the real will transform itself
through the same action into the opposite of the thing-
in-itself, namely the self-in-itself. The self, which
was hitherto always both subject and object at once, is
now for the first time something in itself; the
originally subjective aspect of the self has been
carried over the boundary, and is there intuited as
the thing-in-itself; what remains within the boundary
is the purely objective aspect of the self.

Thus the deduction now stands at the point where
the self and its opposite separate, not just for the
philosopher merely, but for the self itself. The original
duality of self-consciousness is now as it were divided
between the self and the thing-in-itself. From the
present action of the self there is left over, therefore,

not a mere passivity, but two opposites really opposed
to each other, on which the determinacy of sensation
depends; and thereby the problem of how the self comes
to have sensation for itself is first completely solved.
A problem that until now no philosophy could answer, and
least of all empiricism. In passing, when the latter
vainly endeavors to explain the passage of the impression
from the purely passive self into the thinking and
active one, the difficulty of the task is one that he
actually shares with the idealist. For wherever the
passivity may come from, whether from an impression of
the thing outside us, or from the primordial mechanism
of the mind itself, it is still always passivity, and
the transition to be explained is the same. The marvel
of productive intuition resolves this difficulty, and
without this there is no solving it at all. For it is
manifest that the self cannot intuit itself as sensing,
without intuiting itself as opposed to itself, and
simultaneously in limitant and delimited activity--in
that mutual determination of activeness and passiveness
which arises in the manner indicated; save only that
this opposition in the self itself, which only the
philosopher perceives, appears to his object, the self,
as an opposition between itself and something outside
it.
     4. The product of the oscillation between real and
ideal activity is the self-in-itself on the one hand,
and the thing-in-itself on the other, and both are the
factors of the intuition now to be derived. We must
first ask how these two are determined by the action
already inferred.
     a) That the self is determined by this action as a
pure objective, has just been proved. But it only
becomes so in the reciprocal relationship in which it
now stands with the thing-in-itself. For were the
limitant still within it, it would be determined merely
through appearing so to itself, whereas it now is
determined in itself and as it were independently of
itself; exactly as is demanded by the dogmatist, who
in fact only elevates himself to this point of view.
     (It is not a matter of which self is active in this
process, for this self is ideal in its limitation, and
conversely, limited in its ideality, neither subject nor
object alone, since it embraces within itself the whole
((complete)) self; save only that what belongs to the
subject appears as thing-in-itself, and what belongs
to the object, as self-in-itself.)
     b) The thing is, to start with, wholly and solely
determined as the absolute opposite to the self. But
now the self is determined as activity, and so the thing
is likewise determined merely as a counterpart to the
activity of the self. But all setting in opposition

is determinate; it is therefore impossible for the thing
to be opposed to the self without it being simultaneously
limited. Here we discover what it means to say that
the self must also in turn limit the passivity (I). The
passivity is limited by the fact that its condition, the
thing, is limited. The limitation in limitation, which
we saw to arise at the very outset along with limitation
in general, in fact enters consciousness only with the
opposition between self and thing-in-itself. The thing
is determined as an activity opposed to the self, and
hence as the ground of limitation in general; as itself
a limited activity, and hence as the ground of limitation
in particular. Now what limits the thing? The same
boundary which also limits the self. The greater the
amount of activity in the self, the greater the amount
of nonactivity in the thing, and vice versa. Only
through this communal limiting do they both engage in
interaction. That one and the same boundary limits
both self and thing, i.e., that the thing is limited
only so far as the self is, and the self only so far as
the thing is, in short, this interdetermination, in the
present act, of activity and passivity in the self, is
perceived only by the philosopher; in the act that
follows, the self will see it too, but, as might be
expected, in a very different fashion. The limit is
still always the same as that originally posited by the
self itself, save only that it now no longer appears
simply as the boundary of the self, but also as that of
the thing. The thing acquires only so much reality as
was wiped out in the self itself through its original
act. But just as with the self itself, so also will the
thing appear to it as limited without its concurrence,
and, to link this result again to the point we started
from, here too, therefore, the ideal activity becomes
limited in direct consequence of the fact that it oversteps the boundary and is intuited as having done so.
      It may readily be inferred from this how, by this
act,
      c) the limit becomes determined. Since it is
limit for both self and thing at once, its ground can
be no more in the one than in the other; for if it lay
in the self, the latter's activity would not be conditioned by passivity; if it lay in the thing, its
passivity would not be conditioned by activity; in
short, the act would not be what it is. Since the ground
of the limit lies neither in self nor thing, it lies
nowhere; it exists absolutely because it exists, and
is as it is because that is how it is. Hence, in relation to both self and thing it will appear as absolutely
contingent. That item in intuition is the boundary,
therefore, which is absolutely contingent for self and
thing alike; a more accurate determination or account

of it is not yet possible here, and can be given only
in the sequel.
    5. That oscillation, whose residues are the self
and thing-in-itself as opposites, cannot persist, for
by this opposition a contradiction is posited in the self
itself (that self which oscillates between the two).
But the self is absolute identity. As certainly, therefore, as <u>self</u> = <u>self</u> there arises automatically and
necessarily a third activity, in which the two opposites
are brought into a relative equilibrium.
    <u>All</u> activity of the self proceeds from a contradic-
tion therein. For since the self is absolute identity,
it requires no ground determining it to activity other
than a duality in itself, and the persistence of all
mental activity depends upon the continuance, <u>i.e.</u>,
the constant reemergence, of this contradiction.
    Here indeed, the contradiction appears as an opposi-
tion between the self and something outside it, but is
by derivation a contradiction between ideal and real
activity. If the self is to intuit (or sense) itself in
its original confinement, it must simultaneously press
on out beyond the confinement. Restriction, necessity,
compulsion--these are all felt only in opposition to an
unconfined activity. Nor is anything actual in the
absence of imagination. --Thus already with sensation
itself a contradiction is posited in the self. It is
at once confined and pressing out over the boundary.
    This contradiction cannot be got rid of, but nor
again can it persist. Hence it can be unified only by
means of a third activity.
    This third activity is essentially <u>intuitant</u>, for
it is the <u>ideal</u> self that is here thought of as becoming
limited.
    But this intuition is an intuiting of intuition, for
it is an intuiting of sensation. --Sensing is already
itself an intuiting, but an intuiting of the <u>first</u> order
(hence the simplicity of all sensations, the impossibility of defining them, for all definition is synthetic).
The intuiting now derived is thus an intuiting of the
<u>second</u> order, or, what comes to the same, a <u>productive
intuition</u>.

C

Theory of Productive Intuition

Introductory

<u>Descartes</u> the physicist said: give me matter and motion,
and from that I will fashion you the universe. The
transcendental philosopher says: give me a nature made
up of opposed activities, of which one reaches out into

the infinite, while the other tries to intuit itself in
this infinitude, and from that I will bring forth for
you the intelligence, with the whole system of its
presentations. Every other science presupposes the
intelligence as already complete; the philosopher
observes it in its genesis, and brings it into being,
so to speak, before his eyes.

The self is but the ground upon which the intelligence, with all its determinations, is delineated. The
original act of self-consciousness explains to us only
how the self is restricted in regard to its objective
activity, or in its original striving; but not how it
is confined in its subjective activity, or in knowing.
It is productive intuition which first transfers the
original limit into the ideal activity, and is the self's
first step towards intelligence.

The necessity of productive intuition, here
systematically deduced from the entire mechanism of the
self, has got to be derived, as a general condition of
knowing as such, directly from the concept thereof; for
if all knowing borrows its reality from an immediate
cognition, it is this alone that is to be met with in
intuition; whereas concepts, in fact, are merely shadows
of reality, projected through a reproductive power, the
understanding, which itself presupposes a higher power,
having no original outside itself, and which produces
from within itself by a primordial force. Hence an
improper idealism, a system, that is, which turns all
knowledge into illusion, would have to be one which
eliminated all immediacy in our cognition, e.g., by
positing external originals independent of our presentations; whereas a system which seeks the origin of things
in an activity of the mind that is ideal and real at
once, would have, precisely because it is the most perfect idealism, to be at the same time the most perfect
realism. For if the most perfect realism is that which
cognizes things in themselves and immediately, it is
possible only in an order which perceives in things its
own reality merely, confined by its own activity. For
such an order, as the indwelling soul of things, would
permeate them as its own immediate organism and--just
as the master has the most perfect knowledge of his work--
would fathom their inner mechanism from the first.

As against this, the attempt may be made to explain
the evidence of sensory intuition upon the hypothesis
that there is something or other in our intuition which
arrives there through a check or impression. For a
start, however, a check upon the percipient will not
convey to him the object itself, but only the effect
thereof. But now in intuition it is not the mere effect
of an object, but the object itself that is immediately
present. Now as to how the object is annexed to the

impression, one might perhaps try to explain it by way
of inference, were it not that in the intuition itself
we find no trace whatever of an inference or mediation
through concepts such as those of cause and effect, and
were it not the object itself, rather than a mere product of syllogism, that stands before us in intuition.
Alternatively, one might explain the accession of the
object to sensation by means of a productive faculty, set
in motion by an external impulse; but that would never
explain the immediate conveyance into the self of the
external object which is the source of the impression;
and we should then have to derive the impression or check
from a force able to take complete possession of the soul,
and as it were to pervade it. It is thus ever and again
the most characteristic procedure of dogmatism to weave
a veil of mystery about the origin of presentations from
external things; to speak of it as though it were a
revelation, making all further explanation impossible;
or to account for the inconceivable emergence of anything so strange as a presentation from the impress of
an external object by ascribing it to a force, for which,
as for God (the one immediate object of our knowledge,
according to this view), even the impossible is possible.

It seems to have never even remotely occurred to
the dogmatist, that in a discipline such as philosophy
nothing can be presupposed, and that here, indeed, even
those concepts that are otherwise the most common and
familiar require to be deduced before any others. Thus
the distinction between what comes from without and
what comes from within is one that undoubtedly stands
in need of justification and explanation. But in the
very process of explaining it I posit a region of
consciousness where this separation does not yet exist,
and where inner and outer worlds are conceived as interfused. So certain is it that a philosophy, which does
but make it an absolute rule to leave nothing unproved
and without derivation, will arrive, almost without
willing it and through its own mere consistency, at
idealism.

No dogmatist has yet undertaken to describe or
depict the nature and manner of this external influence;
though this, in all fairness, could have been expected,
as necessarily demanded of a theory upon which nothing
less than the whole reality of knowledge depends. One
would have indeed to include here those gradual sub-
limations of matter into spirituality, whereby one thing
only is forgotten, namely that the spirit is everlastingly
an island, never to be reached from matter without a
leap, however roundabout the approaches may be.

There is no holding out long against such demands
with the pretext of absolute unintelligibility, for the
urge to comprehend this mechanism continually recurs,

and if a philosophy, which boasts of leaving nothing
unproved, pretends to have actually discovered this
mechanism, we should be bound to find something unintelligible in the explanation itself. Yet everything
unintelligible therein emerges solely from the common
standpoint, to abandon which is the first condition of
all understanding in philosophy. Anyone, e.g., for whom
in all the activity of the mind there is nowhere anything
unconscious, and no region outside that of consciousness,
will no more understand how the intelligence can forget
itself in its products, than how the artist can be lost
in his work. For him there is nothing other than the
ordinary moral bringing-forth, and nowhere any producing
in which necessity is united with freedom.

   All productive intuition springs from a perpetual
contradiction; the intelligence, which has no other urge
but to revert into its identity, is thereby placed under
a constant compulsion to activity, and is no less bound
and fettered in the manner of its producing than nature
in its engenderings appears to be; so much has already
been partially deduced in the foregoing, and will be
further elucidated by means of the full theory of
intuition.

   In connection with the term 'intuition', it should
be noted that nothing at all of a sensory kind is to be
imported into the concept, as though, for example, seeing
alone were an intuiting, notwithstanding that language
has exclusively credited it with being so; for which,
indeed a reason can be given, and pretty deep it lies.
The thoughtless multitude accounts for seeing by means
of lightrays; but what is a lightray, in fact? It is
itself already a seeing, and the original seeing at
that, namely intuition itself.

   The whole theory of productive intuition proceeds
from the proposition already derived and demonstrated:
in that the out-of-bounds and the in-bounds activities
are related to one another, they are fixed as opposed to
each other, the one as thing, the other as self-in-itself.

   The question might straightway arise at this point,
as to how in fact this ideal activity, posited as
absolutely illimitable, could come to be fixated and
thereby also limited. The answer is that this activity
is not limited as intuitant, or as activity of the self,
for in becoming limited it ceases to be an activity of
the self and is transformed into the thing-in-itself.
This intuiting activity is now itself an intuited, and
thus no longer intuitant. But only the intuitant as
such is illimitable.

   The intuiting activity which replaces it is that
comprised in production, and is for that very reason
at the same time real. As intuitant, the ideal activity
thus bound in with production continues to remain

illimitable. For though limited in the course of
productive intuition, it is limited nonetheless for that
moment only, whereas the real activity is limited continually. Now if it should appear that all producing
on the part of the intellect rests on the contradiction
between the illimitable ideal and the restricted real
activities, the producing will be no less infinite than
that contradiction itself, and along with the ideal
activity that is limited in course of production, a
progressive principle in production will have been
posited. All producing is finite, so far as it goes,
but that which also comes about through this producing
will furnish the condition for a new contradiction, which
will turn into a new producing, and so assuredly ad
infinitum.

If the self did not contain an activity which oversteps every boundary, it would never emerge from its
first producing. It would produce, and be limited in its
producing, for an intuitant outside it, maybe, but not
for itself. Just as the self, to attain to sensation for
itself, must push on out beyond the originally sensed,
so, to be producing for itself, it must transcend every
product. In productive intuition we shall thus be
involved in the same contradiction as with sensation, and
by the same contradiction, productive intuition will
likewise raise itself again for us to a higher power,
just as simple intuition did in sensation.

That this contradiction will have to be an infinite
one, can be shown most briefly as follows:

The self contains an illimitable activity, but it is
not in the self as such, unless posited by the latter
as its own activity. However, the self cannot intuit
it as its own activity without distinguishing itself
therefrom as the subject or substrate of the infinite
activity in question. But by this very act there arises
a new duality, a contradiction between finitude and
infinitude. The self qua subject of this infinite
activity is dynamically (potentia) infinite, but the
activity itself, in being posited as an activity of the
self, becomes finite; but in becoming finite, it once
more becomes extended out over the boundary, yet in
being extended it is also again limited. --And thus
this alternation is prolonged ad infinitum.

The self that is elevated in this manner to an
intelligence is therefore thrown into a perpetual state
of expansion and contraction; but this state is precisely
that of imaging and producing. The activity at work
in this alternation is therefore bound to appear as a
producing activity.

Deduction of Productive Intuition

1. We left our object in a state of oscillation between opposites. In themselves, these opposites are absolutely incapable of unification, and if they can be unified,
it is only through the self's endeavor to unite them, which a-
lone gives them stability and mutual relation to one another.
Both opposites are affected only by the action of the
self, and are to that extent a product of the self, the thing-
in-itself no less than the self, which figures here for the
first time as its own product. --The self, of which the two
are products, elevates itself by that very fact into intelligence. If we think of the thing-in-itself as outside the
self, and the two opposites as therefore in different spheres,
then no unification whatever will be possible between them,
since in themselves they are not unifiable; to unite them,
therefore, there will be need of something higher which en-
compasses them. But this higher principle is the self itself, raised to a higher power, or elevated into intelligence,
and it is of this that we shall be speaking constantly hereafter. For the self that the thing-in-itself is outside of
is only the objective or real self, while that which includes
it is the simultaneously ideal and real, i.e., the intelligent self.

2. These opposites are held together only by an act of
the self. But the latter has no intuition of itself in this
act; thus the acting sinks, as it were, out of consciousness,
and only the opposition remains qua opposition therein. But
it could not even have remained as an opposition in consciousness (the opposites would have destroyed one another), but
for a third activity which has held them apart (opposed) and
by that very fact united them.

That the opposition as such enters consciousness, or
that the two opposites do so as absolute (and not merely
relative) opposites, is the condition of productive intuition. The difficulty is to explain even this. For everything
enters the self only through its act, and so too with this
opposition. But if the latter is posited through an act of
the self, it ceases by that very fact to be absolute. This
difficulty is soluble only along the following lines. The
act itself must be lost from consciousness, for thereafter
only the two members of the opposition (self and thing-in-
itself) will remain behind as in themselves incapable (by
their own power) of unification. For in the original action
they were surely held together only by the act of the self
(and so not by themselves); that act served merely to bring
them to consciousness, and having done this now itself
disappears from consciousness.

The fact that this opposition as such remains behind
in consciousness is sufficient to secure a large territory for consciousness. For now indeed the identity of
consciousness is utterly abolished thereby, not only
for the observer, but for the self itself; the self is

thus led to the same point of observation at which we
ourselves have been stationed from the first, save only
that for the self at this point a number of things must
appear quite otherwise than they did to us. We viewed
the self originally in a conflict of opposing activities.
The self, without knowing of that conflict, has had to
reconcile it involuntarily and, as it were, blindly in
a common construction. In this construction the ideal,
illimitable activity of the self was included as such,
so from that construction only the real activity could
remain behind as limited. At the present juncture, now
that the conflict becomes an object to the self itself,
it has transformed itself for the self-intuiting self
into the opposition between the self (as objective
activity) and the thing-in-itself. Since, therefore, the
intuitant activity is now outside the conflict (which
happens precisely through the self's elevation to intelligence, or through the fact that this very conflict again
becomes an object to the self), it will now become possible for this opposition to be eliminated, for the self
itself, in a common construction. It is also evident,
why the most fundamental opposition for the self itself,
though assuredly not for the philosopher, is that
between self and thing-in-itself.

    3. This intrinsically irreconcilable opposition is
posited in the self only insofar as the latter intuits
it as such; and this intuiting we have also derived
already, though till now we have considered only one part
of it. For in virtue of the original identity of its
nature, the self cannot intuit the opposition without
again importing identity into it, and hence a reciprocal
relation of self to thing and thing to self. Now in that
opposition the thing emerges only as activity, albeit
as an activity opposed to the self. Through the act
of the self this activity is indeed fixated, but only
qua activity. So the thing, as so far derived, is
still always a live and active affair, and not yet the
passive, inert item encountered in appearance. This
we shall never arrive at unless we again import an
opposition, and thence an equilibrium, into the object
itself. The thing-in-itself is pure ideal activity,
in which nothing is recognizable save its opposition
to the real activity of the self. And like the thing,
so the self too is mere activity.

    These opposed activities cannot part company, since
they are in fact united by the common boundary as their
point of contact. But nor, likewise, can they subsist
together, unless they are straightway reduced to a third
item common to both. Not until this happens do they
abdicate as activities. Now the third item that arises
from them can be neither self nor thing-in-itself, but
only a product lying midway between the two. Hence

this product will not figure in intuition as thing-in-
itself, or as an active thing, but merely as the appearance of that thing. The thing, so far as it is active and
a cause of passivity in us, therefore lies beyond the
stage of intuition, or is repressed from consciousness by
productive intuition, which, oscillating as it does
between thing and self, gives birth to something that lies
midway between the two, and in holding them apart is a
common expression of them both.

It is only ourselves, however, and not the self itself, who see this third item to be the object of sensory
intuition, and even for us it is not yet demonstrated, but
has first to be proved.

The proof can be no other than this. The product contains only the content of the productive activity, and
whatever has been incorporated therein by the synthesis
must also allow of again being extracted from it by analysis. In the product, therefore, the traces of both
activities, that of the self no less than that of the
thing, must be discernible.

In order to know how these two activities disclose
themselves in the product, we first have to know how they
are distinguishable as such.

The first activity is that of the self, which originally, i.e., prior to limitation (and this is here for
the first time to be elucidated for the self itself), is
infinite. Now there is in fact no ground for positing the
activity opposed to the self as finite; as surely, indeed,
as the self's activity is infinite, so also must be the
opposing activity of the thing.

But two activities, opposed and external to each
other, simply cannot be thought of as infinite, if both
are positive in character. For between equally positive
activities only relative opposition is possible, that is,
a mere opposition in direction.

(Suppose two equal forces, A, A, exerted upon one
and the same body in opposite directions; both are then
initially positive, so that if they are conjoined together,
a double force results; hence they are not opposed in any
primordial or absolute sense, but simply through their
relationship to the body; once they emerge from this
relationship, both are again positive. Moreover, it is
entirely indifferent which of the two is made positive
or negative. Both are ultimately distinguishable only
through their opposite directions.)

Hence, if the self's activity, like that of the thing,
be in both cases positive, and so opposed only relatively
to the other, they will likewise have to be distinguishable only by their directions. But now both are in fact
posited as infinite, and in infinity there is no direction
at all. Hence the two activities will have originally to
be distinguishable, as in merely relative opposition,

by means of a higher activity. One of them will have to
be not merely the relative, but the absolute negation of
the other; how this is possible has yet to be shown; our
claim is merely that that is how it must be.

(In place of the above-mentioned forces in merely
relative opposition, suppose a pair of forces of which
one = A, the other = -A; -A is then negative from the
beginning and absolutely opposed to A; if I combine them,
the result is not the double force previously obtained,
but a combination expressed as A+ (-A) = A - A. We
may see from this in passing why mathematics does not need
to take note of the difference between absolute and relative opposition, since for purposes of calculation the
formulae a - a and a + (- a) , of which one expresses
relative, the other absolute opposition, have exactly the
same significance. But for philosophy and physics the distinction is all the more important, as will clearly emerge
in the sequel. Nor are A and -A to be distinguished
merely through their opposite directions, since one of
them is negative, not in this relationship only, but
absolutely and by its very nature.)

Applying this to the case under discussion, we find
the self's activity to be intrinsically positive, and the
ground of all positivity. For it has been characterized
as a striving to expand out to infinity. The activity of
the thing would thus have intrinsically to be that which
is absolutely and by nature negative. Were it a striving
to occupy the infinite, it could only be thinkable, on
the contrary, as the limitant of the first activity. In
and for itself it would not be real, and would be capable
of demonstrating its reality only in opposition to the
other, through a constant restriction of the operation
thereof.

And this is in fact the case. What appears to us
from the present standpoint as activity of the thing-in-
itself, is nothing else but the ideal self-reverting activity of the self, and this can only be presented as the
negative of the other. The objective or real activity
subsists for itself and exists, even in the absence of an
intuitant; but the intuitant or limitant activity is
nothing without something to intuit or to limit.

Conversely, it follows from the fact that both activities are absolutely opposed to one another, that they
must be posited in one and the same subject. For only if
two opposed activities inhere in one and the same subject,
can one be the absolute opposite of the other.

(Consider, for example, a body driven upward by a
force = A, proceeding from the earth; owing to the continuous influence of gravity, it will return to earth by
a steady deviation from the straight-line path. Suppose
now, on the one hand, that gravity works by impulse; then
A, and the impulse of gravity B, coming in the opposite

direction, are both positive forces, and opposed only
relatively to one another, so that it is completely arbitrary which of the two, A or B, is taken to be negative.
Suppose, on the other hand, that the cause of gravity lies
in no way outside the point from which force A proceeds;
in that case the two forces A and B will have a common
source, whereupon it is at once evident that one of the
two is necessarily and by origin negative, and such that
if A, the positive, is a force operating through contact,
the negative must be such that it also acts at a distance.
The first case is an example of a purely relative opposition, the second of an absolute one. Which of the two
is adopted is admittedly a matter of indifference for calculation, but not for natural philosophy.)

Thus if two activities have one and the same subject,
the self, it is self-evident that they must be absolutely
opposed to each other; and conversely, if both are absolutely opposed to each other, that they are activities
of one and the same subject.

If the two activities were divided between different
subjects, as might here seem to be the case, since we have
posited one as an activity of the self, the other as an
activity of the thing, then the self's tendency to reach
out to infinity could indeed be restricted by an activity
(of the thing-in-itself) coming in the opposite direction.
In that case, however, the thing-in-itself would have to
be outside the self. But the thing-in-itself is only
outside the _real_ (practical) self; by the magic of intuition
both are united, and posited as activities, not relatively
but absolutely opposed, within one identical subject.

4. The opposed activities that are to be the condition of intuition are now more exactly determined, and
for both we have found characterizations independent of
their directions. The first, that of the self, may be
recognized by its positive nature, the second by the fact
that it can be thought of solely as the limitant of a
positive activity. We now proceed to apply these definitions to the question raised above.

In the common outcome arising from the opposition of
the two activities, the traces of both must be apparent,
and since we know their nature, the product also must admit
of characterization in terms of them.

Since the latter is a product of opposed activities,
it must, for that very reason, be finite.

Since, moreover, it is the common product of opposites,
neither activity can eliminate the other; both together
must emerge in the product, not indeed as identical, but
as what they are, namely _opposed_ activities, maintaining
a mutual equilibrium.

To the extent that they preserve a balance between
them, the two will not cease, indeed, to be activities,
but they will not _appear as_ such. --Let us recall once more

the example of the lever. In order for it to remain in
balance, equal weights must bear upon it at both ends, at
equal distances from the fulcrum. Each individual weight
acts, but cannot achieve its effect (it does not appear
as active); both are confined to the common effect. So
in intuition. The two activities that preserve equilibrium
do not thereby cease to be activities, for the equilibrium
only exists insofar as both are actively opposed to one
another; only the product is static.

But in the product, moreover, since it is to be a
common one, the traces of both activities must also be discernible. The opposite activities will therefore be distinguishable therein, one absolutely positive and tending
to expand to infinity, the other, as absolute opposite of
the first, directed to absolute finitude, and for that
very reason recognizable only as limitant of the positive
activity.

Only because both activities are absolutely opposed
can both also be infinite. Both are infinite only in an
opposite sense. (We get help in explaining this from the
infinity of the number sequence in opposite directions.
A finite quantity as such = 1, can be increased indefinitely
in such fashion that a divisor can still always be found
for it; but if we suppose it increased beyond all limits,
it becomes equal to 1/0, that is, the infinitely large.
The same quantity can be diminished indefinitely, by endlessly dividing it; but if we now suppose the divisor to
increase beyond all limits, the result = 1/∞ , that is, the
infinitely small.)

Thus the first activity, if unrestricted, would produce the positive infinite, and the second, under like conditions, the negative infinite.

In the common product, therefore, we must encounter
the traces of two activities, of which one, in the absence
of limits, would produce the positive infinite, and the
other the negative.

But furthermore, these two activities cannot be ab-
lutely opposed to each other without being activities of
one and the same identical subject. So nor can they be
united in one and the same product without a third activity which synthesizes them both. Besides these two
activities, therefore, there must also emerge in the product the traces of a third synthetic activity opposed
to both of them.

Now that the characteristics of the product have been
deduced in full, it remains only to demonstrate that they
all come together in what we speak of as matter.

Deduction of Matter

1. The two activities, which maintain equilibrium
in the product, can appear only as fixed, static activities,
that is, as <u>forces</u>.
The first of these forces will be by nature positive,
so that if unrestricted by any opposing force it would
expand out to infinity. --That matter possesses such an
infinite expansive force will be given only a transcendental proof. As surely as the first of the two activities
from which the product is constructed tends, by its nature,
to strive into the infinite, so surely must the first factor of the product be also an infinite expansive force.
Left to itself, this latter force, which is concentrated
in the product, would now expand <u>ad infinitum</u>. That it is
actually retained in a finite product, is explicable only
through an opposing, negative, restraining force, which
must likewise display itself as the counterpart in the
common product to the limiting activity of the self.
Thus if the self could reflect at this present stage
upon its construction, it would find the latter to be a
composite of two forces maintaining an equilibrium, of which
one on its own would produce the infinitely large, while
the other in its unrestricted form would reduce the product
to the infinitely small. --However, at its present stage
the self is not yet reflective.
2. Till now we have had regard only to the opposite
natures of the two activities and of the forces corresponding to them; but upon their opposite natures their opposite directions also depend. We can therefore raise the
question, how two forces come to be distinguished even
in their mere directions, a problem that will lead us to
a closer determination of the product, and will open the
road to a new enquiry; for it is undoubtedly a query of
great importance, to ask how forces that are thought of as
operating from one and the same point can act in opposite
directions.
The first of the two activities was assumed to be
headed originally towards the positive infinite. But in
infinity there are no directions. For direction is determination, yet determination = negation. The positive activity will therefore have to appear in the product as an
activity intrinsically quite lacking in direction, and
for that very reason headed in all directions. It must
be noted once more, however, that this omnidirectional
activity is in fact only distinguished as such from the
standpoint of reflection, for in the moment of production
the activity is nowhere distinguished from its direction,
and how the self makes this distinction on its own account
will be the topic of a special enquiry. The question now

arises, as to what direction distinguishes the activity in
the product that is opposed to the positive. What we shoul
expect in advance, namely that if the positive activity
embraces all directions, the other will have only one direc
tion, can be rigorously proved. --The concept of expansiveness is contained in that of direction. No expansiveness,
no direction. Now since the negative force is absolutely
opposed to the expansive force, it must appear, therefore,
as a force operating against all direction, which if unrestricted would constitute an absolute negation of all
direction in the product. But the negation of all directio
is the absolute boundary, the mere point. So this activity
will appear as one that endeavors to bring back all expansion to a mere point. This point will indicate its directio
and hence it will have but one direction, towards this poin
Picture the expansive force as operating out from the commo
midpoint C in all directions, CA, CB, etc.; then in contrast, the negative or attractive force will push back
from all directions toward the one point C. --But here too
it remains true of this direction what we recalled concerning the directions of the positive force. Here too activity and direction are absolutely one; the self itself
does not distinguish them.

Just as the directions of the positive and negative
activities are not distinguished from the activities themselves, so equally the directions are not distinguished
from one another. How the self arrives at making this distinction, whereby it first singles out space as space, and
time as time, will be the subject of a later enquiry.

3. The most important question that now remains for
us in regard to the relationship of the two forces is this:
how in fact can activities of opposing directions be
united in one and the same subject? How two forces emanating from different points can work in opposite directions,
it is possible to understand; it is less easy to see this
of two forces emanating from one and the same point. If
CA, CB, etc. are the lines on which the positive force
acts, then the negative force will have to operate in the
opposite sense, that is, in the directions AC, BC, etc.
Suppose now the positive force to be limited at A; then if
the negative force, to operate at point A, had first to
traverse all the intermediate points between C and A, it
would be absolutely indistinguishable from the expansive
force, for it would be acting in exactly the same direction
as the latter. Now since it works counter to the positive
force in the opposite direction, the reverse will in fact
hold of it, that is, it will act immediately, and without
traversing the individual points between C and A, upon
point A, and set a limit to line A.

So while the expansive force acts only in continuous
fashion, the attractive or retarding force, by contrast,
will operate immediately, or at a distance.

The relationship of the two forces will be determined as follows. --Since the negative force operates immediately upon the point of limitation, there will be nothing <u>within</u> that point save the expansive force; but beyond that point the attractive force working in opposition to the expansive force (albeit from the same source) will necessarily extend its operation <u>ad infinitum.</u>

For since <u>it is</u> a force that acts <u>immediately</u>, so that distance is nonexistent for it, it must be thought of as acting far and wide, and thus <u>ad infinitum</u>.

The relationship of the two forces is thus now the same as that of the objective and subjective activities in abstraction from production. --Just as the activity pent within the boundary, and that which reaches to infinity beyond it, are merely the factors of productive intuition, so also it is with the repulsive and attractive forces (of which one is pent within the limiting point, while the other goes to infinity, although the common boundary between them is a boundary for the latter only <u>in relation to the former</u>); they are divided by the common boundary (which is absolutely contingent to both) and are merely the factors for the construction of matter, not the constructive principle itself.

The constructive principle can only be a third force, which synthesizes both, and corresponds to the synthetic activity of the self in intuition. Only by means of this third synthetic activity was it intelligible how the two activities, as absolutely opposed to each other, could be posited in one and the same identical subject. The force corresponding to this activity in the object will thus be that whereby these two absolutely opposite forces are posited in one and the same identical subject.

(Kant, in his <u>Metaphysical First Principles of Natural Science</u>, speaks of attraction as a pervasive force, but this he does only because he already takes attraction to be gravitation ((and thus not in its pure sense)), so that he only requires two forces for the construction of matter, while we deduce three of them to be necessary. --Attraction in the pure sense, considered, that is, as a mere factor in the construction, is certainly a force that operates immediately at a distance, but not a pervasive force, since where there is nothing, there is nothing to pervade. It first acquires the property of pervasiveness on being incorporated into gravitation. Gravitation itself is not identical with attraction, though the latter is necessarily included therein. Nor is gravitation a simple force, as attraction is, but, as will emerge from our deduction, a composite force.)

With gravitation, the truly productive and creative force, the construction of matter is first completed, and it now merely remains for us to draw the main conclusions from this construction.

Corollaries

It is a demand that can quite justifiably be made of a transcendental enquiry, that it should explain why matter must necessarily be intuited as extended in three dimensions, of which, so far as we know, no explanation has hitherto been attempted; we therefore deem it necessary to append here a deduction of the three dimensions of matter, directly founded upon the three basic forces appertaining to the construction of matter.

According to the investigations detailed above, three stages must be distinguished in the construction of matter.

a) The first stage is that in which the two opposing forces are thought of as united in one and the same point. The expansive force will be able to operate outwards from this point in all directions, though these latter will be distinguished only by means of the opposite force, which alone furnishes the limiting point, and hence also the point of direction. But these directions are not to be confused, say, with dimensions, for a line, in whatever direction it be drawn, always has but one dimension, namely that of length. The negative force gives the intrinsically directionless expansive force a determinate direction. But now it has been demonstrated that the negative force acts, not mediately but immediately, upon the limiting point. Let us suppose, therefore, that from point C, as the common source of both forces, the negative force operates immediately on the limiting point of the line, which limit may to start with still remain wholly indeterminate; then, owing to its action at a distance, nothing whatever of the negative force will be encountered up to a certain distance from C, the positive force alone being dominant; but then some point A will occur on the line at which both forces, the positive and the negative approaching in the opposite direction, stand in mutual equilibrium, and this point will thus be neither positive nor negative, but wholly neutral. From this point on, the dominance of the negative force will increase, until at some determinate point B it gains the ascendency, at which juncture, therefore, the negative force alone prevails, and the line, for that very reason, is limited absolutely. Point A will be the common limit of the two forces; point B, the limiting point of the whole line.

The three points located on the line just constructed, C, between which and A the positive force is alone dominant, A, the mere equilibrium point of both forces, and lastly B, where only the negative force prevails, are the same as those that are in fact discriminated in the magnet.

Hence, without our having purposed it, and along with the first dimension of matter, namely length, we have also deduced magnetism, and from this a number of important conclusions can now be drawn, whose further elaboration

cannot be presented in this book. It emerges, for
example, from this deduction, that in magnetic phenomena
we see matter still at the first stage of construction,
where the two opposing forces are united in one and the
same point; that magnetism, accordingly, is a function,
not of any particular matter, but of matter in general,
and is thus an authentic category of physics; that the
three points which nature has preserved for us in the
magnet, while they are obliterated in other bodies,
are none other than the three points deduced a priori
which pertain to the real construction of length; that
magnetism as such is therefore the general constructor
of length, etc. I merely add the remark that this
deduction also throws a light for us on the physics of
magnetism, which perhaps might never have been obtained
from experiment, namely that the positive pole (point
C above) is the seat of both forces. For that negative
M appears to us only at the opposite point B is a
necessary fact, since the negative force can only act
at a distance. Given this one proviso, the three points
in the magnetic line are necessary. Conversely, the
existence of these three points in the magnet proves
that the negative force is one that acts at a distance,
just as the whole coincidence between our a priori
constructed line and that of the magnet proves the
correctness of our entire deduction.

    b)   In the line just constructed, point B is the
limit of the line as such, point A the common boundary
of the two forces. A limit is posited as such by the
negative force; but now if, as ground of limitation,
the negative force is itself limited, there arises a
limitation of limitation, and this falls at point A, the
common boundary of the two forces.

    Since the negative force is no less infinite than
the positive, the limit at A will be no less contingent
for it than for the positive force.

    But if A is contingent in regard to both forces,
we can also think of the line CAB as divided into two
lines, CA and AB, separated from each other by the
boundary A.

    This stage, which presents the two opposite forces
as completely external to each other and separated by
the boundary, is the second in the construction of
matter, and the same as that represented in nature by
electricity. For if ABC represents a magnet whose
positive pole is A, its negative C, and its neutral
point B, the schema of electricity at once arises for
me by my representing this one body as separated into
AB and BC, of which each represents one of the two
forces exclusively. The strict demonstration of this
claim is, however, as follows.

    So long as the two opposite forces are thought of
as united in one and the same point, nothing can result

save the line above constructed, since the direction of
the positive force is so far determined by the negative
that it can perforce go only towards the one point at
which the boundary falls. The opposite will happen,
therefore, as soon as the two forces are parted from
each other. Let C be the point at which both forces
are united. If we suppose this point stationary, then
round about it is a countless set of points to which it
could move, if it were capable of purely mechanical
motion. But now at this point there is a force which
can move in all these directions at once, namely the
expansive force, originally directionless, and thus
capable of all directions. This force will thus be
able to pursue all these directions at once, but in
every single line that it describes will nevertheless
be unalterably capable of following just this one
direction, so long as the negative force is not separated
therefrom; it will thus also operate in all directions
only in the pure dimension of length. As soon as the
two forces are completely distinct, the opposite will
happen. For no sooner does point C shift (in the
direction CA, for example) than already, at the next
position it occupies, it is surrounded by innumerable
points, to all of which it can move. The expansive
force, now wholly given over to its tendency to spread
in all directions, will therefore again throw out lines
in all directions from every point along line CA; these
will form angles with CA and thus the dimension of
length will be supplemented by that of breadth. The
same, however, also holds of all the lines which point
C, still supposed stationary, radiates in the other
directions, so that none of these lines will now continue to represent mere length.

Now that this stage of construction will be represented in nature by electricity, is evident from the
fact that, unlike magnetism, the latter does not act
in merely linear fashion, seeking and guided by length,
but adds to the pure length of magnetism the dimension
of breadth, in that it spreads over the whole surface
of a body to which it is conveyed; yet no more acts in
depth than does magnetism, since, as we know, it seeks
merely length and breadth.

c) As surely as the two now completely separated
forces are originally forces of one and the same point,
so surely must their cleavage occasion a striving in
both for a return to unity. But this can come about
only by means of a third force, which can intervene
among the two opposed forces and in which these may
interpenetrate. This mutual interpenetration of the
two forces by means of a third first endows the product
with impenetrability, and by this property adds to the
two earlier dimensions a third, namely thickness,

whereby the construction of matter is first completed.

In the first stage of construction, the two forces, though united in one subject, were yet separated, so that, in the above-constructed line CAB, CA is positive force only, and AB only negative; in the second stage they are actually divided among different subjects. In the third, both are so far united into a common product, that there is no point in the entire product at which both forces will not be simultaneously present, in such wise that now the whole product is neutral.

This third stage of construction is evinced in nature through the chemical process. For that the two bodies in a chemical process represent only the original opposition of the two forces is evident from the fact that they mutually interpenetrate, which only forces can be thought to do. But that two bodies should represent the original opposition is again unthinkable unless in each of them one of the two forces secures absolute predominance.

It is through the third force, wherein the two opposites so interpenetrate that the whole product is at every point attractive and repulsive force at once, that the third dimension is first added to the other two; and in just the same fashion, the chemical process is the fulfillment of the first two, of which one seeks length only, and the other only length and breadth, until finally the chemical process operates in all three dimensions at once, wherein, for that very reason, a genuine interpenetration is also alone possible.

If the construction of matter runs through these three stages, it may be expected, a priori, that the three stages in question will also be more or less distinguishable in individual natural bodies; it is even possible to determine a priori the position in the series at which any one of these stages must especially emerge or disappear; for example, that the first stage must be distinguishable only in the most rigid bodies, whereas it is utterly unrecognizable in liquids; which actually yields an a priori principle for the distinguishing of natural bodies, e.g., into liquid and solid, and for establishing an order among them.

In place of the more special expression of chemical process, whereby every process whatever is included, so far as it transforms into a product, we may seek a general expression instead. If so, we shall have to take note in the first place that according to the principles so far derived, the condition of the real product is essentially a trinity of forces; and hence that a process must be sought a priori in nature, in which this trinity of forces is recognizable above all others. Such a process is galvanism, which is not a single process, but the general expression for all processes that transform into a product.

There will doubtless be no reader who in the course of
our enquiry has not made the following observation.

In the first epoch of self-consciousness we could
distinguish three acts, and these seem to reappear in
the three forces of matter and in the three stages of
its construction. These three stages of construction
give us three dimensions of matter, and these latter,
three levels in the dynamic process. It is very natural
to hit upon the idea that it is always just one and the
same trinity that recurs among these various forms. To
develop this idea and gain a complete grasp of the
connection so far merely surmised, a comparison of the
three acts of the self with the three stages in the
construction of matter will not be devoid of usefulness.

Transcendental philosophy is nothing else but a
constant raising of the self to a higher power; its
whole method consists in leading the self from one level
of self-intuition to another, until it is posited with
all the determinations that are contained in the free
and conscious act of self-consciousness.

The first act, from which the whole history of
intelligence sets forth, is the act of self-consciousness
insofar as it is not free but still unconscious. The
same act, which the philosopher postulates from the very
outset, when thought without consciousness, yields the
first act of our object, the self.

In this act the self is for us, indeed, but not for
itself, both subject and object at once; it presents,
as it were, that point we noted in the construction of
matter, at which the two activities, the originally
unlimited and the limitant, are still united.

The result of this act is again for us only, not
for the self itself, a limitation of the objective
activity by the subjective. But the limiting activity,
as itself illimitable and acting at a distance, must
necessarily be thought of as striving out beyond the
point of limitation.

In this first act, therefore, exactly the same
determinations are contained as those which also distinguish the first stage in the construction of matter.

In this act there really does occur a common construction out of the self as object and as subject,
but this construction does not exist for the self itself.
Hence we were driven on to a second act, which is a
self-intuiting of the self in this state of limitation.
Since the self cannot be aware of its limitation as
having been posited by itself, this intuiting is merely
a finding, or sensing. Since, therefore, the self is
not conscious in this act of its own activity, whereby
it is limited, there is at once and immediately

posited along with sensation--not for the self, but
certainly for us--the contrast between self and thing-
in-itself.

Stated in other terms, this amounts to saying that
in this second act there is a separation--not for the
self, but for us--of the two activities originally
united therein into two entirely different and mutually
external activities, namely into that of the self on the
one hand, and that of the thing on the other. The
activities, which are originally those of an identical
subject, are divided between different subjects.

Hence it becomes clear that the second stage we
assume in the construction of matter, namely the stage
where the two forces become forces of different subjects,
is exactly the same for physics as this second act of
intelligence is for transcendental philosophy. It is
also now evident that already with the first and second
acts a start has been made with the construction of
matter, or that the self, without knowing it, is already
from the first act onwards engaged, as it were, upon the
construction of matter.

A further remark, which shows us more closely yet
the identity of the dynamic and the transcendental, and
affords us a glimpse of the far-reaching interconnections
stemming from the present point, is as follows. This
second act is the act of sensation. Now what, then, is
it that becomes an object to us through sensation?
Nothing else but quality. But all quality is simply
electricity, a proposition that is demonstrated in
natural philosophy. But electricity is precisely that
whereby we designate in nature this second stage in
construction. One might therefore say that what sensation is in the realm of intelligence, electricity is in
nature.

The identity of the third act with the third stage
of the construction of matter really requires no proof.
Thus it is obvious that in constructing matter the self
is in truth constructing itself. The third act is that
by means of which the self as sensing becomes an object
to itself. But this is incapable of derivation unless
the two activities, so far completely separated, are
exhibited in one and the same identical product. This
product, namely matter, is thus a complete construction
of the self, though not for the self itself, which is
still identical with matter. If the self in the first
act is intuited only as object, and in the second only
as subject, it now becomes objectified in the third act
as both at once--for the philosopher, of course, not
for itself. For itself it is objectified in this act
as a subject only. That it appears merely as matter
is necessary, since in this act it admittedly is a
subject-object, but without intuiting itself as such.

The concept of the self that the philosopher starts
from is that of a subject-object which is conscious of
itself as such. Matter is not so conscious, and through
it, therefore, the self, likewise, does not become
objectified as a self. But now transcendental philosophy is completed only when the self becomes an object
to itself just as it does to the philosopher. Hence
also the circuit of this science cannot be closed with
the present epoch.

The result of the comparison so far instituted is
that the three stages in the construction of matter really
do correspond to the three acts in the intelligence. So
if these three phases of nature are actually three stages
in the history of self-consciousness, it is evident
enough that really all forces of the universe ultimately
relate back to presentative forces, a principle underlying the idealism of Leibniz, which, properly understood, does not in fact differ from transcendental
idealism. When Leibniz calls matter the sleeping state
of monads, or when Hemsterhuis speaks of it as con-
gealed mind, there lies in these statements a meaning
very easy to discern from the principles now put forward. Matter is indeed nothing else but mind viewed
in an equilibrium of its activities. There is no need
to demonstrate at length how, by means of this elimina-
tion of all dualism, or all real opposition between
mind and matter, whereby the latter is regarded merely
as mind in a condition of dullness, or the former, conversely, as matter merely in becoming, a term is set to
a host of bewildering enquiries concerning the relationship of the two.

There is equally little need of any further discussion to show that this view leads to far more elevated
notions of the nature and dignity of matter than any
others; for example, atomism, which constructs matter
out of atoms, without considering that we advance not a
step thereby towards its true nature, since the atoms
themselves are just matter.

The construction of matter deduced a priori provides the basis for a general theory of natural phenomena, in which there is hope of being able to dispense
with all the hypotheses and fictions which an atomistic
physics will never cease to require. Before even the
atomistic physicist actually arrives at the explanation
of a natural phenomenon, he is obliged to make a mass
of assumptions, e.g., concerning materials to which he
assigns, quite arbitrarily and without the smallest
evidence, a multitude of properties, simply because he
can use just these and no others for his explanation.
But once it is established that the ultimate causes of
natural phenomena can never be investigated by the aid
of experience, there is nothing for it but either to

renounce knowing them altogether, or to invent them as
atomistic physics does, or else to discover them
a *priori*, which is the sole source of <u>knowledge</u> remaining to us apart from experience.

From Productive Intuition to Reflection

Introductory

The first epoch closes with the self's elevation to
intelligence. The two activities, wholly separated and
located in quite different spheres, are, by the third
that intervenes upon them, again posited in one and the
same product. By this intervention in both of a third
activity, the activity of the thing again also becomes
an activity of the self, which, by that very fact, is
itself elevated into an intelligence.

But the self, in its intuitive capacity, is also
completely fettered and bound in its producing, and
cannot be both intuitant and intuited at once. The
production is thus totally blind and unconscious. In
accordance with the now familiar method of transcendental philosophy, the question now arises, therefore, how
the self, which has so far been intuitant and intelligent
only for us, becomes this also for itself, or intuits
itself as such. But now no ground whatever can be
thought of, which would determine the self to intuit
itself as productive, unless in the production itself
there lies a ground whereby the ideal activity of the
self that is involved in producing is driven back upon
itself, and is thereby led to transcend the product.
The question as to how the self recognizes itself as
productive is thus the same as asking how it is able
to tear itself free from its production and to transcend the latter.

Before embarking upon the solution of this problem
itself, the following remark will serve to give a preliminary idea of the content of the next epoch.

The whole topic of our enquiry is simply the elucidation of self-consciousness. All acts of the self that
we have so far derived, or will derive henceforth, are
but the intermediate stages through which our object
attains to self-consciousness. Self-consciousness
itself is a determinate act, and so all these inter-
mediaries must also be determinate acts. But through
every determinate act a determinate product arises for
the self. Now the self's concern was not with the
product, but with itself. It seeks to intuit, not the
product, but itself in the product. Now it would,
however, be possible, and is, as we shall soon see,
actually necessary, that in the very act of striving
to intuit itself in production the condition of a new
product should arise for the self; and so on indefinitely, were it not for the addition of a new and
hitherto unknown limitation, such that there is no

seeing how the self, having once launched into production, should ever again emerge from it, since the
condition of all producing, and the mechanism thereof,
is constantly reinstated.

Hence, in trying to explain how the self gets
clear of production, we shall in fact involve our object
in a whole series of productions. We shall thus be able
to resolve the main problem of this epoch only in a
very indirect fashion, and only so long as there will
arise for our object, instead of what we sought, something entirely different, until we finally break out of
this circle, as it were, by an act of reflection occurring with absolute spontaneity. Between this point of
absolute reflection and the present point of consciousness there lies as an intermediate stage the whole
multiplicity of the objective world, its products and
phenomena.

Since our whole philosophy proceeds from the standpoint of intuition, not that of reflection, occupied,
for instance, by Kant and his philosophy, we shall also
derive the now incipient series of acts of the intelligence as acts, and not, say, as concepts of acts, or
as categories. For how these acts attain to reflection
is the problem for a later epoch of self-consciousness.

D

Problem:

To explain how the self comes to intuit itself as
productive

Solution

I

After the self has once become productive, we must
renounce the idea that it should intuit itself as a
simple activity. But that it should intuit itself as
producing, cannot be conceived unless directly through
production there should arise for it a further ideal
activity, whereby it intuits itself therein.

Thus it will meanwhile be assumed as a hypothesis
merely, that the self has an intuition of itself in its
producing, in order thereby to find the conditions of
such an intuition. If these conditions are actually
to be found in consciousness, we shall thereupon conclude that such an intuition does indeed take place,
and will try to discover its outcome.

The first thing we can establish in this matter
is the following: if the self is to intuit itself as

producing, it must necessarily distinguish itself at the same time from itself insofar as it is not producing. For in that it intuits itself as producing, it undoubtedly regards itself as a determinate; but this it cannot do without opposing to itself something else, whatever the latter may be. --

To facilitate the enquiry, we ask straightaway what in fact this nonproductive element in the self will be, to which the productive element must be opposed? Here this much, at least, can already be discerned. Insofar as it produces, the self is not a simple, but a compound activity (in the sense in which one speaks, for example, of a compound motion in mechanics). The nonproductive element in the self must therefore be opposed to the productive as a simple activity.

Moreover, in order to be opposed to each other, the productive activity and this simple activity must at the same time again coincide in a higher concept. In relation to the latter, both must appear as one activity, and their difference, therefore, as something merely contingent. It will have to appear that, if something be posited, the two activities are different, and if something be not posited, both are identical.

There will have, furthermore, again to be three activities in the self, one simple, one compound, and a third which divides them from each other and relates them together. Now this third activity must necessarily itself be a simple one, for without that it could not distinguish the combination for what it is. This simple activity, to which the combination is related, is therefore at once the relating activity, and, if the latter be characterized, it is also that which is related.

But now the relating activity can be no other than the ideal activity we postulated earlier, reemerging directly through production. This, precisely because it is ideal, is directed solely to the self itself, and is nothing else but that simple intuitant activity which we posited from the outset in the self.

The ground of relation of the two activities would thus be, that they are both intuitant, while the ground of difference would be that one is a simple intuitant activity, the other a compound one.

If both activities are to be posited as intuitant, both must have originated from a single principle. The condition under which both are different must thus appear as contingent in relation to that principle. This contingency is common to both; what is contingent, therefore, for the productive activity is also contingent for the simple one. Now can we find a contingent element in production which could simultaneously form the common boundary of both activities?

To discover this, let us turn the question round.

What, then, is the essential, necessary element in
production? The necessary is that which is the condition of producing as such, and the contingent or
accidental will therefore be the opposite, and hence
that which restricts or limits production.

    That which restricts production is the activity, in
opposition to the self, of the thing-in-itself. But this
cannot be contingent for production, for it is a necessary condition of producing. It is not, therefore, the
restricting factor itself that will be contingent, but
the restricting of that restriction.

    To be more explicit: the thing-in-itself's
activity explains for me in general only a restriction
of the now productive activity, but not the contingency
of this restriction, or that it is this one in particular.
The activity of the thing-in-itself is, in and for itself,
no more limited than that of the self.

    That it is the thing-in-itself's activity which
limits the self is explicable in that it is opposed
thereto; but that it limits the self in a particular
fashion, which itself is not possible unless it be likewise limited--this can no longer be derived from the
opposition in question. It could, after all, be opposed
to the self without being so in this particular way.

    The necessary factor in production therefore lies
in the opposition as such; the contingent, in the limit
of this opposition. But this is nothing else but the
communal boundary lying between self and thing. The
boundary is common, that is, it is a boundary no less
for the thing than for the self.

    Combining our conclusions, we obtain the following
result. The two intuitant activities, in principle
identical, are differentiated by the contingent boundary
of the self and the thing-in-itself; or, that which is
the boundary of self and thing is also the boundary of
these two intuitant activities.

    The simple intuitant activity has merely the self
itself as its object; the compound, both self and thing
together. The latter, for this very reason, partly
oversteps the boundary, or is both inside and outside
the boundary at once. But now the self is only a self
within the boundary, for beyond that boundary it has
transformed itself, for itself, into the thing-in-
itself. The intuition that oversteps the boundary
therefore goes at the same time beyond the self as
such, and to that extent appears as outer intuition.
The simple intuitant activity remains within the self,
and can to that extent be termed inner intuition.

    The relationship of the two intuitant activities
is thus as follows. The sole boundary between inner
and outer intuition is that between self and thing-in-
itself. Once remove it, and inner and outer intuition

merge into one. Outer sense begins at the point where
inner sense leaves off. What appears to us as the
object of outer sense is merely a boundary point of inner
sense, and hence both of them, outer and inner, are also
in origin identical, for outer sense is merely inner
sense subjected to a limit. Outer sense is necessarily
also inner, though by contrast, inner is not necessarily
also outer. All intuition is in principle intellectual,
and hence the objective world is merely the intellectual
world appearing under restrictions. --

The outcome of the whole enquiry consists in the
following. If the self is to intuit itself as producing,
inner and outer sense must <u>firstly</u> part company therein,
and <u>secondly</u> there must be a relation of each to the
other. The question at once arises, therefore, as to
what the relating factor of the two intuitions will be.

The relating factor is necessarily something common
to both. But now inner intuition had nothing in common
with outer intuition as such, though conversely, outer
intuition certainly had something in common with inner,
for outer sense is also inner sense. Thus the relating
factor of outer and inner sense is itself once more
inner sense.

Here we first begin to grasp how the self may be
able to arrive at opposing outer and inner sense to
itself, and at relating them to one another. For this
in fact would never happen, if the relating factor, inner
sense, were not itself incorporated in outer intuition,
as the sole active and constructive principle therein;
for if outer sense is inner sense under limitation, we
are obliged, in contrast, to posit inner sense, as
such, as originally illimitable. Inner sense is thus
nothing else but the illimitable tendency of the self,
posited therein from the very outset, to self-intuition;
and at this point is distinguished only for the first
time as inner sense, and thus as the same activity which,
in the foregoing act, was immediately limited by its
overstepping of the boundary.

If the self is to recognize itself in outer intuition as intuitant, it must needs relate outer intuition
to the now reinstated ideal intuition, which now appears,
however, as inner intuition. But the self is itself
nothing other than this ideal intuition, for the simultaneously ideal and real intuition is something quite
different; hence the relating element, and that to
which it relates, will in this act be one and the same.
Now outer intuition could indeed be related to inner,
for the two are different and yet again there is a
ground of identity between them. But the self cannot
relate outer intuition to inner, <u>qua</u> inner, for it
cannot in one and the same act relate outer intuition
to itself, and in doing so, simultaneously reflect

again upon itself as the ground of relation. Thus it
could not relate outer intuition to inner, qua inner,
for, according to presumption, it would itself be
nothing else but inner intuition; and were it to acknowledge inner intuition as such, it would have again to
be something other than this.

In the foregoing act, the self was a producer,
but producer and produced lapsed into one; the self and
its object were one and the same. We now seek an act
in which the self shall recognize itself as producing.
If this were possible, no trace at all of an intuited
would evince itself in consciousness. But productive
intuition, if it were recognized, would be recognized
as such only in contrast to inner intuition. But now
inner intuition itself would not be acknowledged as
inner, precisely because the self in this act would be
nothing else but inner intuition, and hence even outer
intuition could not be acknowledged as such, and since
it can be recognized only as outer intuition, it could
not be acknowledged as intuition at all. There would
accordingly be nothing left of this whole act in consciousness, save on the one side the intuited (detached
from the intuition) and on the other the self as ideal
activity, though this latter is now inner sense.

In empirical consciousness there is no trace whatever of an outer intuition, qua act, nor should there
be; it is, however, most important to enquire how in such
a consciousness the object and an inner sense as yet
unlimited and wholly free, for example, in the pro-
jecting of schemata, etc., can coexist together. --The
thing-in-itself likewise makes no more appearance in
consciousness than does the act of outer intuition;
repressed from consciousness by the sensory object, it
is simply an ideal explanatory ground of consciousness,
and, like the acts of the intelligence itself, lies, for
intelligence, beyond consciousness. As ground of
explanation, the thing-in-itself needs only a philosophy
that stands a few steps higher than empirical consciousness. Empiricism will never ascend to this level.
By the thing-in-itself, which he introduced into
philosophy, Kant has at least provided the first impulse
which could carry philosophy beyond ordinary consciousness, and has at least shown that the ground of the
object that appears in consciousness cannot itself
again lie in consciousness; but he never even considered
clearly, let alone explained, that this ground of
explanation lying beyond consciousness is in the end
no more than our own ideal activity, merely hypostatized
into the thing-in-itself.

II

The outcome of the relationship hypothetically assumed
would be, on the one side, the <u>sensory object</u> (separated
from intuition as an act), and on the other, <u>inner sense</u>.
Both together engender a self having sensation with
consciousness. For what we call inner sense is nothing
else but the consciously sensing element in the self.
In the original act of sensation the self had sensation
without having it for itself, that is, it was sensing
without consciousness. Through the act just derived,
of which indeed, for the reasons given, nothing can
remain in the self save the sensory object on the one
hand and inner sense on the other, it is evident that
through productive intuition the self <u>comes to have
sensation with consciousness</u>.

In accordance with the sufficiently familiar procedure of transcendental philosophy, the question of how
the self recognizes itself as producing must now therefore be framed as follows: <u>how the self becomes to itself
an object as having sensation with consciousness?</u> Or,
since sensation with consciousness and inner sense are
the same, how the self also becomes to itself an object
as inner sense?

Thus the whole course of the enquiry will have as
its object the act of relation just derived (I), and
must try to make this latter intelligible.

It is easy to perceive the following. The self
can distinguish itself as having sensation with consciousness only by opposing the object, as merely
intuited and thus without consciousness, to itself as
the conscious (having sensation with consciousness).

Now the object, transcendentally regarded, is
nothing else but outer or productive intuition itself.
Only the self cannot become conscious of this intuition
as such. The object must thus be opposed to inner sense
precisely as outer sense was opposed thereto. But the
opposition of the two intuitions, inner and outer,
merely engendered the boundary lying between them.
Hence the object is an object only insofar as it is
bounded by the same limit whereby inner and outer
sense were distinguished, which now therefore is no
longer the boundary between inner and outer sense, but
the boundary dividing the consciously sensing self from
the wholly unconscious object.

Thus the self cannot oppose the object to itself
without recognizing the boundary as a boundary. So
how then is the latter determined? --As contingent in
either respect, for the thing no less than for the self.
But to what extent is it, in fact, a boundary for the
self? It is not indeed a limit to activity, but rather
to the passivity in the self, a passivity, of course,

in the real and objective self. The self's passivity
was limited by the very fact that its ground was posited
in a thing-in-itself, which itself was necessarily a
limited affair. But that which is boundary for the
thing-in-itself (the ideal activity), is boundary of the
passivity of the real self, not its activity, for this
is already restricted by the thing-in-itself as such.

As to what the boundary of the thing may be, that
question now answers itself. Self and thing are so
opposed, that what is passivity in the one is activity
in the other. So if the boundary limits the passivity
of the self, it necessarily sets a limit to the activity
of the thing, and only to that extent is it the common
boundary of them both.

Thus the boundary, too, can only be recognized as
such if it is recognized as bounding the activity of the
thing. The question arises, how we are to conceive of
this.

The boundary is to set limit to the activity of the
thing, and it is to be contingent, not only to the self
merely, but equally so to the thing. If it is contingent
to the thing, the latter must originally, and in and for
itself, be unlimited activity. Hence the fact that the
thing's activity is limited must be inexplicable from
its own nature, and hence explicable only from a ground
external to it.

Where are we to look for this ground? In the self?
But from our present standpoint, this explanation will
simply not do any longer. That the self should unconsciously be the cause once more of this limitation of
the thing (the ideal activity) and thereby of its own
passivity--that is, as will soon appear, of its own
particular limitation--is something of which the self
itself can know nothing. So the ground of limitation of
the thing's activity, and hence indirectly of the limited
passivity of the self, can be sought by the self itself
nowhere but in something that now lies wholly outside
consciousness, but yet intervenes in the present phase
of consciousness. As surely, therefore, as the self
must acknowledge the boundary as a boundary, so surely
must it also overstep the boundary, and seek its ground
in something that now no longer falls within consciousness.
This unknown, which we shall meanwhile describe as A,
therefore lies necessarily beyond the producing of the
present object, which we may designate as B. Thus while
the self was producing B, A must already have existed.
So in the present phase of consciousness, nothing can
any longer be changed in A; it is, so to speak, out of
the hands of the self, for it lies beyond the current
act of the latter, and is unalterably determined for
the self. Once A is posited, B too must be posited
just so and no otherwise as it is now in fact posited.

For A contains the ground of its determinate limitation.
But the self is now no longer conscious of this
ground A. The determinate limitation of B will thus
indeed be a contingent one for the self, since it is
unaware of the ground thereof, whereas for us, who do
know of this, it is a necessary limitation. --
A further remark by way of explanation: --the
particular determinacy of B is to have its ground in an
A which now lies wholly outside consicousness. But
that this A is this particular one may perhaps have its
ground in something else again, lying still further back,
and so perhaps back ad infinitum, unless indeed we light
upon a general ground which determines the whole series.
Now this general ground can be nothing else but what we
termed at the very outset the limitation within limitation; at present we have not yet fully derived this, but
so far as we can already see here, its ground rests
solely upon that common boundary between ideal and real
activity. --
If the self is to recognize the boundary between
itself and the object as contingent, it must recognize
this as conditioned by something that lies wholly outside the present phase. It therefore feels itself
driven back to a stage of which it cannot be conscious.
It feels itself driven back, for it cannot in fact go
back. There is therefore in the self a state of incapacity, a state of constraint. That which contains
the ground of the specific limitedness of B is already
present in actuality and independently of the self.
In regard to A there will thus occur in the self only
an ideal producing, or a reproducing. But all reproducing is free, since it is a wholly ideal activity.
A must indeed be precisely so determined that it contains the ground of the specific limitedness of B;
hence, in reproducing A, the self will admittedly not
be materially free, but will be so formally. By contrast, in the producing of B it was free neither formally nor materially, for once A existed it was bound
to produce B precisely as determined in that fashion,
and could not produce anything else in its stead. Hence
the self here is in one and the same act at once formally free and formally constrained. The one is conditioned by the other. In regard to B the self could
not feel itself constrained, if it were not able to
revert to an earlier stage, where B did not yet exist
and it felt itself free in regard thereto. But
conversely also, it would not feel itself driven back
if it did not feel itself constrained in the present
stage.
The state of the self at the present juncture is
thus briefly as follows. It feels itself driven back
to a stage of consciousness to which it cannot, in

fact, return. The common boundary of self and object,
the ground of the second limitation, forms the boundary
between the present stage and a past one. The feeling
of being thus driven back to a stage that it cannot in
reality return to is the feeling of the present. Thus at
the first stage of its consciousness the self already
finds itself trapped in a present. For it cannot oppose
the object to itself without feeling itself restricted
and committed, as it were, to a single point. This
feeling is no other than that which we describe as self-
awareness. All consciousness begins with it, and by it
the self first posits itself over against the object.

In self-awareness, inner sense, that is, sensation
combined with consciousness, becomes an object to itself.
It is for that very reason entirely different from
sensation, into which there necessarily enters something
different from the self. In the previous act, the self
was inner sense, but without being so for itself.

But now how, then, does the self become an object
to itself as inner sense? Simply and solely through the
fact that time arises for it (not time insofar as it is
already externally intuited, but time as a mere point, a
mere limit). In that the self opposes to itself the
object, there arises for it the feeling of self-awareness, that is, it becomes an object to itself as pure
intensity, as activity which can extend itself only in
one dimension, but is at present concentrated at a single
point; but in fact this unidimensionally extensible
activity, when it becomes an object to itself, is time.
Time is not something that flows independently of the
self; the self itself is time conceived of in activity.

Now since in this act the self opposes to itself the
object, the latter will have to appear to it as the negation of all intensity, that is, will have to appear to
it as pure extensity.

Thus the self cannot oppose the object to itself
without inner and outer intuition not only separating
themselves within the self, but also becoming, as such,
objects.

But now the intuition whereby inner sense becomes
an object to itself is time (though we are speaking here
of pure time, i.e., time in its total independence of
space); the intuition whereby outer sense becomes an
object to itself is space. Hence the self cannot oppose
the object to itself without on the one hand inner sense
becoming an object to it, through time, and on the other,
outer sense becoming an object, through space.

III

In the first construction of the object, inner and outer
sense were involved together. The object appears as

pure extensity only when outer sense becomes objectified
to the self, because it is in fact inner sense itself
to which outer sense is objectified; hence the two can
no longer be united, which was not so, however, in the
original construction. Thus the object is neither merely
inner nor merely outer sense, but both of them at once,
in such a way that each is reciprocally restricted by
the other.

Hence, to determine the object more accurately than
hitherto as the union of both forms of intuition, we
must distinguish still more strictly than has yet been
done the opposing members of the synthesis.

So what, then, is inner sense, and what is outer--
both considered in their unrestricted form?

Inner sense is nothing else but the self's activity
driven back into itself. If we consider inner sense as
absolutely unrestricted by outer, the self will be in
its highest state of feeling, its whole illimitable
activity concentrated, as it were, upon a single point.
If, on the contrary, we consider outer sense as unrestricted by inner, it will be the absolute negation
of all intensity, the self will be wholly dissolved,
there will be no resistance therein.

Inner sense, considered in its unrestrictedness,
will thus be represented by the point, the absolute
boundary, or by the image of time in its independence
of space. For time, considered in and for itself, is
merely the absolute boundary, and hence the first synthesis of time with space, which so far, however, has
not yet been derived at all, can be expressed only by
the line, or by the expanded point.

The opposite of the point, or absolute extensity,
is the negation of all intensity, viz., infinite space,
likewise the dissolved self.

Hence, in the object itself, that is, in producing,
space and time can only arise together and unseparated
from each other. Both are opposed to each other,
precisely because they mutually restrict each other.
Both, for themselves, are equally infinite, though in
opposing senses. Time becomes finite only through space,
space only through time. That one becomes finite through
the other means that one is determined and measured
through the other. Hence the most basic measure of
time is the space traversed by a uniformly moving body
therein, and the most basic measure of space is the
time that a uniformly moving body requires in order to
traverse it. Both therefore show themselves as
absolutely inseparable.

But now space is nothing else but objectified outer
sense, and time nothing else but objectified inner sense,
so what holds of space and time is also true of outer
and inner sense. The object is outer sense determined

by inner. Extensity is thus not merely spatial size
in the object, but extensity determined by intensity,
in a word, what we call <u>force</u>. For the intensity of a
force can only be measured by the space in which it can
diffuse itself without becoming equal to zero. Just as,
conversely, this space is again determined by the size
of that force for inner sense. So what corresponds in
the object to inner sense is intensity, and what corresponds to outer, extensity. But intensity and extensity are mutually determined by each other. The object
is nothing else but fixated, merely present time, and
yet time is fixed simply and solely by the space that is
occupied, and the occupancy of space is determined simply
and solely by the amount of time, which is not itself
in space but is <u>extensione prior</u>. So that which <u>deter-</u>
<u>mines</u> the occupancy of space has a mere existence in
<u>time</u>, and that which, conversely, fixes <u>time</u> has a mere
existence in <u>space</u>. But now that in the object which
has mere existence in time, is precisely that whereby
the object belongs to inner sense, and the magnitude
of the object for inner sense is determined solely by
the common boundary of inner and outer sense, which
boundary appears as absolutely contingent. Hence that
in the object which corresponds to inner sense, or has
magnitude merely in time, will appear as the absolutely
contingent or accidental; while that, on the other hand,
which corresponds in the object to outer sense, or has
magnitude in space, will appear as the necessary or the
substantial. Hence, just as the object is extensity and
intensity at once, so likewise is it also <u>substance and</u>
<u>accident</u> at once; both are inseparable therein, and
only through both together is the object completed.
     That which is substance in the object has only
magnitude in space, and that which is accident, magnitude only in time. Time is fixed through the occupancy of space, and space occupied in determinate
fashion through magnitude in time.
     If now, armed with this result, we return to the
question from which this enquiry began, the outcome is
as follows. --The self was obliged to oppose the object
to itself in order to recognize it as an object. But
in this opposition, outer and inner sense became objects
for the self, that is, for us, as philosophers, space
and time could be distinguished in the self, and substance and accident in the object. --That substance and
accident were distinguishable therefore rested simply
on the fact that the one has only being in time ascribed
to it, and the other only being in space. Only through
the accidents of intuition is the self restricted to
time as such, for substance, since it only has being
in space, also has a being wholly independent of time,
and leaves the intelligence wholly unrestricted in
regard to time.

Since, then, in this manner, and through the act of
the self deduced in the foregoing, space and time have
become, for the philosopher, distinguishable in the
self, and substance and accident in the object, we now
ask, according to our established method, how space and
time, and thereby substance and accident, also become
distinguishable for the self itself?

Time is merely inner sense becoming an object to
itself, and space is outer sense becoming an object
thereto. Thus if both are again to become objects,
this can only take place through a higher, that is, a
productive, intuition. Both are intuitions of the self,
which can only again become objects to the self inasmuch
as they emerge out of the self. Now what do we mean
by "out of the self"? The self at the present juncture
is simply inner sense. So what is out of the self is
that which exists only for outer sense. Space and time
alike can thus become objects to the self only through
production, that is, since the self has stopped producing
(being now merely inner sense), only through the fact
that it now starts producing again. --But now in this
producing space and time, no less than inner and outer
sense, are synthetically united. Hence even by this
second producing we should have gained nothing: we
should again stand towards it precisely as we stood
with the first, unless, say, this second producing
were opposed to the first, so that by means of this
opposition to the first it immediately became an object
to the self. --But that the second producing should be
opposed to the first is conceivable only if the first
is in some sense restrictive of the second. --Hence,
that the self as such should start producing again can
in no case have its ground in the first producing, for
this is merely the restricting factor of the second,
and presupposes something to be restricted, or a
material for restriction; the ground must lie, rather,
in the intrinsic infinitude of the self.

The first producing cannot therefore be the ground
of a transition from present producing to a subsequent
one on the part of the self as such, but only of the
fact that the succeeding object is produced with this
particular degree of limitation. In a word, only the
accidental features in the second producing can be
determined by the first. We designate the first producing as B, and the second as C. Now if B contains
only the ground of the accidental in C, it can only be
something accidental in B whereby that in C is determined. For that C is limited by B in this particular
manner is possible only if B itself is limited in a
particular way, that is, by virtue merely of that which
is accidental in B itself.

To facilitate the enquiry, and so that its goal

will be seen right away, let it be observed that we are
approaching the deduction of the causal relation. Since
this is in fact a point from whence it is easier than
in many other cases to discern the manner in which
categories are deduced in transcendental idealism, we
may be permitted to prefix a general remark about our
procedure.

We deduce the causal relation as the necessary
condition under which alone the self can recognize the
present object as an object. If the presentation in
intelligence as such were static, if time remained fixed,
the intelligence would not only contain no manifold of
presentations (as would, of course, be the case), but
even the present object would not be recognized as
present either.

The succession in the causal relation is a necessary
one. From the very outset there can be no thought of an
arbitrary succession among presentations. The choice
which occurs, for example, in construing the individual
parts of a whole as those of an organism or an artifact,
is itself ultimately grounded in a causal relation.
Whatever part of the former I start from, I shall always
be driven back from one to another, and from this one
to that, because in an organism everything is reciprocally
cause and effect. Admittedly, this is not the case with
an artifact, for here no part is cause of another, but
each in fact presupposes the other in the productive
understanding of the maker. So is it everywhere, where
otherwise the succession of presentations appears
arbitrary, for example, in construing the individual
parts in inorganic nature, in which there is likewise
a general interplay of all the parts.

All categories are modes of action, whereby objects
themselves first come about for us. There is no object
for the intelligence in the absence of a causal relation, and the relation is for that very reason inseparable from objects. If we judge that $\underline{A}$ is the cause of
$\underline{B}$, this is to say that the succession occurring between
them is not only present in my thoughts, but lies in
the objects themselves. Neither $\underline{A}$ nor $\underline{B}$ could exist
at all, if they were not in this relation. Here,
therefore, we have not only succession as such, but a
succession that is the condition of the objects themselves. Now what, then, in idealism, can be understood
by this contrast between that which exists in thought
merely, and that which exists in the objects themselves? That the succession is objective, means, for
the idealist, that its ground lies, not in my free and
conscious thinking, but in my unconscious act of producing. That the ground of this succession does not
lie in us means that we are not conscious of this
succession before it takes place; its occurrence and

the awareness thereof are one and the same. The succession must come before us as inseparable from the
appearances, just as the appearances present themselves
as inseparable from the succession. For experience,
therefore, the result is the same, whether the succession be linked to the things, or the things to the
succession. The judgment of common sense is merely that
both are absolutely inseparable. It is thus in fact
completely illogical to attribute the succession to an
act of the intelligence, while the objects, by contrast,
are held to arise independently thereof. At least we
should proclaim both, the succession no less than the
objects, to be equally independent of our presentations.

Let us revert to the connection. We now have two
objects, B and C. And what, in fact, was B? It was
substance and accident inseparably united. So far as
it is substance, it is nothing else but fixated time
itself, for by the fact that time is fixed for us, substance arises for us, and vice versa. So if there is
also a sequence in time, substance itself must again
be that which persists through time. And substance,
accordingly, can neither come to be nor pass away. It
cannot come into being, for if we posit something as
doing so, a moment must have preceded in which it did
not yet exist; but that moment must itself have been
fixed, and so in it there must have been something that
persisted. Hence, what now comes into being is only a
determination of the permanent, not the permanent itself,
which is always the same. Equally little can substance
disappear, for if something disappears, a permanent of
some kind must remain behind, whereby the moment of
disappearance is fixed. Hence that which disappeared
was not the permanent itself, but merely a determination
thereof.

If therefore, no object can engender or abolish the
substance of another, it will in fact be only the accidental in the subsequent object that can be determined
by the preceding one, and conversely, it will be only
the accidental in the later object whereby the accidental in the first is determined.

Now in that B determines something accidental in
C, substance and accident are separated in the object;
substance persists, while the accidents change--space
abides, while time passes, and so both become objects
to the self in separation. But by this very fact the
self also finds itself translated into a new condition,
namely into that of an involuntary succession of presentations, and it is to this state that our reflection
must now turn.

"The accidental in B contains the ground of an
accidental in C." --This, however, is known only to
us, who contemplate the self. But now the intelligence

itself must also recognize the accidental in B as the
ground for that in C; yet this is not possible unless
both B and C are opposed in one and the same act, and
again related to one another. That they are both opposed
is obvious, for B is repressed from consciousness by
C and retreats into time past; B is the cause, C the
effect, B the restricting factor, C the restricted. But
how both can be related to each other is not intelligible, since the self is now nothing else but a succession
of primary presentations, of which one represses another.
(On the same grounds whereby the self is driven from B
to C, it will also be driven from C to D, and so on.)
Now it was indeed established that only accidents can
come and go, not substances. But then what is substance?
It is itself no more than the fixation of time. Hence
even substances cannot endure (for the self, needless
to say, since the question how substances may somehow
persist for themselves is wholly without meaning);
for time is now not fixated at all, but in flux (again,
not in itself, but only for the self), and so substances
cannot be fixated, since the self itself is not fixed,
being now nothing save this succession itself. --
     This state of the intelligence, in which it is just
a succession of presentations, is in fact a merely
intermediate condition, assumed therein only by the
philosopher, since it necessarily passes through this
state into the following. --
     Assuredly, substances must endure, if an opposition
between C and B is to be possible. It is, however, impossible for the succession to be fixed unless it be
through the very fact that opposing directions enter
into it. The succession has but one direction. This
one direction, abstracted from the succession, is what
constitutes time, which, outwardly intuited, has but
one dimension.
     But opposing directions could enter into the suc-
cession only if the self, while it is driven from B to
C, is simultaneously driven back again upon B; for then
the opposing directions will cancel one another, the
succession will be fixated, and thereby also the substances. But now the self can undoubtedly be driven
back from C to B only in a manner similar to that
whereby it was driven from B to C. Exactly, that is, as
B contained the ground of a determination in C, so must
C, in turn, contain the ground of a determination in B.
But now this determination in B cannot have existed
before C did, for the accidental in C is supposed, after
all, to contain the ground of it; C, however, arises for
the self as this particular determinate only at the
present moment. C as a substance may, indeed, have
already existed previously, but of this the self knows
nothing just now; C arises for it absolutely in arising

for it as this particular determinate, and hence that determination in B, of which C is to contain the ground, must likewise come into being only at this moment. Hence, in that one and the same indivisible moment in which C is determined by B, B too must conversely be determined by C. But now B and C have been opposed to one another in consciousness, so that a positing in C must necessarily be a nonpositing in B, and vice versa, of such a kind that if the determining of C by B is taken to be positive, that of B by C must be posited as the negative of this.

It scarcely needs pointing out that by way of the foregoing we have derived all the determinations of the relation of reciprocity. No causal relation whatsoever can be thought of without reciprocity, for no relation of effect to cause is possible, i.e., the above-required opposition is impossible, unless the substances, as substrates of the relationship, are fixated by each other. But this they cannot be unless the causal relation is a reciprocal one. For if the substances are not in reciprocity, both can admittedly be posited in consciousness, but only in the sense that one is posited if the other is not, and vice versa; not, however, in the sense that, in the same indivisible moment in which one is posited, the other is likewise; though this is necessary, if the self is to recognize both as standing in the causal relation. This condition, that both of them--not just one and then the other, but both at once-- are posited, can only be conceived if each is posited through the other, that is, if each is the ground of a determination in the other which is proportional and opposite to the determination posited in itself; that is, if both are in reciprocity with one another.

Through reciprocity the succession is fixated; it becomes a present, and by this the simultaneity of substance and accident in the object is again restored; B and C are at once both cause and effect. As cause, each is substance, for it can be known as a cause only insofar as it is intuited as persisting; as effect it is accident. Through reciprocity, therefore, substance and accident are again synthetically united. The possibility of cognizing the object as such is therefore governed, for the self, by the necessity of the succession and the reciprocity; the former abolishes the present (so that the self may go on beyond the object); the latter, however, reinstates it.

B and C are thus at one and the same moment the reciprocal ground of determinations in one another; but it has yet to be shown that they are thereby also simultaneous outside this moment. For the intelligence itself this simultaneity holds only for a moment; for since it produces continually, and no ground has so

far been given whereby the producing itself should again
be limited, the intelligence is repeatedly carried away
in the stream of succession. So how it arrives at
accepting a simultaneity of all substances in the world,
that is, a universal reciprocity, is not yet explained
thereby.

Along with reciprocity, the concept of coexistence
is also simultaneously derived. All simultaneity occurs
only through an act of the intelligence, and coexistence
is merely the condition of the primordial succession of
our presentations. Substances are nothing distinct from
coexistence. That they are fixated as substances means
that coexistence is posited, and conversely, coexistence
is nothing else but a mutual fixating of substances by
one another. If now this act of the intelligence is
reproduced ideally, that is, with consciousness, there
arises for me thereby space, as the mere form of coexistence or simultaneity. In general, it is first through
the category of reciprocity that space becomes the form
of coexistence; under the category of substance it emerges
only as the form of extensity. Thus space itself is
nothing else but an act of the intelligence. We can
define space as time suspended, and time, by contrast,
as space in flux. In space, regarded on its own account,
everything is merely concurrent, just as in time, rendered objective, everything is sequential. Hence both,
space and time, can become objects only in succession as
such, since in the latter space is static, while time
flows. Synthetically united, both space and time,
rendered objective, are manifested in reciprocity.
Simultaneity is, in fact, this union; adjacency in
space is transformed, once the determination of time is
added, into a simultaneity. And so too, once the determination of space is added, with successiveness in time.
--Time alone has a fundamental direction, though the
point which gives it direction lies in the infinite;
but precisely because it has this basic direction, only
one direction is in fact distinguished therein. Space
originally has no direction, for in it all directions
mutually cancel one another; as the ideal substrate of
all succession it is itself absolute rest, absolute
want of intensity, and to that extent nothing. --What
has hitherto made philosophers doubtful in regard to
space is simply that it possesses all the predicates
of nothing, and yet cannot be regarded as nothing.
Precisely because space originally has no direction,
every direction is contained in it, when once direction
has entered into it at all. But now in virtue merely
of the causal relation there is but one direction; I
can only go from A to B, and not back again from B to
A, and it is not until we introduce the category of
reciprocity that all directions become equally possible.

The foregoing enquiries contain the complete deduction of the categories of relation, and, since there are initially no others but these, the deduction of all categories--for the philosopher, to be sure, not for the intelligence itself (for how the latter arrives at recognizing them as such can only be explained in the epoch that is to follow). If we examine the table of categories given by Kant, we find that the first two in each group are always opposed to each other, and that the third is the union of them both. --The relation of substance and accident, for example, served to determine but a single object; through that of cause and effect a multiplicity of objects is determined; and through reciprocity these too are united once more into one object. --In the first relation something is posited as a unity, which is abolished again in the second, and recombined synthetically only in the third. Moreover, the two first categories are merely ideal factors, and only the third that evolves from them is the real. In the original consciousness, therefore, or in the intelligence itself, insofar as it is implicated in the mechanism of presentation, there can emerge neither the individual object as substance and accident, nor even a pure causal relation (containing, that is, succession in one direction); it is only by means of the category of reciprocity that the object first becomes at once substance and accident, and cause and effect, for the self. Insofar as the object is a synthesis of inner and outer sense, it necessarily stands in connection with a moment past and a moment to follow. In the causal relation this synthesis is dissolved, in that the substances persist for outer sense, whereas for inner sense the accidents pass away. But the causal relation itself cannot be recognized as such unless both the substances involved therein are again combined into one, and so this synthesis proceeds, up to the idea of nature, wherein all substances are at last combined into one, which is in reciprocity only with itself.

With this absolute synthesis, all involuntary succession among presentations will be fixated. But since we as yet discern no ground whereby the self should ever break wholly out of the succession, and since we comprehend only relative syntheses, but not the absolute one, we can see in advance that the presentation of nature as the absolute totality, in which all oppositions are resolved and all succession of causes and effects is united into an absolute organism, is possible, not through the original mechanism of presentation, which merely carries it on from one object to the next, and within which all synthesis is purely relative, but rather by means only of a free act of the intelligence, though this itself we do not as yet comprehend.

In the course of the present enquiry we have deliberately left a number of individual points undiscussed, so as to make for less interruption in the sequence of the deduction; but we now need to turn our attention to them. Thus till now, for example, we have merely presupposed that intelligence itself contains the ground of a continual producing. For that the self as such embarked on producing could not have had its ground in the first producing; there must have been a ground for it in the intelligence as such. This ground must already be contained in the first principles given earlier.

The self is neither originally productive, nor is it even so by choice. It is a primary opposition, whereby the essence and nature of intelligence are constituted. But now the self originally is a pure and absolute identity, to which it must constantly seek to return; yet the return to this identity is yoked to the original duality, as to a condition never wholly overcome. Now as soon as the condition of producing, namely duality, is given, the self must produce, and is compelled to do so, as surely as it is an original identity. So if there is a continual producing in the self, this is possible only in that the condition of all producing, that original conflict of opposing activities in the self, is reestablished ad infinitum. But now this conflict was to end in productive intuition. But if it is really ended, the intelligence goes over utterly and completely into the object; it is an object, but not an intelligence. The intelligence is such only so long as this conflict continues; once it is ended, it is no longer intelligence but matter, an object. As surely, therefore, as all knowledge as such depends on that opposition between intelligence and the object, so surely can the opposition be resolved in no single object. How then indeed it arrives at a finite object is utterly inexplicable unless every object is only apparently single, and can be produced only as a part of an infinite whole. But that the opposition is resolved only in an infinite object can be envisaged only if it is itself an infinite opposition, so that mediating terms of the synthesis are alone possible, and the two outermost factors of the opposition can never, in fact, merge into one another.

But is it not also possible to show, in fact, that the opposition must be infinite, since the conflict of the two activities it depends on is necessarily an eternal one? The intelligence can never extend itself into the infinite, for it is prevented from doing so by its striving to return back into itself. It is, however, equally incapable of an absolute return into

itself, for from this it is prevented by the tendency
to infinitude. Here, therefore, no mediation is possible, and every synthesis is but a relative one.

If it be desired, however, that the mechanism of
producing should be more exactly specified, we shall be
able to think of it only in the following manner. Faced,
on the one hand, with the impossibility of overcoming
the absolute opposition, and with the necessity of doing
so on the other, a product will ensue, but in it the
opposition cannot be absolutely, but only partially, overcome; outside the opposition that is resolved by this
product, there will lie another that is still unresolved,
though this too can be overcome in a second product.
Hence every product that arises, in virtue of the fact
that it gives only a partial resolution of the infinite
opposition, will become the condition of a subsequent
product, which, since it still only partially removes
the opposition, becomes the condition of a third. All
these products will be subordinated one to another, and
all of them ultimately to the first, since every preceding
product sustains the opposition which is the condition
of the one following. If we reflect that the force
corresponding to the productive activity is the true
synthesizing force of nature, namely gravitation, we
shall be persuaded that this subordination is none other
than the subordination of celestial objects one to
another, as it occurs in the universe; a subordination
such that the organization of these bodies into systems,
where one is conserved in its being by the next, is
nothing else but an organization of the intelligence
itself, which throughout all these products is continually in search of the absolute point of equilibrium
with itself, albeit that this point lies at infinity.

But now even this explanation of the mechanism
whereby the intelligence produces immediately involves
us in a new difficulty. All empirical consciousness
begins with a present object, and already on first
becoming conscious the intelligence sees itself involved
in a determinate succession of presentations. But now
the individual object is possible only as part of a
universe, and succession, in virtue of the causal
relation, itself already presupposes not only a multiplicity of substances, but a reciprocity, or a dynamic
simultaneity of all substances. The contradiction is
therefore this, that the intelligence, insofar as it
becomes conscious of itself, can intervene only at a
specific point in the order of succession, and hence,
in becoming self-conscious, must already presuppose a
totality of substances, and a universal reciprocity
among substances, as conditions of a possible succession independent of itself.

This contradiction is soluble only by a distinction

between the absolute and the finite intelligence, and
serves at the same time as a new proof that, without
knowing it, we have already displaced the self and its
producing into the second or determinate form of limitation. The more exact working-out of this relationship
is as follows.
     That a universe, i.e., a universal interplay of
substances, exists at all, is necessary, if the self
as such is originally restricted. In virtue of this
original restrictedness, or, what comes to the same,
in virtue of the original conflict of self-consciousness,
the universe arises for the self, not gradually, but
through one absolute synthesis. But this original or
primary restrictedness, which assuredly can be explained
from self-consciousness, does not explain for me the
particular restrictedness which can no longer be
explained from self-consciousness, and to that extent
is therefore not explicable at all. The particular,
or, as we shall also call it in future, the secondary
restrictedness, is precisely that by virtue of which the
intelligence, at the very outset of empirical consciousness, must appear to itself as in a present, as held
fast in a particular moment of the time series. Now
what emerges in this series of the second restrictedness is all posited already through the first, only
with this difference, that by the latter everything is
posited at once, and the absolute synthesis arises for
the self, not by an assemblage out of parts, but as a
whole; nor does it arise in time, for all time is first
posited through that synthesis, whereas in empirical
consciousness the whole in question can only be engendered through a gradual synthesis of parts, and so only
through successive presentations. Now insofar as the
intelligence is not in time, but is eternal, it is
nothing else but that absolute synthesis itself, and
to that extent has neither begun, nor can it cease, to
produce; but insofar as the intelligence is limited, it
can also appear only as intervening upon the successive
series at a particular point. Not indeed, as if the
infinite intelligence were different from the finite,
and as though there existed an infinite intelligence
outside, as it were, the finite one. For if I take
away the particular restrictedness of the finite
intelligence, it is the absolute intelligence itself.
If I posit this restrictedness, the absolute intelligence
is by that very fact suspended as absolute, and is now
a merely finite one. Nor is the relationship to be
pictured as though the absolute synthesis and this
incursion upon a particular point in its evolution
were two different acts; rather it is that in one and the
same original act there arises at once for the intelligence both the universe, and the particular point of

evolution to which its empirical consciousness is
attached; or more briefly, there arise through one and
the same act, for the intelligence, both the first and
the second types of restriction, of which the latter
appears incomprehensible only because it is posited along
with the first, yet without being derivable therefrom
in its determinacy. This determinacy will thus appear
as the contingent, absolutely and in every respect,
which the idealist can account for only by an absolute
act of the intelligence, whereas the realist explains
it by what he calls destiny or fate. It is, however,
easy to see why, to the intelligence, the point from
which its consciousness begins must appear as determined wholly without its concurrence; for just because
it is at this point that consciousness, and with it
freedom, first arise, whatever lies beyond this point
must appear as totally independent of freedom.

　　We are now so far advanced in the history of the
intelligence that we have already confined it to a
specific succession, into which its consciousness can
enter only at a particular point. The enquiry above-
instituted was concerned only with the question, how
the intelligence has been able to enter into this
succession; since we have now discovered that for it
the second restrictedness must also arise along with the
first, we see in consequence that at the first onset
of consciousness we could find it no otherwise than as
we have in fact found it, namely as involved in a
particular successive series. As a result of these
enquiries, the proper task of transcendental philosophy
has been much illuminated. Everyone can regard himself
as the object of these investigations. But to explain
himself to himself, he must first have suspended all
individuality within himself, for it is precisely this
which is to be explained. If all the bounds of individuality are removed, nothing remains behind save the
absolute intelligence. If the bounds of intelligence
are also once more suspended, nothing remains but the
absolute self. The problem now is simply this: how
the absolute intelligence is to be accounted for by an
act of the absolute self, and how, in turn, by an act
of the absolute intelligence, we may explain the whole
system of restrictedness which constitutes my individuality. But now if all limits are taken away from
the intelligence, what is there still left as explanatory ground of a determinate action? I observe that even
if I deprive the self of all individuality, including
the very limits by virtue of which it is an intelligence,
I still cannot eliminate the basic character of the self,
namely that to itself it is at once subject and object.
Hence, in itself and by its own nature, before ever it
is restricted in particular ways, the self, by the very

fact that it is an object to itself, is originally
restricted in its acting. From this first or original
restrictedness of its acting, there arises immediately
for the self the absolute synthesis of that infinite
conflict which is the ground of the restrictedness in
question. Now if the intelligence were to remain one
with the absolute synthesis, there would indeed be a
universe, but there would be no intelligence. If an
intelligence is to exist, it must be able to emerge from
this synthesis, in order to engender it again with consciousness; but this is impossible, however, unless there
enters into this first restrictedness a second or
particular one, which can now no longer consist in the
fact that the intelligence intuits a universe at large,
but rather that it views the universe precisely from
this particular point. So the difficulty which at first
sight seemed insoluble, namely that everyhing which exists
is to be explicable from an act of the self, and yet
that the intelligence can enter only at a particular point
of a succession already determined beforehand, is resolved
by the distinction between the absolute and the determinate intelligence. The succession into which your
consciousness has entered is not determined by you,
insofar as you are this individual, for to that extent
you are not the producer, but yourself belong to the
product. The succession in question is but the development of an absolute synthesis, wherewith everything
which happens or will happen is already posited. That
you picture just this particular succession is necessary,
in that you are this particular intelligence. It is
necessary that this series appears to you as a predetermined series independent of yourself, which you
cannot produce afresh. Not that it is as if it had
somehow elapsed of itself; for that what lies beyond
your consciousness should appear to you as independent
of yourself, is precisely what constitutes your
particular limitation. Take this away, and there is no
past; posit the latter, and it is just as necessary and
just as real--no more, that is, and no less--as the
limitation. Beyond the particular limitation lies the
sphere of the absolute intelligence, for which nothing
has begun, nor does anything become, since everything,
for it, is simultaneous, or rather, it is itself everything. Thus the boundary between the absolute intelligence, unaware of itself as such, and the conscious
intelligence, is simply time. For pure reason there is
no time, for it is everything, and everything at once;
for reason insofar as it is empirical, everything comes
into being, and what arises for it is all merely successive.
        Now before we pursue the history of the intelli-
gence from this point onwards, we must turn our attention

again to some more exact determinations of this succession which are given to us along with the deduction
thereof; from these, as might be expected in advance,
there are numerous other conclusions that we shall be
able to draw.

a)   The successive series is, as we know, nothing
else but the evolution of the original and absolute synthesis; so what emerges in this series is already determined in advance thereby. With the first limitation,
all the determinations of the universe are posited;
with the second, by virtue of which I am this intelligence, all the determinations under which this object
enters my consciousness.

b)   This absolute synthesis is an act which takes
place outside all time. With every empirical consciousness, time, as it were, begins all over again; by the
same token, every empirical consciousness presupposes
a time as having already elapsed, for it can begin only
at a determinate point in the evolution. Hence, for the
empirical consciousness, time can never have begun, and
for the empirical intelligence there is no beginning in
time, save that through absolute freedom. To that extent
one can say that every intelligence, not for itself, to
be sure, but objectively regarded, is an absolute beginning in time, an absolute point that is pitched and
posited, as it were, into a timeless infinity, and from
which all infinitude in time now first commences.

It is a very common objection to idealism, that
presentations of outward things come to us quite involuntarily, that we can do nothing whatever about this,
and that, so far from producing them, we are obliged,
rather, to accept them as they are given to us. But
that presentations must appear to us thus is a consequence to be drawn from idealism itself. In order that
it may intuit the object in general as an object, the
self must posit a past moment as a ground of the present,
and the past therefore arises ever and again through the
action of the intelligence only, and is necessary only
insofar as this regression of the self is necessary.
But the reason why nothing in the present moment can
arise for me, save what actually does arise for me now,
is to be sought wholly and solely in the infinite consistency of the mind. An object with these and no
other determinations can only arise for me now, because
in the preceding moment I had produced an object containing the ground of just these and no other determinations. How the intelligence should be able to see
itself, through one production, involved at once in an
entire system of things, can be shown by analogy with
innumerable other cases, in which reason, by the sole
power of its consistency, sees itself precipitated by
a single presupposition into the most complex of systems,

even where the presupposition is an entirely arbitrary
one. There is, for example, no more complicated system
than that of gravitation, which has required for its
development the highest exertions of the human mind; and
yet it is an exceedingly simple law which has led the
astronomer into this labyrinth of motions, and again
guided him out of it. Our decimal system is without
doubt a wholly arbitrary one, and yet, by that one
presupposition, the mathematician sees himself plunged
into consequences which (as, for example, with the
remarkable properties of decimal fractions) perhaps
not one of them has yet completely developed. --
     In its present producing the intelligence is there-
fore never free, because it has been producing in the
preceding moment. Through the first producing the freedom of producing is, as it were, forfeited forever. But
in fact there is no first producing for the self; for
that the intelligence appears to itself as though it
had absolutely begun to form presentations, is in any
case a feature merely of its particular restrictedness.
Remove this, and it is eternal, and has never begun to
produce. If it be judged that the intelligence has begun
to produce, it is always itself that judges thus, according to a specific law; whence it follows, indeed, that
the intelligence has begun to have presentations for
itself, but never that it has done so objectively or in
itself.
     It is a question that the idealist cannot escape,
how he in fact arrives at assuming a past, or what serves
him as a guarantee for this? The present is explicable
to everyone in virtue of his own producing, but how
does he come to assume that he was something before he
produced? Whether there has been a past-in-itself is
a question no less transcendent than the question whether
there is a thing-in-itself. The past <u>exists</u> only through
the present, and so exists for everyone as such only
through his own original restrictedness; take away the
latter, and everything that has happened, like everything now occurring, is the production of the one
intelligence, which has not had a beginning, nor will
cease to exist. --
     If one seeks to determine, through time as such, the
<u>absolute</u> intelligence, which has absolute rather than
<u>empirical</u> eternity, then it is everything that is, and
was, and will be. But the <u>empirical</u> intelligence, in
order to be something, that is, to be a determinate,
must cease to be everything and cease to be outside
time. Originally there exists for it only a present,
and through its infinite striving the present instant
becomes an earnest of the future, but this infinitude
is now no longer absolute, that is, timeless, but an
empirical infinitude engendered through succession of

presentations. The intelligence strives, indeed, at
every moment to exhibit the absolute synthesis; as
Leibniz says, the soul brings forth at every moment the
presentation of the universe. But since it is unable
to do so through an absolute act, it attempts to show
it forth through a successive progression in time.

c) Since time, in and for itself, or originally,
betokens a mere limit, it can be outwardly intuited,
that is, united with space, only as the fluxion of a
point, i.e., as a line. But a line is the original
intuition of motion; all motion is intuited as motion
only insofar as it is intuited as a line. Hence the
original succession of presentations, outwardly intuited,
is motion. But now since it is the intelligence which
seeks merely its own identity throughout the whole
successive sequence, and since this identity would be
abolished at every moment through the transition from
one presentation to the next, if the intelligence did
not continually seek to restore it, the transition from
presentation to presentation must occur by a magnitude
that is constant, i.e., of which no part is absolutely
the smallest.

Now it is time in which this transition occurs,
and hence time will be such a magnitude. And since all
original succession appears outwardly in the intelligence as motion, the law of constancy will thus be a
basic law of all motion.

The same property will be shown in the same manner
to hold of space.

Since the succession and all changes in time are
nothing else but evolutions of the absolute synthesis,
whereby everything is determined in advance, the ultimate
ground of all motion must be sought in the factors of
that synthesis itself; but now these factors are none
other than those of the original opposition, and hence
the ground of all motion will likewise require to be
looked for in the factors of that opposition. This
original opposition can be but momentarily abolished
only in an infinite synthesis and in the finite object.
The opposition arises anew at every moment, and is at
every moment again annulled. This reengendering and
reabolition of the opposition at every moment must be
the ultimate ground of all motion. This principle,
which is basic to a dynamic physics, has its place,
like all basic principles of the subordinate sciences,
in transcendental philosophy.

IV

In the succession above described, the intelligence has
to do, not with the succession, for the latter is
wholly involuntary, but rather with itself. It seeks

itself, but in so doing actually flees from itself.
Once it has been displaced into this succession, it
can no longer intuit itself otherwise than as active
in the succession. But now we have already deduced a
self-intuition of the intelligence within the succession,
by way, that is, of reciprocity. But hitherto we have
been able to make reciprocity intelligible only as a
relative, not as an absolute synthesis or intuition of
the <u>whole</u> succession of presentations. It is now utterly
beyond conception, how the whole succession can become
an object unless a limiting of the succession is to take
place.

Here, therefore, we see ourselves driven into a
third phase of limitation, which thrusts the intelligence
into a sphere still narrower than any of the preceding,
but one we must put up with, if only in order to postulate. The first restriction of the self was that it
became an intelligence at all; the second, that it had
to start out from a present moment, or could intervene
only at a particular point in the succession. Though
from that point at least, the series could proceed to
infinity. But now if this infinitude is not in turn
restricted, there is absolutely no seeing how the
intelligence may step out from its own producing and
intuit itself as productive. Hitherto, the intelligence
and the succession itself have been one; now it must
oppose the succession to itself, in order to intuit
itself therein. The succession, however, runs only to
change among the accidents, whereas the intuiting of the
succession requires that the substantial element therein
be intuited as persisting. But the substantial element
in this infinite succession is nothing else save the
absolute synthesis itself, which did not come to be, but
is eternal. The intelligence, though, has no intuition
of the absolute synthesis, that is, of the universe,
unless the latter become finite to it. The intelligence,
therefore, is also unable to intuit the succession unless
the universe comes to be limited for it in intuition.

But now the intelligence can no more cease to produce than it can cease to be an intelligence. Hence
this succession of presentations will not be capable of
limitation for it, unless it be again an infinite
succession within this limitation. To make this clear
at once, there is in the external world a constant sequence of changes, which do not, however, lose themselves
in the infinite, but are restricted to a specific circle,
into which they constantly revert. This sequence of
changes is thus at once both finite and infinite; finite,
because it never oversteps a certain limit; infinite,
because it constantly returns back into itself. The
circular line is the original synthesis of finitude
and infinity, into which even the straight line must

be resolved. The succession only appears to proceed in
a straight line, and constantly flows back into itself.
     But the intelligence must intuit the succession as
returning into itself; by means of this intuition a new
product will undoubtedly arise for it, and thus again
it will never arrive at intuiting the succession, for
instead of the latter there arises for it something
entirely different. The question is, what the nature
of this product will be.
     One may say that organic nature furnishes the most
obvious proof of transcendental idealism, for every
plant is a symbol of the intelligence. For the plant,
indeed, the material that it appropriates or incorporates
into itself under a particular form is already preformed
in the natural environment; but whence then is material
to come to the intelligence, since it is absolute and
alone? Since, therefore, it produces the material no
less than the form from out of itself, it is the absolutely organic. In the original succession of presentations it appears to us as an activity which is unceasingly
at once both cause and effect of itself; cause, insofar
as it produces; effect, insofar as it is the produced.
Empiricism, which has everything entering the intelligence from without, in fact explains the nature of
intelligence in purely mechanical fashion. Yet if the
intelligence is organic at all, as indeed it is, it has
also framed to itself outwardly from within everything
that is external for it, and that which constitutes the
universe for it is merely the grosser and remoter organ
of self-consciousness, just as the individual organism
is the finer and more immediate organ thereof.
     A deduction of organic nature has primarily four
questions to answer.
     1. Why is an organic nature necessary at all?
     2. Why is a graduated sequence in organic nature
necessary?
     3. Why is there a difference between living and
nonliving organization?
     4. What is the basic character of all organization?
1.   The necessity of organic nature is deducible in the
following manner.
     The intelligence must intuit itself in its produc-
tive transition from cause to effect, or in the succession of its presentations, insofar as this returns into
itself. But this it cannot do, without making the
succession permanent, or representing it as static.
A self-reverting succession, statically represented, is
in fact organization. The concept of organization does
not exclude all notion of succession. Organization is
merely succession confined within limits and presented
as fixed. The expression of organic configuration is
rest, although this constant reproducedness of the static

figure is possible only through a continuous inward
flux. As surely, therefore, as the intelligence, in
the original succession of presentations, is at once
both cause and effect of itself, and as surely as this
succession is a limited one, the succession must become
objectified to it as organization, which is the first
solution of our problem, as to how the intelligence
intuits itself as productive.
2.   But now within its limits the succession is again
infinite. The intelligence is thus an endless endeavor
towards self-organization. Thus everything in the entire
system of the intelligence will also strive towards
organization, and the general drive towards this will
have to extend over its external world. Hence a
graduated sequence of organization will also be necessary. For insofar as it is empirical, the intelligence
has a continual endeavor at least to bring forth in
succession the universe which it cannot depict by means
of an absolute synthesis. The serial order in its
original presentations is therefore nothing else but a
successive depiction or development of the absolute
synthesis, save only that by virtue of the third
restriction, even this development can obtain only up
to a certain limit. This evolution, limited and intuited
as limited, is organization.
    Organization in general is therefore nothing else
but a diminished and as it were condensed picture of the
universe. But now the succession is itself gradual,
that is, it cannot wholly develop itself in any single
moment. But the further the succession advances, the
further the universe also develops. In proportion, therefore, as the succession proceeds, organization too will
achieve a greater extension, and depict within itself
a larger portion of the universe. This will thus provide a graduated sequence running parallel to the development of the universe. The law of this sequence is that
organization constantly enlarges its scope as the
intelligence constantly extends it. If this extension,
or the evolution of the universe, were to go on to
infinity, organization too would go on ad infinitum;
the limit of the one is also the limit of the other.
    The following may serve by way of elucidation. The
deeper we descend into organic nature, the narrower
becomes the world which organization depicts within
itself, and the smaller the portion of the universe
that condenses into organization. The vegetable kingdom is assuredly the narrowest, since a multitude of
natural changes simply do not fall within its sphere.
Broader already, though still very restricted, is the
sphere of changes exhibited among the lowest orders of
the animal kingdom, in that, for example, the noblest
senses, those of sight and hearing, still lie dormant,

and even touch, that is, receptivity for the immediately
present, is scarcely operative. --What we call sensation
in animals does not refer, say, to a power of acquiring
presentations through impressions from without, but
merely to their relationship with the universe, which
may be broader or more confined. But the view we have to
take of animals as such may be gathered from this, that
through them there is designated in nature that stage
of consciousness at which our deduction presently stands.
--If we move upwards in the scale of organization, we
find that the senses gradually develop in that order
in which, by means of them, the world of the organizations is enlarged.[1] The sense of hearing, for example,
appears far earlier, since by means of it the world of
the organism is extended only to a very short distance.
The godlike sense of vision is much later to emerge,
since by means of it the world is expanded to an extent
which even the imagination is unable to encompass.
Leibniz betrays so great a reverence for light that for
this reason alone he attributes higher presentations to
animals, that they are receptive to light-impressions.
Although even where this sense, with its associated
structures, appears, it remains always uncertain how
far the sense itself extends, and whether even for the
highest organizations the light is not simply light.
3.   Organization as such is succession hampered and,
as it were, coagulated in its course. But now the
intelligence was to intuit, not merely the succession of
its presentations as such, but itself, and itself as
active in the succession. If it is to become an object
to itself as active in the succession (externally, of
course, for the intelligence is now merely outwardly
intuitant), it must intuit the succession as sustained
by an inner principle of activity. But now the internal succession, outwardly intuited, is motion. Hence
the intelligence will be able to intuit itself only in
an object that has an internal principle of motion within
itself. But an object such as this is said to be alive.
Hence the intelligence must intuit itself, not merely
qua organization as such, but as a living organization.
But now it appears from this very deduction of life,
that the latter must be common to all organic nature,
and hence that there can be no distinction between living
and nonliving organizations in nature itself. Since the
intelligence is to intuit itself as active in the succes-
sions throughout the whole of organic nature, every
organization must also possess life in the wider sense
of the word, that is, must have an inner principle of

[1]In regard to this law, I must refer to Herr
Kielmeyer's discourse on the relationships of the organic
powers, where it is set forth and demonstrated.

motion within itself. The life in question may well
be more or less restricted; the question, therefore:
whence this distinction? reduces itself to the previous
one: whence the graduated sequence in organic nature?

But this scale of organization merely refers to
different stages in the evolution of the universe.
Precisely as the intelligence, by means of the succession, constantly tries to depict the absolute synthesis,
so likewise will organic nature constantly appear as
struggling towards universal organism and at war against
an inorganic nature. The bounds of the succession in the
presentations of the intelligence will also be the
bounds of organization. But now there must be an absolute boundary to the intuiting of the intelligence; this
boundary, for us, is light. For although it extends
our sphere of intuition almost into the immeasurable,
the light-boundary cannot be the boundary of the universe,
and it is no mere hypothesis that beyond the world of
light there shines with a radiance unknown to us a world
which no longer falls within the sphere of our intuition. --So now if the intelligence intuits the evolution
of the universe, so far as this falls within its intuition, in terms of an organization, it will intuit this
latter as identical with its own self. For it is the
intelligence itself, which through all the labyrinths
and convolutions of organic nature seeks to reflect back
itself as productive. But in none of the subordinate
organizations is the world of the intelligence depicted
to the full. Only on attaining to the most perfect
organization, into which its entire world contracts,
will it recognize this organization as identical with
itself. Hence the intelligence will appear to itself,
not merely qua organic as such, but as standing at the
summit of organization. It can regard the other organizations only as intermediate stages, throughout which
the most perfect gradually extricates itself from the
fetters of matter, or by way of which it becomes completely an object to itself. Hence also it will not
concede to the other organizations a like dignity with
its own.

The limit of its world, or what comes to the same,
the limit of the succession of its presentations, is
also, for the intelligence, the limit of organization.
Hence, what we have called the third restrictedness
consists in the fact that the intelligence must appear
to itself as an organic individual. Through the
necessity of intuiting itself as an organic individual
its world, for it, becomes wholly limited, and conversely, through the fact that the succession of its
presentations is a limited one, it itself becomes an
organic individual.
4.   The basic character of organization is that,

excluded, as it were, from mechanism, it subsists not
merely as cause or effect, but through itself, since it
is at once both cause and effect of itself. We began
by defining the object as substance and accident, but
it could not be intuited as such without also being
cause and effect, and conversely, it could not be intuited
as cause and effect unless substances were fixated. But
where, then, does substance begin, and where does it
leave off? A simultaneous existence of all substances
transforms all of them into one, comprehended only in
eternal reciprocity with itself; this is the absolute
organization. Organization is thus the higher power of
the category of reciprocity, which, viewed universally,
leads to the concept of nature or of universal organization, in relation to which all individual organizations
are again themselves accidents. The basic character of
organization is therefore that it be in reciprocity with
itself, at once both producer and product, and this
concept is the principle of the whole theory of organic
nature, whence all further determinations of organization can be derived a priori.

Since we now stand at the summit of all production,
namely at the organic, we are accorded a retrospect over
the whole series. We can now distinguish in nature
three orders of intuition: The simple, that of stuff,
which is posited therein through sensation; the second,
that of matter, which is posited through productive
intuition; and lastly the third, which is characterized
by organization.

Now since organization is merely productive intuition of the second order, the categories for the construction of matter as such, or of general physics, will
also be categories of organic construction and of the
theory of organic nature, save only that they must likewise be thought of therein as raised to a higher power.
Moreover, just as the three dimensions of matter are
determined by these three categories of general physics,
so also are the three dimensions of the organic product
determined by the three categories of the organic. And
if galvanism, as stated, is the general expression of
process going over into product, and if magnetism,
electricity and chemical force, raised to a higher
power with the product, yield the three categories of
organic physics, we shall have to envisage galvanism
as the bridge whereby these universal forces of nature
pass over into sensibility, irritability and formative
urge.

The basic character of life, in particular, will
consist in this, that it is a sequence, reverting into
itself, fixated, and sustained by an inner principle;
and just as intellectual life, whose image it is, or the
identity of consciousness, is sustained only by the

continuity of presentations, so life is sustained only
by the continuity of internal motions; and just as the
intelligence, in the succession of its presentations,
constantly struggles to achieve consciousness, so life
must be thought of as engaged in a constant struggle
against the course of nature, or in an endeavor to uphold
its identity against the latter.

Having answered the main questions that can be asked
of a deduction of organic nature, we turn our attention
further to one particular result of this deduction, namely
that in the scale of organizations there must necessarily
emerge one which the intelligence is obliged to intuit
as identical with itself. Now if the intelligence is
nothing else but an evolution of original presentations,
and if this succession is to be exhibited in the organism,
then that organization which the intelligence must recognize as identical with itself will at every moment be
the perfect expression of its inner nature. Now where
the changes in the organism that correspond to presentations are lacking, those presentations likewise cannot
become an object to the intelligence. If we wish to
speak transcendently, the man born blind, for example,
certainly has a presentation of light for an observer
outside him, since all that is required for this is the
power of internal intuition, it being merely that this
presentation does not become an object for him; although,
from a transcendental viewpoint, this presentation really
does not exist in him, since nothing exists in the self
which it does not itself intuit therein. The organism
is the condition under which alone the intelligence can
distinguish itself, as substance or subject of the
succession, from the succession itself, or under which
alone this succession can be something independent of
the intelligence. That it now appears to us as though
there were a transition from the organism into the
intelligence, whereby an affection of the former brings
about a presentation in the latter, is a mere illusion,
because we can indeed know nothing of the presentation
before it becomes an object to us through the organism:
the affection of the latter therefore precedes the presentation in consciousness, and must thus appear, not as
conditioned thereby, but rather as the condition thereof.
Not the presentation itself, though certainly the consciousness thereof, is conditioned by the affection of
the organism, and if empiricism restricts its claim
to the latter point, no objection can be made to it.

If then, one may speak of a transition at all,
where in fact there are not two opposing objects, but
properly only one, we may rather refer to a transition
from the intelligence into the organism than to a movement in the opposite direction. For since the organism
itself is but a mode of intuition on the part of the

intelligence, everything in the latter must necessarily
become an object to it immediately in the organism. It
is merely this necessity of intuiting everything within
us, and hence also the presentation as such, and not just
the object thereof, as located outside us, which underlies the whole so-called dependence of the mental on the
material. As soon, for example, as the organism is no
longer a perfect reflex of our universe, it also serves
no longer as an organ of self-intuition, that is, it is
ailing; we feel <u>ourselves</u> to be ill only because of
this absolute <u>identity of</u> the organism with ourselves.
However, the organism is itself ill only according to
natural laws, that is, according to laws of the intelligence itself. For the intelligence in its producing
is not free, but restricted and compelled by laws. So
when, by natural laws, my organism is obliged to be ill,
I am also necessitated to intuit it as such. The feeling
of sickness arises through nothing else but a loss of
identity between the intelligence and its organism;
whereas the feeling of health, if one can indeed speak
of a wholly empty sensation as a feeling, is the feeling of a total absorption of the intelligence in the
organism, or, as an excellent writer expresses it, of
the transparency of the organism for the spirit.

     To this dependence, not of the mental itself, but
of the consciousness of the mental upon the physical,
there belongs also the waxing and waning of the intellectual powers along with the organic, and even the
necessity of appearing to ourselves as having been
born. I, as this particular individual, did not exist
at all before I intuited myself as this, nor shall I
be this same person, once the intuition ceases. Since,
by the laws of nature, there is necessarily a time at
which the organism, as a fabric gradually destroying
itself through its own energies, must cease to reflect
the external world, the absolute loss of identity between
organism and intelligence, which in sickness is only
partial, namely death, is thus a natural event itself
falling within the original series of the intelligence's
presentations.

     What holds of the intelligence's blind activity,
namely that the organism is the constant expression
thereof, will also have to hold of free activity, if
there is any such in the intelligence--a thing we have
so far not derived. Hence, to every voluntary succession of presentation in the intelligence free movement
in its organism will have to correspond, wherein is
included not merely so-called voluntary movement in the
narrow sense, but also demeanor, speech, and in short
everything that is the expression of an inner state.
But how a freely engendered presentation of the
intelligence passes over into an outward motion--a

question belonging to practical philosophy and touched
on here only because it is in fact answerable solely
according to the principles just laid down--requires a
solution entirely different from the converse question,
how a presentation in the intelligence can be conditioned
by a change in the organism. For insofar as the intelligence produces unconsciously, its organism is immediately identical with it, in such a way that what it
intuits externally is reflected by the organism without
further mediation. For example, it is necessary according to natural law that under such-and-such a configuration, e.g., of the general causes of stimulation, the
organism should appear to be ill; these conditions being
given, the intelligence is no longer free to envision
the conditioned or not; the organism becomes ill, because the intelligence is obliged to perceive it thus.
But insofar as it is freely active, the intelligence
becomes distinct from its organism, so that a presenting
on the part of the former is not immediately followed
by something existent in the latter. A causal relation
between a free activity of the intelligence and a
motion in its organism is no more conceivable than the
converse relationship, since the two are not opposed
really at all, but only ideally so. Hence there is
nothing for it but to posit a harmony between the intelligence, so far as it is freely active, and so far as
it intuits unconsciously--and this harmony is necessarily a preestablished one. To be sure, even transcendental idealism has no need at all of a predetermined
harmony in order to explain how changes in the organism
conform to involuntary presentations; yet it does need
one to explain the coincidence of organic changes with
voluntary presentations. Nor does it require a preestablished harmony like that of Leibniz, as commonly
expounded, holding immediately between the intelligence
and the organism; but rather a harmony between the free
and the unconscious producing activities, since only
the latter is needed to explain a passage from the
intelligence into the external world.

Yet how such a harmony itself may be possible, we
can neither discern, nor do we even need to discern it,
so long as we occupy the ground we are on at present.

V

From the relationship, now wholly deduced, of the intelligence to the organism, it is evident that in the
present stage of consciousness the intelligence is
absorbed in its organism, which it intuits as wholly
identical with itself, and so once more fails to attain
to intuition of itself.

But now at the same time, owing to the fact that

its whole world is drawn together, for the intelligence, in the organism, the circle of production is closed for it. So the last act whereby complete consciousness is posited in the intelligence (and to find this was our only task; everything else which occurred in solving this problem arose for us only incidentally, as it were, and with no more intention than for the intelligence itself), must fall altogether outside the sphere of producing; that is, the intelligence itself must break away entirely from producing if consciousness is to come about, which can undoubtedly occur once more only through a series of acts. Now before we are able to derive these acts themselves, it is necessary to have at least a general acquaintance with the sphere covering those acts which are opposed to producing. For that such acts must be opposed to producing is already to be inferred from the fact that they are to set limits thereto.

We ask, therefore, whether perchance in the foregoing sequence, any act opposed to producing has emerged for us? --In deducing the series of productions whereby the self gradually arrived at intuiting itself as productive, we certainly found no activity whereby the intelligence divorced itself utterly from producing, though the positing of every derived product in the intelligence's own consciousness could indeed be explained only through a constant reflecting of the intelligence upon the produced; save only that through every act of reflection the condition of a new producing arose for us. In order to explain the progressive sequence in producing, we therefore had to posit an activity in our object, whereby it strives on beyond every individual act of producing, though the very effect of its so doing is to involve it repeatedly in new productions. We can therefore know in advance that the series of acts we have now postulated belongs in the sphere of reflection as such.

But producing is now at an end for the intelligence, so that it cannot return into that sphere by any new act of reflection. The reflecting that we shall now deduce must therefore be entirely different from that which constantly ran parallel to the act of producing; and if, indeed, as is perfectly possible, it should be necessarily accompanied by a producing, this producing, in opposition to the necessary sort will be a free one. And conversely, if the reflection that accompanied production without consciousness was a necessary one, so much the more will that which we now seek be a free one. By means of it the intelligence will set limits, not simply to its own individual producing, but to producing absolutely and as such.

The contrast between producing and reflecting will become most apparent in that what we have hitherto

viewed from the standpoint of intuition will appear
quite differently to us from the standpoint of reflection.
      Thus we now have at least a general and preliminary
knowledge of the sphere which embraces as such that
series of acts whereby the intelligence breaks loose
entirely from producing, namely the sphere of free
reflection. And if this free reflection is to stand
connected with what has been derived earlier, its ground
must lie immediately in the third restrictedness, which
will drive us into the epoch of reflection, precisely
as the second restrictedness drove us into that of
producing. Though till now we find ourselves still
wholly unable to exhibit this connection in fact, and
can only maintain that it will exist.

GENERAL NOTE UPON THE SECOND EPOCH

An understanding of the whole interconnection of the
series of acts derived in the foregoing epoch depends
upon a proper grasp of the difference between what we
have called the first or original, and the second or
specific, restrictedness.
      The original limit was in fact posited already
in the self in the first act of self-consciousness,
through the ideal activity, or, as it later appeared to
the self, through the thing-in-itself. But now it was
simply the objective or real self that was limited
through the thing-in-itself. However, the self, so soon
as it is producing, that is, throughout the whole second
period, is no longer merely real, but ideal and real
at once. So the now productive self cannot feel itself
limited as such by the original boundary, and not least
because that boundary has now gone over into the
object; the latter, indeed, is the common representation
of self and thing-in-itself, wherein that original
restrictedness posited through the thing-in-itself must
therefore also be sought, just as it has also actually
been exhibited therein.
      So if now the self still feels itself to be limited,
it can do so only qua producing, and this again can
come about only by means of a second boundary, which
must serve to limit the thing no less than the self.
      But now this boundary was to set limits to the
passivity in the self, though this it does only for
the real and objective self, while for that very reason
it bounds the activity of the ideal or subjective self.
That the thing-in-itself is limited is to say that the
ideal self is limited. It is therefore evident that,
through producing, the boundary has actually gone over
into the ideal self. The same boundary which limits
the ideal self in its activity, limits the real self

in its passivity. Through the opposition between ideal
and real activity as such the first restrictedness is
posited; while through the measure or limit of this
opposition, which, no sooner is it recognized as opposition, as happens, in fact, in productive intuition,
than it must necessarily be a determinate opposition,
the second restrictedness is posited.

Thus without knowing it, the self, immediately on
becoming productive, was subjected to the second form
of restriction, that is, even its ideal activity became
limited. For the intrinsically illimitable self this
second restrictedness must necessarily be absolutely
contingent. That it is absolutely contingent means
that it has its ground in an absolutely free action of
the self itself. The objective self is bounded in this
particular fashion, because the ideal self has acted in
just this particular way. But that it should have acted
thus itself presupposes already a determinacy in the
latter. Hence this second limit must appear to the
self as at once dependent on, and independent of, its
activity. This contradiction is soluble only on the
assumption that this second restrictedness is merely a
present one, and thus must have its ground in a past
act of the self. Insofar as we reflect on the fact
that the boundary is a present one, it is independent
of the self; insofar as we reflect on the fact that it
exists at all, it is posited through an act of the
self itself. This restrictedness of the ideal activity
can thus appear to the self only as a restrictedness
of the present; thus immediately through the fact that
the self comes to have sensitivity with consciousness,
time arises for it as an absolute limit, whereby it
becomes an object to itself as having sensation with
consciousness, that is, as inner sense. But now in the
preceding act (that of producing) the self was not
merely inner sense, but--though this is admittedly
visible only to the philosopher--both inner and outer
sense at once, for it has at once both ideal and real
activity. Hence it cannot become an object to itself
as inner sense without outer sense simultaneously
becoming an object to it, and if the former is intuited
as an absolute boundary, the latter can be intuited
only as activity infinite in all directions.

As an immediate result, therefore, of the bounding
of the ideal activity in production, inner sense becomes
an object to the self through time in its independence
from space, and outer sense an object through space in
its independence from time; both, therefore, enter
consciousness, not as intuitions, of which the self
cannot become conscious, but merely as items intuited.

But now time and space themselves must again become
objects for the self, which constitutes the second

intuition of this epoch, whereby a new determination is
posited in the self, namely the succession of presentations; it is in virtue of this that there is no first
object at all for the self, since it can originally
become conscious only of a second object through opposition to the first as that which restricts it; and by
this means, therefore, the second restrictedness is
posited completely in consciousness.

But now the causal relation itself must again
become an object for the self, which comes about
through reciprocity, the third intuition in this epoch.

Hence the three intuitions of this epoch are none
other than the basic categories of all knowledge, namely
those of relation.

Reciprocity is itself not possible without the
succession itself again becoming a limited one for the
self; and this takes place through organization, which,
insofar as it betokens the highest point of production,
and is the condition of a third form of restriction,
compels the transition to a new series of acts.

In the series of synthetic acts that have so far been
derived, we have encountered none whereby the self might
have arrived directly at a consciousness of its own
activity. But now since the circle of synthetic acts
is closed and totally exhausted by the foregoing deductions, the act or series of acts, whereby consciousness
of the derived is posited in the self itself, cannot be
synthetic, but only analytic in nature. The standpoint
of reflection is therefore identical with that of analysis, and from it, accordingly, no act can be found in
the self which has not already been posited synthetically
therein. But how the self itself attains to the standpoint of reflection is something that has neither been
explained until now, nor is perhaps explicable at all
in theoretical philosophy. In discovering that act
whereby reflection is posited in the self, the synthetic
thread will again be united, and from that point on
will undoubtedly extend into the infinite.

Since the intelligence, so long as it is intuitant,
is one with the intuited and in no way distinct therefrom, it will be unable to arrive at any intuition of
itself through the products until it has separated
itself from the products; and since in itself it is
nothing else but the determinate mode of action whereby
the object arises, it will be able to arrive at itself
only by separating its acting as such from that which
arises for it in this acting, or, what comes to the
same, from the items produced.

Till now we have been quite unable to tell whether
such a separation in the intelligence is possible at
all, or whether it occurs; assuming that it does, the
question is, what will the intelligence contain?

This separating of the act from the product is
referred to in ordinary usage as abstraction, which
therefore appears as the first condition of reflection.
So long as the intelligence is nothing distinct from
its acting, no consciousness thereof is possible.
Through abstraction itself it becomes something different from its producing, which latter, for that very
reason, however, can now no longer appear as an acting,
but only as a product.

But now the intelligence, i.e., this acting, and
the object are originally one. The object is this
particular one, because the intelligence has produced
precisely thus and not otherwise. The object on the
one hand, and the acting of the intelligence on the

other, since they both exhaust each other and are alike
in all respects, will thus again coincide in one and the
same consciousness. --That which arises for us, when we
separate the acting as such from the outcome, is called
the concept. The question as to how our concepts conform to objects has therefore no meaning from a transcendental viewpoint, inasmuch as this question presupposes an original difference between the two. In the
absence of consciousness, the object and its concept,
and conversely, concept and object, are one and the
same, and the separation of the two first occurs with
the emergence of consciousness. A philosophy which
starts from consciousness will therefore never be able
to explain this conformity, nor is it explicable at all
without an original identity, whose principle necessarily lies beyond consciousness.

In producing as such, where the object still has no
existence whatever as an object, the act itself is
identical with what arises therein. This state of the
self can be elucidated by reference to similar cases,
where no external object as such makes entry into consciousness, although the self does not cease to produce
or intuit. In sleep, for example, the original producing is not suspended; it is a state of free reflection,
simultaneously interrupted by the consciousness of
individuality. Object and intuition are completely
lost in each other, and for that very reason neither one
nor the other exists in the intelligence for itself.
The intelligence, were it not everything solely for
itself, would in this state be intuitant for an intelligence outside itself, but it is not so for itself, and
therefore is not so at all. Such is the state of our
object, as so far derived.

So long as the act of producing does not become an
object to us, uncontaminated by and separated from the
product, everything exists only within us, and without
this separation we should indeed believe that we intuited
everything purely in ourselves. For that we must intuit
objects in space still does not explain the fact that
we intuit them outside ourselves, since we could also
intuit space purely within us, and originally we do
indeed intuit it purely in ourselves. The intelligence
is present where it intuits; how, then, does it now come
to intuit objects outside itself? There is no seeing
why the whole of the external world does not appear to
us in the manner of our organism, in which we believe
ourselves to be immediately present wherever we have
sensation. Just as, even after external things have
detached themselves from us, we do not as a rule intuit
our organism as in any way outside us, unless it is
distinguished from us by a special abstraction, so
also we could not view objects as distinct from us

without an original abstraction. That they therefore
loose themselves, as it were, from the mind, and take
their place in space outside us, is possible as such only
through the separation of the concept from the product,
i.e., of the subjective from the objective.

But now if concept and object originally coincide
so far that neither of them contains more or less than
the other, a separation of the two is utterly inconceivable without a special act whereby they become opposed
in consciousness. Such an act is that which is most
expressively denoted by the word judgment (Urteil),[1]
in that by this we first have a separation of what was
hitherto inseparably united, the concept and the
intuition. For judgment is not a comparison of concept
with concept, say, but of concepts with intuitions.
The predicate as such is not distinguished from the
subject, for there is in fact an identity of the two
posited in judgment itself. Hence a separation of
subject and predicate is possible as such only in
that the former represents the intuition and the latter
the concept. In judgment, therefore, concept and object
have first to be opposed, and then again related to each
other, and set equal one to another. But now this
relating is possible solely through intuition. Only
this intuition cannot be the same as productive intuition, for otherwise we should not have advanced a step
further; it must, on the contrary, be a mode of intuition hitherto quite unknown to us, which first requires
to be deduced.

Since object and concept are thereby to be related
to one another, this mode of intuition must be such as
to border upon the concept on one side, and upon the
object on the other. Now since the concept is the mode
of action whereby the object of intuition arises as
such, and thus the rule according to which the object
as such is constructed, whereas the object is not the
rule, but the expression of the rule itself, an act must
be found in which the rule itself is intuited as an
object, or in which, conversely, the object is intuited
as a rule of construction as such.

An intuition of this type is schematism, of which
everyone can learn only from his own inner experience,
and which, for purposes of recognition and the guidance
of experience, can only be described and separated from
everything else that resembles it.

The schema must be differentiated no less from the
image than from the symbol, with which it is very
commonly confounded. The image is always so determined
in every respect, that a complete identity of image and

[1]Suggesting "primal division" (Tr.).

object wants only the specific region of space wherein
the latter is located. The schema, by contrast, is not
a presentation determinate in all its aspects, but
merely an intuition of the rule whereby a specific object
can be brought forth. It is an intuition, and so not a
concept, for it is that which links the concept with the
object. But nor is it an intuition of the object itself, being merely an intuition of the rule whereby such
an object can be brought forth.
    The nature of the schema can be explained most
clearly from the example of the craftsman, who has to
fashion an object of specific form in accordance with a
concept. What can be conveyed to him, in effect, is
the concept of the object, but it is uttelry inconceivable that, without any external pattern, the form
associated with the concept should gradually emerge
under his hands, if he did not have an inner, though
sensorily intuited rule, which guides him in the making.
This rule is the schema, which contains nothing in any
way individual, and is equally little to be identified
with a general concept, whereby an artist could create
nothing. Following this schema, he will first bring
forth merely a raw sketch of the whole, proceeding from
thence to the fashioning of the individual parts, until
gradually, in his inner intuition, the schema approximates to the image, which again accompanies him, until
simultaneously with the fully emergent determination of
the image, the work of art itself is also brought to
completion.
    In the commonest exercise of the understanding, the
schema figures as the general link whereby we recognize any object as of a certain sort. If, as soon as
I see a triangle, of whatever kind you please, I judge
in the same moment that this figure is a triangle, that
presupposes the intuition of a triangle as such, which
is neither obtuse nor acute nor right-angled, and would
be no more possible by means of a mere concept of a
triangle than by means of a mere image thereof; for
since the latter is necessarily a determinate thing, the
congruence of the actual with the merely imagined
triangle, if it were to occur, would be purely for-
tuitous, which is insufficient for the formation of
a judgment.
    We may infer from this very necessity of a schema-
tism, that the whole mechanism of language will rest
upon it. Suppose, for example, that a man wholly
unacquainted with technical concepts knows only certain specimens or particular strains of a given animal;
nevertheless, as soon as he sees an individual of a
strain as yet unknown to him within this species, he
will still judge that it belongs to that type; he cannot
do this by means of a general concept, for whence,

indeed, is he to obtain this latter, seeing that even scientists frequently find it extremely difficult to agree upon the general concepts of a given species?

The application of the theory of the original schematism to enquiry into the mechanism of primeval languages, and of the earliest conceptions of nature, whose relics are preserved for us in the mythologies of ancient peoples, and lastly to the critique of scientific language, whose expressions almost all betray their origin in schematism, would provide the clearest evidence of how pervasive this operation is in all the concerns of the human mind.

To complete everything that can be said about the nature of the schema, it still remains to be observed, that it is for concepts precisely what the symbol is for Ideas. The schema, therefore, is always and necessarily related to an empirical object, either actual or yet to be brought forth. Thus of every organic shape, for example, such as the human, a schema alone is possible, whereas, for example, there are merely symbols of beauty, eternity, and the like. Now since the aesthetic artist works only from Ideas, and yet on the other hand requires once more a mechanical art, to present the art object under empirical conditions, it is obvious in consequence that for him the graduation from the Idea to the object is a replica of that of the mechanical artist.

Now that the concept of a schema is completely specified (it is in fact the sensorily intuited rule for the bringing forth of an empirical object), we can revert to a summary of our enquiry.

Our purpose was to explain how the self arrives at intuiting itself as active in producing. This was explained through abstraction; the mode of action whereby the object arises had to be separated from the outcome itself. This was effected through judgment. But judgment itself was impossible without schematism. For in judgment an intuition is equated with a concept; that this may happen, requires that there be something that forms a link between the two, and this is no other than the schema.

But now through this power of abstracting from the individual object, or what comes to the same, through the power of empirical abstraction, the intelligence will never arrive at detaching itself from the object; for by the schematism itself, concept and object are again united. Hence this power of abstraction presupposes a higher power in the intelligence itself, such that the result thereof may come to be posited in consciousness. If empirical abstraction is to be fixated at all, it can come about only through a power in virtue of which we distinguish from the object itself, not merely the

mode of action whereby the particular object arises, but
the mode of action whereby the object as such comes into
being.

II

In order to characterize this higher abstraction more
precisely, we now need to ask,
a) what becomes of intuition, when everything conceptual
is removed from it (for in the object intuition and
concept are originally united, but now we are to abstract
from the mode of action as such, and thus remove everything conceptual from the object).
          In every intuition a twofold distinction must be
made, between intuiting as such, or insofar as it is
essentially an act, and the determinant of intuition,
which makes it the intuition of an object, in a word,
the concept of the intuition.
          The object is this particular one, because I have
acted in this particular way, but this determinate mode
of action is in fact the concept, and thus the concept
determines the object; hence the concept originally
takes precedence over the object itself, not in time,
to be sure, but in status. The concept is the determinant, the object the determinate.
          Thus the concept is not, as is commonly alleged,
the universal, but rather the rule, the restrictive
factor, the determinant of the intuition; and if the
concept can be called undetermined, it is so only
insofar as it is not the determinate but the determinant.
It is thus the intuiting, or producing, that is universal, and it is only because a concept enters into this
intrinsically indeterminate intuiting that it becomes
the intuition of an object. The common explanation of
the origin of concepts, if it is not to be merely an
explanation of the empirical origin thereof, namely
that whereby the concept is said to arise for me because I suppress the particular in a number of individual
intuitions, and retain only the general, can be readily
exposed in all its superficiality. For in order to carry
out this operation, I must undoubtedly compare these
intuitions with one another; but how do I achieve this,
unless I am already guided by a concept? For how, then,
do we know that these individual objects given to us
are of the same sort, unless the first has already become
a concept for us? Thus this empirical procedure of
apprehending what is common to many individuals already
itself presupposes the rule of apprehension, i.e., the
concept, and hence a power of abstraction higher than
this empirical one.
          We therefore distinguish in the intuition the
intuiting itself, and the concept or determinant of the

intuiting. In the original intuition both are united.
Hence if, by the higher abstraction, which in contrast
to empirical abstraction we wish to call transcendental,
everything conceptual is to be removed from intuition,
the latter becomes, as it were, free, for all restrictedness enters it only through the concept. Divested of
the latter, intuiting therefore becomes an undetermined act, completely and in every respect.

If intuition becomes wholly indeterminate, absolutely
without concepts, nothing else remains of it save the
general intuiting itself, which, if it is itself intuited
once more, is space.

Space is conceptless intuiting, and thus in no way
a concept that might have been first abstracted, say,
from the relationships of things; for although space
arises for me through abstraction, it is still no
abstract concept either in the sense that categories
are, or in the sense that empirical or specific concepts are; for if there was a specific concept of space,
there would have to be many spaces, instead of which
there is but one infinite space, which is presupposed
by every limitation in space, that is, by every individual
space. Since space is merely an intuiting throughout,
it is necessarily also an intuiting into the infinite,
such that even the smallest part of space is still itself an intuiting, that is, a space and not, say, a mere
boundary; and this alone is the basis for the infinite
divisibility of space. Geometry, although it draws
all its proofs solely from intuition, and yet does so
no less generally than from concepts, ultimately owes
its existence entirely to this property of space; and
this is so generally admitted, that no further demonstration of it is needed here.

b)   What becomes of the concept when everything intuitive is removed from it?

In that, by transcendental abstraction, the original schematism is done away with, it follows that if
conceptless intuition arises at one extreme, an intuitionless concept must come about at the other. If the
categories, as deduced in the preceding epoch, are determinate intuition-forms of the intelligence, then if they
are divested of intuition, pure determinacy alone must
remain behind. It is this that is designated by the
logical concept. Hence, if a philosopher begins by
adopting merely the standpoint of reflection or analysis, he will also be able to deduce the categories as
no more than purely formal concepts, and thus to
deduce them simply from logic. But apart from the
fact that the different functions of judgment in logic
are themselves in need of a further derivation, and
that so far from transcendental philosophy being
abstracted from logic, the latter has to be abstracted

from the former, it is in any case a pure deception to
believe that the categories, once separated from the
schematism of intuition, continue to remain as real
concepts; for, divested of intuition, they are purely
logical concepts, connected with intuition, yet no
longer concepts proper, but true forms of intuition.
The inadequacy of such a derivation will betray itself
through still other deficiencies, e.g., that it cannot
uncover the mechanism of the categories, the special
any more than the general, though it is evident enough.
Thus it is certainly a striking feature of the so-called
dynamic categories, that each of them has its correlate,
whereas with the so-called mathematical categories this
is not the case. Yet this peculiarity is very easily
accounted for, once we know that in the dynamic categories inner and outer sense are still unseparated,
whereas of the mathematical categories one belongs only
to inner, and the other only to outer sense. Again,
the occurrence, throughout and in every class, of three
categories, of which the first pair are opposed, while
the third is a synthesis of the two, shows that the
general mechanism of the categories rests upon a higher
opposition, no longer perceived from the standpoint of
reflection, and therefore requiring the existence of a
higher viewpoint, lying further back. Since, moreover,
this opposition runs through all the categories, and
it is one type that underlies them all, there is
undoubtedly also but one category, and since from the
original mechanism of intuition we could derive only
the single category of relation, it is to be expected
that this one category will be primary, which a closer
inspection does indeed confirm. If it can be shown
that prior to reflection, or beyond it, the object is
in no wise determined by the mathematical categories, it
being in fact only the subject that is so determined,
whether it be as intuiting or as feeling, just as, for
example, the object is one, not indeed in itself, but
only in relation to the simultaneously intuitant and
reflecting subject; and if it can be shown, in contrast,
that already in the first intuition, and without a
supervening reflection, the object must be determined
as substance and accident: Then it surely follows
from that, that the mathematical categories are as such
subordinated to the dynamic, or that the latter precede the former; and hence, for this very reason, the
mathematical categories can only present separately
what the dynamic present as united, namely that the
categories arising merely from the viewpoint of
reflection, so long as here too there has been no
preceding opposition of outer and inner sense, as
happens in the categories of modality, also belong
merely to inner sense or to outer, and so can likewise

have no correlate. The proof might be effected more
briefly by considering that in the original mechanism
of intuition the first two categories emerge only by
way of the third; the third of the mathematical categories, however, always already presupposes reciprocity,
in that, for example, we can neither think of a universe
of objects without a general reciprocal presupposing
of objects by one another, nor even of a limiting of the
individual object without viewing objects as mutually
limited by one other, that is, in a universal reciprocal relation. Hence, of the four classes of categories,
only the dynamic are left as fundamental, and if it can
further be shown that even those of modality cannot be
categories in the same, that is, an equally fundamental
sense as those of relation, then only the latter remain
as the sole basic categories. But now in the original
mechanism of intuition no object actually presents
itself as possible or impossible, in the way that every
object figures as substance and accident. Objects first
appear as possible, actual and necessary only through
the highest act of reflection, which has not even been
deduced at all so far. These terms express a mere relation of the object to the cognitive faculty as a whole
(to inner and outer sense), of such a kind that neither
through the concept of possibility, nor even through
that of actuality, is any determination whatever posited
in the object itself. This relating of the object to
the whole cognitive faculty is, however, indubitably
first possible only when the self has completely
divorced itself from the object, i.e., from its ideal
and real activity alike, and that is to say by means of
the highest act of reflection. In reference to this
act the categories of modality can thus again be called
the highest, just as can those of relation in regard
to the synthesis of productive intuition; but from this
it is evident, indeed, that they are not original categories appearing in course of the primary intuition.

III

Transcendental abstraction is the condition of judgment,
but not judgment itself. It explains merely how the
intelligence arrives at separating object and concept,
but not how it again unites them both in the judgment.
How the intrinsically quite intuitionless concept and
the intrinsically quite conceptless intuition of space
again unite into the object, is inconceivable without an
intermediary. But that which mediates as such between
concept and intuition is the schema. Hence transcendental abstraction will also be superseded again by a
schematism, which in distinction from that deduced
earlier we shall term transcendental schematism.

The empirical schema was explained as the sensorily intuited rule whereby an object can be brought forth empirically. The transcendental schema will thus be the sensory intuition of the rule whereby an object can be brought forth as such, or transcendentally. Now insofar as the schema contains a rule, to that extent it is merely the object of an inner intuition; while insofar as it is a rule for the construction of an object, it must in fact be intuited externally, as something delineated in space. Thus the schema is, as such, an intermediary between inner and outer sense. Hence the transcendental schema will have to be explained as that which mediates most fundamentally between inner and outer sense.

But the most fundamental intermediary of inner and outer sense is time, not insofar as it is _merely_ inner sense, that is, an absolute boundary, but insofar as it itself again becomes an object of outer intuition; time, therefore, insofar as it is a line, _i.e._, a magnitude extended in one direction.

We linger upon this point, in order to determine more exactly the real character of time.

Seen from the standpoint of reflection, time is merely a form of intuition of inner sense, since it comes about only in regarding the succession of our _presentations_, which from this point of view exists solely in ourselves; whereas the _coexistence_ of substances, which is the condition of _inner and outer_ sense, we can only intuit outside us. From the standpoint of intuition, on the other hand, time at the outset is already an _outer_ intuition, since from that point of view there is _indeed_ no difference between _presentations_ and _objects_. So although time, for reflection, is merely an inner form of intuition, for intuition it is both at once. From this property of time we may discern, among other things, why, though space is the substrate of geometry only, time is the substrate of the whole of mathematics, and why all of geometry, even, can be reduced to analysis; and this in turn explains the relation between the geometrical method of the ancients and the analytical method of the moderns, whereby, though the two are opposed to each other, exactly the same results are nonetheless obtained.

This property of time, whereby it appertains at once to both outer and inner sense, is the sole ground for its role as the universal link between concept and intuition, or as transcendental schema. Since the categories are originally types of intuition, and hence not separated from the schematism--a separation which first occurs through transcendental abstraction--it will be evident from this,
1. that time already enters originally into productive

intuition, or the construction of the object, as was
also demonstrated in the preceding epoch;
2. that from this relation of time to pure concepts on
the one hand, and to pure intuition, or space, on the
other, the entire mechanism of the categories must allow
of being derived;
3. that if by transcendental abstraction the original
schematism is done away with, an altogether different
view of the original construction of the object must
also come about; and this, since the abstraction in
question is the condition of all consciousness. Hence,
through the very medium it must traverse to attain to
consciousness, productive intuition loses its character.
    A few examples may serve to elucidate this latter
point.

    In every change there is a transition from one state
into its contradictory opposite, as, for example, when a
body switches from movement in direction $\underline{A}$ to movement in
direction $\backsim \underline{A}$. In the self-identical intelligence, with
its constant striving for identity of consciousness,
this combination of contradictorily opposite states is
possible only through the schematism of time. Intuition
produces time as constantly in transition from $\underline{A}$ to $\backsim \underline{A}$,
in order to mediate the contradiction between opposites.
By abstraction, the schematism, and with it time, are
abolished. There is a well-known sophism whereby the
ancient sophists contest the possibility of communicating
motion. Take, they say, the last instant at which a
body is at rest, and the first at which it moves; there
is no intermediate between the two. (This is also perfectly true from the standpoint of reflection.) Hence,
if a body is set in motion, this happens either at the
last instant of its rest, or the first instant of its
motion; but the former is impossible, because it is
still at rest, and the latter impossible, because it is
already in motion. This sophism is originally resolved
through productive intuition; to solve it for reflection, the artificial concepts of mechanics are devised;
but reflection can conceive the transition of a body,
e.g., from rest to motion, i.e., the union of contradictorily opposing states, only as mediated by an infinity;
productive intuition has been abolished for it, yet the
latter alone can picture an infinite in the finite,
that is, a quantity in which, though itself finite, no
indefinitely smaller part is possible; and so reflection
finds itself obliged to interpolate between these two
states an infinity of discrete portions of time, each
of which is infinitely small. But now this transition,
e.g., from one direction into its opposite, still has to
occur in a finite time, albeit through endless intermediate steps, which is originally possible, however,
only by means of continuity; and hence the movement

itself, which is communicated to the body in an instant,
can only be a solicitation, since otherwise an infinite
velocity would be generated in a finite time. All these
peculiar notions are made necessary only by the abolition
of the original schematism of intuition. But so far as
motion as such is concerned, a construction of it from
the standpoint of reflection is utterly impossible, since
between any two points on a line an infinity of others
must be supposed. Hence even geometry postulates the
line, that is, demands that reflection itself bring it
forth in productive intuition, which it certainly would
not do if the genesis of a line could be conveyed through
concepts.

From time's property of being a transcendental
schema, it is self-evident that it is no mere concept,
such as might be abstracted either empirically or transcendentally. For everything that time could be abstracted
from already presupposes it as a condition. But were it
a transcendental abstraction like the concepts of the
understanding, then, just as there are, for example, many
substances, so equally there would have to be many times;
yet there is but one time; what we speak of as different
times are merely different partitions of absolute time.
Hence, too, there can be no demonstration from mere concepts of any axiom of time, e.g., that two times cannot
exist separately or simultaneously, or of any proposition of arithmetic that rests wholly upon the form of
time.

Having now deduced the transcendental schematism,
we also find ourselves in a position to exhibit completely the entire mechanism of the categories.

The first category underlying all the others, the
only one whereby the object is already determined in
production, is, as we know, that of relation, which,
since it is the sole category of intuition, will be
alone in presenting inner and outer sense as still united.

The first category of relation, that of substance
and accident, betokens the first synthesis of inner and
outer sense. But now if the transcendental schematism
be removed from the concepts of both substance and
accident, nothing remains save the merely logical concepts of subject and predicate. If, on the other hand,
we remove all concepts from both, substance remains only
as pure extensity, or space, and accident only as
absolute boundary, or time, insofar as it is simply inner
sense and is wholly independent of space. But now how
the in itself wholly intuitionless concept of the logical subject, or the equally intuitionless concept of the
logical predicate, can become in the one case substance,
and in the other, accident, is explicable only by the
fact that the determination of time is added to them both.

But this determination is first added through the

second category, for only through the second (deduced by us as the intuition of the first) does that which in the first is inner sense become time for the self. Hence the first category as such is intuitable only through the second, as has been shown at the proper juncture; the ground of this, which appears here, is that only through the second do we add the transcendental schema of time.

Substance is intuitable as such only by being intuited as persisting in time, but it cannot be intuited as persistent unless time, which has so far designated only the absolute boundary, flows (extends itself in one dimension), which in fact comes about only through the succession of the causal sequence. But conversely, too, that any succession occurs in time is intuitable only in contrast to something that persists therein, or, since time arrested in its flow = space, that persists in space, and this in fact is substance. Hence these two categories are possible only mutually through one another, that is, they are possible only in a third, which is reciprocity.

From this deduction the following two propositions can be abstracted as a matter of course, whereby the mechanism of all the other categories becomes intelligible:

1. The opposition obtaining between the first two categories is the same as that originally obtaining between space and time;

2. The second category in each class is necessary only because it appends the transcendental schema to the first. --

Not for the purpose of anticipating something as yet underived, but in order to clarify these two propositions by further employment, we set forth their application to the so-called mathematical categories, although these have not yet been deduced as such.

We have already pointed out that these are not categories of intuition, in that they arise solely from the standpoint of reflection. But concurrently with reflection, the unity of outer and inner sense is at once abolished, and the one basic category of relation thereby divided into two opposites, of which the first designates only that in the object which pertains to outer sense, while the other expresses only that in the object which belongs to outwardly intuited inner sense.

If then, to begin with the first, we remove everything intuitive from the category of unity, which stands first in the class of quantity, we are left only with logical unity. If this is to be combined with intuition, the determination of time must be added. But now quantity combined with time is number. Hence only by way of the second category (that of plurality) does the determination of time come to be appended. For only with a given plurality does numbering begin. Where there is

only one, I do not number. Only through multiplicity
does unity become a number. (That time and plurality
first enter together is also apparent from the fact that
only through the second category of relation, namely
that whereby time first arises for the self in outer
intuition, is a multiplicity of objects determined.
Even in the arbitrary succession of presentations, a
multiplicity of objects only arises for me in that I
apprehend them one after another, i.e., apprehend them
simply and solely in time. In the number series, only
through multiplicity does 1 become a unity, that is,
an expression of finitude as such. This can be shown
as follows. If 1 is a finite number, there must be a
possible divisor for it, but $1/1 = 1$; hence 1 is divisi-
ble only by 2, 3, etc., that is, by plurality as such;
without this it is $1/0$, i.e., the infinite.)
     But just as unity is unintuitable without plurality,
so plurality is unintuitable without unity, and so both
mutually presuppose one another, that is, both are
possible only through a third that is common to them.
     The same mechanism now appears in the categories
of quality. If I remove from reality the intuition of
space, which is effected by transcendental abstraction,
nothing remains for me save the mere logical concept of
position as such. If I again combine this concept with
the intuition of space, I obtain the filling of space;
but there is no intuiting of this without some degree,
that is, without having a magnitude in time. But the
degree, that is, the determination by time, is first
added only through the second category, that of negation.
So again the second is necessary here simply because the
first only becomes intuitable by means of it, or because
it appends to the latter the transcendental schema.
     This may perhaps be clarified as follows. If I
think the real in objects to myself as unrestricted, it
will spread out to infinity, and since intensity, as
shown, stands in converse relation to extensity, nothing
remains save infinite extensity devoid of all intensity,
namely absolute space. If, on the other hand, we think
of negation as the unrestricted, nothing remains save
infinite intensity without extensity, that is, a point,
or inner sense insofar as it is merely inner sense. So
if I take the second category away from the first, I am
left with absolute space; if I take the first away from
the second, I am left with absolute time (i.e., time
merely as inner sense).
     Now in the original intuition neither concept, nor
space, nor time arises for us alone and separately, but
rather all are given at once. Just as our object the
self conjoins these three determinations unconsciously,
and of itself, to the object, so likewise have we fared
in the deduction of productive intuition. Through

transcendental abstraction, which consists, in fact,
in the annulment of that third thing which binds intuition, only the intuitionless concept and the conceptless intuition could remain to us as constituents
thereof. From this standpoint, the question, how the
object is possible, can be formulated only as follows:
how wholly intuitionless concepts, which we find in us
as concepts a priori, come to be so indissolubly conjoined with the intuition, or can so pass over into it,
that they are utterly inseparable from the object? Now
since this transition is possible only through the
schematism of time, we conclude that time, too, must
have already entered into that original synthesis. There
is thus a complete change in the order of construction
that we followed in the preceding epoch, in that it is
transcendental abstraction which alone enables us to set
forth with clear consciousness the mechanism of the
original synthesis.

IV

Transcendental abstraction was postulated as the condition of empirical abstraction, and this as the condition
of judgment. Hence this abstraction lies at the basis
of every judgment, even the most commonplace, and the
capacity for transcendental abstraction, or the capacity
for a priori concepts, is as necessary to every intelligence as self-consciousness itself.

But the condition does not come to consciousness
prior to the conditioned, and transcendental abstraction
is submerged in the judgment, or in empirical abstraction,
which together with its outcome is thereby elevated into
consciousness.

Now however in fact transcendental abstraction, along
with its result, again comes to be posited in consciousness, we can know that in ordinary consciousness nothing
of either appears necessarily and that if anything thereof
does appear, it is utterly contingent; and we may thus
conjecture it in advance to be possible only through
an action which in relation to ordinary consciousness can
no longer be necessary (for otherwise even its result
would have always and necessarily to be found therein);
hence the action must be one which follows from no other
in the intelligence itself (but rather, as it were, from
an action outside it), and this action is thus an
absolute one for the intelligence itself. The ordinary
consciousness may attain to awareness of empirical
abstraction and what results therefrom; for this is
taken care of, indeed, by transcendental abstraction.
But the latter, perhaps precisely because everything
that emerges in empirical consciousness as such is
posited by means of it, will itself no longer attain

to consciousness necessarily, and if it does attain
thereto, will appear there only in a contingent fashion.
    But now it is obvious that only by also becoming
conscious of transcendental abstraction could the self
first elevate itself absolutely, for itself, above the
object (for through empirical abstraction it only breaks
loose from the determinate object); and that only by
elevating itself above any object, could it recognize
itself as an intelligence. But now this act is an
absolute abstraction, and precisely because it is
absolute, can no longer be explained through any other
in the intelligence; and hence at this point the chain
of theoretical philosophy breaks off, and there remains
in regard to it only the absolute demand: there shall
appear such an act in the intelligence. But in so saying,
theoretical philosophy oversteps its boundary, and
crosses into the domain of practical philosophy, which
alone posits by means of categorical demands.
    Whether and how this act be possible is a question
that no longer falls within the scope of the theoretical
enquiry; but there is one question it still has to answer. --Supposing hypothetically that such an act exists
in the intelligence, how will the latter find itself,
and how will it find the world of objects? Undoubtedly
through this act there arises for it precisely what was
already posited for us through transcendental abstraction,
and thus in ourselves taking a step into practical philosophy, we bring our object right up to the point that
we are leaving, in going over into the practical.
    By an absolute act the intelligence elevates itself
above everything objective. Everything objective would
disappear for it in this act, if the original restrictedness did not persist; but the latter must persist, for
if the abstraction is to occur, then that from which
abstraction is made cannot cease to exist. Now in the
abstracting activity, the intelligence feels itself
absolutely free, and yet at the same time, as by an
intellectual gravitation, pulled back into the intuition
by the original restrictedness; and hence first in this
very act it comes to be limited for itself as an
intelligence; no longer merely as real activity, as in
sensation, nor merely as ideal activity, as in productive
intuition, but as both together, that is, as an object.
It appears to itself as limited through productive
intuition. But the intuition, qua act, has been submerged in consciousness, and only the product has
remained. That it recognizes itself as limited through
productive intuition is equivalent to saying that it
recognizes itself as limited by the objective world.
So here for the first time the objective world and the
intelligence confront one another in consciousness
itself, just as we find it in consciousness through the
primary philosophic abstraction.

The intelligence can now fixate transcendental abstraction, though this already occurs through freedom, and a special direction of freedom at that. This explains why a priori concepts do not make an appearance in every consciousness, and do not figure always and necessarily in any. They can emerge, but they do not have to do so.

Through transcendental abstraction, everything is separated that was united in the original synthesis of intuition, and so all this, though always through freedom, will come to be separated, for the intelligence, as an object. Time, for example, will be separated from space and from the object, space will appear as the form of coexistence, and objects as each having its position in space reciprocally determined one by another; but in all this the intelligence finds itself entirely free in regard to the object from which the determination proceeds.

In general, however, its reflection is directed either to the object, whereby there arises for it the already deduced category of intuition or relation.

Or else it reflects upon itself. If it simultaneously both reflects and intuits, there arises for it the category of quantity, which, conjoined with the schema, is number; though the latter, for that very reason, is not a primary category.

If it simultaneously both reflects and senses, or if it reflects upon the degree to which time is filled for it, there arises for it the category of quality.

Or finally, through the highest act of reflection, it reflects simultaneously upon the object and on itself, insofar as it is at once both real and ideal activity. If it reflects simultaneously on the object and on itself as real (free) activity, there arises for it the category of possibility. If it does so upon the object and on itself as ideal (limited) activity, it thereby obtains the category of actuality.

And here again it is only through the second category that the determination of time is added to the first. For, by what was deduced in the preceding epoch, the limitation of the ideal activity consists precisely in the fact that it recognizes the object as contemporaneous. Hence an object is actual if it is posited in a determinate instant of time, and possible, on the other hand, if it is posited and as it were thrown into time generally, by the activity that reflects upon the real.

If the intelligence also goes on to unite this further contradiction between real and ideal activity, there arises for it the concept of necessity. The necessary is that which is posited in all time; but all time is the synthesis for time generally and for particular time, because that which is posited in all

time is posited no less determinately than in the
particular case, and yet no less freely than in time
generally.

The negative correlates of the categories of this
class do not behave like those of relation, since in
fact they are not correlates, but contradictory opposites
of the positive categories. Nor, indeed, are they genuine categories, i.e., concepts whereby an object of
intuition would be determined even for reflection; on
the contrary, if the positive categories of this class
are the highest for reflection, or the syllepsis of all
others, these negative ones, conversely, are the absolute
opposite of the whole body of categories.

Since the concepts of possibility, actuality and
necessity arise through the highest act of reflection,
they are necessarily also those wherewith the entire
arch of theoretical philosophy terminates. But that
these concepts already stand on the road leading from
theoretical to practical philosophy will by now be
already partly foreseen by the reader, and in part will
be recognized more clearly still, as we now proceed to
erect the system of practical philosophy.

GENERAL NOTE UPON THE THIRD EPOCH

The final enquiry which must conclude the whole of theoretical philosophy is undoubtedly that concerning the
distinction between a priori and a posteriori concepts,
which can hardly be made clear, indeed, in any other way
but by exhibiting their origin in the intelligence itself.
The peculiarity of transcendental idealism in regard to
its doctrine is precisely this, that it can also demonstrate the so-called a priori concepts in respect of
their origin; a thing that is only possible, indeed, in
that it transports itself into a region lying beyond
ordinary consciousness. A philosophy that confines
itself to the latter, on the other hand, is able, in
fact, to discover these concepts only as present and,
so to speak, lying there, and thereby involves itself
in the insoluble difficulties by which the defenders
of these concepts have long since been confronted.

In that we project the origin of the so-called a
priori concepts beyond consciousness, where we also
locate the origin of the objective world, we maintain
upon the same evidence, and with equal right, that our
knowledge is originally empirical through and through,
and also through and through a priori.

All our knowledge is originally empirical, precisely because concept and object arise for us unseparated and simultaneously. For were we originally to
have a knowledge a priori, there would first have to

arise for us the concept of the object, and then the object itself in conformity thereto, which alone would permit a genuine a priori insight into the object. Conversely, all that knowledge is called empirical which arises for me wholly without my concurrence, as happens, for example, in a physical experiment whose result I cannot know beforehand. But now all knowledge of objects originally comes to us in a manner so far independent of us, that only after it is there do we devise a concept thereof, but cannot give out this concept as itself again furnished by the wholly involuntary intuition. All knowledge is thus originally purely empirical.

But precisely because our whole knowledge is originally through and through empirical, it is through and through a priori. For were it not wholly our own production, our knowledge would either be all given to us from without, which is impossible, since if so there would be nothing necessary and universal in our knowledge; or there would be nothing left but to suppose that some of it comes to us from outside, while the rest emerges from ourselves. Hence our knowledge can only be empirical through and through in that it comes wholly and solely from ourselves, i.e., is through and through a priori.

Insofar, that is, as the self produces everything from itself, to that extent everything--not just this concept or that, or merely the form of thought, even, but the whole of our knowledge, one and indivisible-- is a priori.

But insofar as we are not aware of this producing, to that extent there is nothing a priori in us, and everything, in fact, is a posteriori. To become aware of our knowledge as a priori in character, we have to become aware of the act of producing as such, in abstraction from the product. But in course of this very operation, we lose from the concept, in the manner deduced above, everything material (all intuition), and nothing save the purely formal can remain behind. To that extent we do indeed have concepts a priori, and purely formal ones at that, but these concepts also exist only insofar as we conceive, insofar as we abstract in that particular fashion, and emerge, therefore, not automatically, but by a special exercise of freedom.

Hence there are a priori concepts without there having to be innate concepts. It is not concepts that are innate in us, but our own nature and the whole of its mechanism. This nature is a specific one, and acts in a specific manner, though quite unawares, for it is itself nothing else but this acting: the concept of this acting is not in it, for otherwise it would have had originally to be something distinct therefrom, and if the concept entered it, it would first do so by way of a new act, which took that first act as its object.

Given, however, that original identity of acting and being which we think in the concept of the self, it becomes quite impossible to entertain, not merely the idea of innate concepts, whose abandonment had already long been necessitated by the discovery that in all concepts there is something active, but also the claim still commonly made, that these concepts are present as original dispositions, for the latter rests solely upon the notion of the self as a special substrate, distinct from its acts. For whoever tells us that he is unable to think of any act without a substrate, admits in so doing that this supposed substrate of thought is itself a mere product of his imagination, and thus again merely his own thinking, which he is thereby compelled to presuppose as independent, and so on backwards ad infinitum. It is a mere illusion of the imagination to believe that, after one has removed from an object the only predicates it possesses, something of it, we know not what, must still remain behind. Thus nobody, for example, will say that impenetrability is implanted into matter, for impenetrability is matter itself. Why, then, do people talk of concepts that are implanted into the intelligence, seeing that these concepts are the intelligence itself? --The Aristotelians compared the soul to a blank tablet, upon which the lineaments of external things are first of all engraved. But if the soul is not a blank tablet, is it then, on that account, simply an inscribed one?

If a priori concepts are dispositions in us, we further have need of an external impact in order to bring these dispositions out. The intelligence, on this view, is a sleeping power upon which external things operate, so to say, as causes to arouse its activity, or as stimuli. The intelligence, however, is not a sleeping power that has first been actuated, for if so it would have to be something other than activity, would have to be activity conjoined with a product, much as the organism is, in being an intuition of the intelligence already endowed with potentiality. Moreover, that unknown from which the impact proceeds, once stripped of all concepts a priori, has no objective predicates left to it at all, and one would thus have to posit this x in an intelligence of some sort; as Malebranche did, who would have us see all things in God, or the sagacious Berkeley, who speaks of light as a converse of the soul with God; though these are ideas which need no refutation for a generation that does not even understand them.

Thus if a priori concepts were taken to include certain original dispositions of the self, one would be justified in continuing to advance the view that maintains all concepts to arise from external

impressions; not, indeed, as if anything intelligible
can be thought in doing so, but rather because then, at
least, there would be unity and wholeness in our knowledge. --Locke, the chief proponent of this view, contends against the figment of innate concepts which he
attributes [sic] to Leibniz, who was very far from holding it, but does not notice that it is equally unintelligible either to have Ideas originally implanted in the
soul, or to suppose them first implanted there by objects;
nor does it ever occur to him to ask, not only whether
in this sense there are any innate Ideas, but whether
there is any Idea at all of such a kind that it could be
an impression on the soul, or equally, where it could
come from?

     All these confusions are resolved by the one princi-
ple, that in origin our knowledge is no more a priori
than it is a posteriori, since this whole distinction is
made simply and solely in regard to philosophic consciousness. For the same reason, namely that in origin
(that is, in regard to the object of philosophy, the
self) our knowledge is neither one nor the other, it can
also not be partly the one and partly the other, a
view which in fact renders impossible all truth or
objectivity of a priori knowledge. For in that it completely abolishes the identity of presentation and
object, seeing that effect and cause can never be
identical, it must maintain either that things accom-
modate themselves like some shapeless stuff to those
original forms in ourselves, or conversely, that those
forms are governed by the things, whereby they lose all
necessity. Nor is this all; for the third possible
presupposition, whereby the objective world and the
intelligence are presented in the manner of two clocks
which, while knowing nothing of each other and being
completely separated, agree together in that each goes
regularly on its own, maintains a claim that is utterly
superfluous and violates a cardinal principle of all
explanation: namely that what can be explained by one
thing should not be explained by many; not to mention
the fact that even this objective world, lying quite
outside the presentations of the intelligence, can
still, since it is the expression of concepts, exist
once more only through and for an intelligence.

Part Four

System of Practical Philosophy according to the

Principles of Transcendental Idealism

We think it not unnecessary to warn the reader in advance
that what we here seek to establish is, not a moral
philosophy of any kind, but rather a transcendental
deduction of the thinkability and explicability of moral
concepts as such; also, that we shall conduct this
enquiry into that aspect of moral philosophy which
falls within the scope of transcendental philosophy at
the highest level of generality. This we shall do by
tracing back the whole to a few principles and problems,
while leaving the application to particular problems to
the reader himself, who in this way may most easily discover, not only whether he has grasped our transcendental
idealism, but also, which is the main thing, whether he
has equally learned to make use of this type of philosophy as an instrument of enquiry.

    <u>First Proposition. Absolute abstraction</u>, i.e.,
<u>the beginning of consciousness, is explicable</u> only through
<u>a self-determining, or an act of the intelligence upon</u>
<u>itself.</u>

    <u>Proof</u>. We presume that the meaning of the term
<u>absolute abstraction</u> is already understood. It is the
act whereby the intelligence raises itself absolutely
above the objective. Since this act is an absolute one,
it cannot be conditioned by any of the preceding acts,
and thereby the concatenation of acts, wherein each
succeeding one is necessarily made through that which
preceded it, is as it were broken off, and a new
sequence begins.

    That an act does not follow from a preceding act of
the intelligence means that it cannot be explained from
the intelligence, insofar as it is this particular one,
and insofar as it acts in a particular way; and since
it must be explicable as such, it is so only from the
absolute in the intelligence itself, from the ultimate
principle of all action therein.

    That an act is explicable only from the ultimate
in the intelligence itself must (since this latter is
nothing else but its original duality) mean the same as
this: the intelligence must determine itself to this
act. Thus the act is admittedly explicable, though
not from a determinacy of the intelligence, but from an
immediate self-determining.

    But an act whereby the intelligence determines
itself is an act upon itself. Hence absolute abstraction is explicable only from such an act of the
intelligence upon itself, and since absolute abstraction

is the beginning of all consciousness in time, the first beginning of consciousness is also explicable only from such an act, which is what we had to prove.

Corollaries

1. This self-determining of the intelligence is called <u>willing</u>, in the commonest acceptation of the term. That <u>in every</u> willing there is a determining of self, or at least that it appears to be an act of this sort, is something that everyone can demonstrate for himself through inner intuition; whether this appearance is truthful or deceptive is of no concern to us here. Nor indeed are we speaking of any determinate act of will, in which the concept of an object would already be present, but rather of a transcendental self-determining, or of the original act of freedom. But what this self-determination may be is inexplicable to anyone who does not know of it from his own intuition.
2. If this self-determination is the original act of will, it follows that it is only through the medium of willing that the intelligence becomes an object to itself.
     The act of the will is thus the complete solution to our problem of how the intelligence recognizes itself as intuiting. Theoretical philosophy was brought to completion by three major acts. In the first, the still unconscious act of self-awareness, the self became a subject-object, without being so for itself. In the second, the act of sensation, only its objective activity became an object to it. In the third, that of productive intuition, it became an object to itself as sensing, that is, as a subject. So long as the self is producing merely, it is never objective as a self, precisely because the intuitant is always directed upon something other than itself, and, as that for which everything else is objective, does not become objective itself; so that throughout the whole epoch of production we could never reach the point at which the producer, the intuitant, became an object to itself as such; productive intuition alone could be raised to a higher power (<u>e.g.</u>, through organization), but not the self-intuition <u>of</u> the self itself. Only in willing is the latter also first raised to a higher power, for by this the self becomes an object to itself as the <u>whole</u> which it is, that is, as at once both subject and object, or as that which produces. This producing function detaches itself, as it were, from the purely ideal self, and now can never again become ideal, but is the external and absolute objective for the self itself.
3. Since, through thé act of self-determination, the

self becomes an object to itself qua self, the question
remains as to how this act may be related to that
original act of self-consciousness, which is likewise
a self-determining, although it does not bring about
the same result.

By what has preceded we are already supplied with
a mark of distinction between the two. The first act
contained only the simple opposition between determinant
and determinate, which corresponded to that between
intuitant and intuited. In the present act we no longer
have this simple opposition; instead, the determinant
and determinate are collectively confronted by an
intuitant, and both together, the intuited and intuitant of the first act, are here the intuited.

The ground of this distinction was as follows. In
that first act the self as such first came to be, for it
is nothing else but that which becomes an object to
itself; hence in the self there was as yet no ideal
activity, which could simultaneously reflect upon what
was emerging. In the present act the self already
exists, and it is a question only of its becoming an
object to itself as that which it already is. Objectively regarded, indeed, this second act of self-determination is therefore just the same, in fact, as the
first and original one, save with this difference only,
that in the present act the whole of the first becomes
an object to the self, whereas in the first act itself
only the objective element therein did so.

Here, no doubt, is also the most suitable place to
review simultaneously the oft-repeated question, by
what common principle do theoretical and practical
philosophy hang together?

It is autonomy which is commonly placed at the
summit only of practical philosophy, and which, enlarged
into the principle of the whole of philosophy, turns out,
on elaboration, to be transcendental idealism. The
difference between the primordial autonomy, and that
which is dealt with in practical philosophy, is simply
this: by means of the former the self is absolutely
self-determinant, but without being so for itself--the
self both gives itself the law and realizes it in one
and the same act, wherefore it also fails to distinguish
itself as legislative, and discerns the laws in its
products, merely, as if in a mirror. By contrast, in
practical philosophy the self as ideal is opposed, not
to the real, but to the simultaneously ideal and real,
yet for that very reason is no longer ideal, but
idealizing. But for the same reason, since the simultaneously ideal and real, that is, the producing self,
is opposed to an idealizing one, the former, in practical philosophy, is no longer intuitant, that is, devoid
of consciousness, but is consciously productive, or
realizing.

Thus practical philosophy rests entirely upon the duality of the self that both idealizes (projects ideals) and realizes. Now realizing is assuredly also a producing, and thus the same with that which in theoretical philosophy constitutes intuition, save with this difference, that here the self produces consciously, just as in theoretical philosophy, conversely, the self is also idealizing, save only that in this case concept and act, projection and realization, are one and the same.

From this contrast between theoretical and practical philosophy a number of significant conclusions can at once be drawn, of which we here give only the most important.

a) In theoretical philosophy, _i.e._, prior to consciousness, the object arises for me exactly as it does in practical philosophy, _i.e._, subsequent to consciousness. The difference between intuition and free action is merely this, that in the latter case the self is productive for itself. The _intuitant_, as always when it simply has the self as its object, is _purely ideal_, whereas the _intuited_ is the _whole_ self, that is, the self that is simultaneously _ideal_ and real. That which acts in us when we act freely is the same that intuits in us; or the intuitant and the practical activity are one--the noteworthy outcome of transcendental idealism, which throws a flood of light upon the nature of intuition and action alike.

b) The absolute act of self-determination was postulated in order to explain how the intelligence becomes intuitant for itself. After the oft-repeated experience that we have had on this point, it cannot astonish us if through this act also we see the emergence for us of something quite different from what we expected. Throughout the whole of theoretical philosophy we have seen the endeavor of the intelligence, to become aware of its action as such, persistently miscarry. The same is also the case here. But upon this very miscarriage, upon the very fact that complete consciousness arises simultaneously for the intelligence in that it intuits itself as producing, rests the further fact, that for it the world becomes really objective. For by the very fact that the intelligence intuits itself as producing, the purely ideal self separates itself from that which is at once ideal and real, and so is now wholly objective and completely independent of the purely ideal. In the same intuition the intelligence becomes consciously productive, but it is supposed to become conscious of itself as productive without consciousness. This is impossible, and for that reason only does the world appear to it as really objective, that is, as present without its own concurrence. The intelligence will not now cease

to produce, but it produces consciously, and so here
there begins an entirely new world, which from this
point on will extend ad infinitum. The first world, if
we may so express it, that is, the world brought about
through unconscious production, now falls, as it were,
behind consciousness, together with its origin. The
intelligence will thus never be able to recognize
directly that it produces this world out of itself just
as much as it does the second world, whose gestation
begins with consciousness. Just as, from the original
act of self-consciousness, a whole nature developed,
so, from the second act, that of free self-determination,
a second nature will come forth, whose derivation is
the entire topic of the enquiry that follows.

Until now we have reflected only upon the identity
of the act of self-determination with the original act
of self-consciousness, and upon the one mark of distinction between them, namely that the former is conscious
whereas the latter is not. There is, however, yet
another distinction of great importance to which further attention must be paid, namely that the original
act of self-consciousness falls altogether outside time,
whereas the present act, which marks, not the transcendental, but the empirical starting point of consciousness, necessarily occurs at a particular phase of consciousness.

But now every action of the intelligence which
occurs for it at a particular juncture in time is, in
consequence of the original mechanism of thought, an
action that has necessarily to be explained. Yet it is
likewise beyond question that the act of self-determination here referred to is not to be explained from any
preceding act in the intelligence; for we were indeed
driven back upon it as a ground of explanation, i.e.,
ideally, but not really, or in such a way that it
resulted necessarily from a preceding act. --In gen-
eral--to recall the fact in passing--so long as we were
following the intelligence in its producing, every subsequent act was conditioned by that which preceded it;
as soon as we forsook that sphere, the order reversed
itself completely and we had to infer from the conditioned to the condition, so that it was inevitable
that we should eventually find outselves driven back
upon something unconditioned, i.e., inexplicable. But
this cannot be, in virtue of the intelligence's own
laws of thought, and as surely as the act in question
occurs at a particular juncture in time.

The contradiction here is that the act has to be
at once both explicable and inexplicable. For this
contradiction a mediating concept must be found, a
concept that has hitherto entered not at all for us
within the scope of our acquaintance. In resolving

this problem we proceed as we have done in the solution of other problems, namely in such a way as to define the task with ever-increasing accuracy--until the one possible solution remains behind.

That an act of the intelligence is inexplicable means that it cannot be explained from any preceding action, and since we at present know of no other act besides that of producing, this means that it is not to be explained by any prior producing on the part of the intelligence. To say that the act is not explicable from a producing is not to say that it is inexplicable absolutely. However, since the intelligence contains nothing at all save what it produces, this something, if it is not a producing, cannot be contained therein; and yet it has got to be so contained, since an act in the intelligence has to be explained thereby. Hence the act has to be explicable from something that both is and is not a producing on the part of the intelligence.

This contradiction can be mediated in no other way save the following: This something which contains the ground of free self-determination must be a producing on the part of the intelligence, although the negative con-dition of this producing must lie <u>outside</u> it; the former, because nothing enters the intelligence save through its own action; the latter, because in and for itself this act is not to be explicable from the intelligence itself. Conversely, the negative condition of this something <u>outside</u> the intelligence must be a deter-mination in the intelligence itself, doubtless a nega-tive one; and since the intelligence is but an act, it will have to be a nonaction of the intelligence.

If this something is conditioned by a nonaction, and by a particular nonaction of the intelligence at that, it is therefore something that can be excluded and made impossible by an action of the latter, and is thus itself an action, and even a particular one. The intelligence is thus to intuit an action as resulting, and as with all other intuiting by means of a producing in the intelligence, there must therefore be no immedi-ate influence exerted upon the latter, there must be no positive condition of its intuiting lying outside it, it must remain as always entirely closed up within itself; and likewise, on the other hand, it must not be the cause of this action, but must merely contain the negative condition thereof, and to that extent the action has to take place in complete independence of the intelligence. In a word, this act must not be the direct ground of a producing in the intelligence, but again, conversely, the intelligence must not be a direct ground of the action, and likewise the <u>presentation</u> of such an act in the intelligence, as an act independent of it, and the <u>act itself</u>, outside

it, must coexist, as though the one were determined
by the other.

Such a relationship is conceivable only through a
preestablished harmony. The act outside the intelligence comes about entirely on its own; the intelligence
contains only the negative condition thereof, that is,
if it had behaved in a certain fashion, this act would
not have taken place; but by merely not acting it still
does not become the direct or positive ground of the
act, for by the mere fact of its not acting, this act
would still not have occurred unless there had been
something else outside the intelligence which contained
the ground of that act. Conversely, the idea or concept of the act arrives in the intelligence entirely on
its own, as though there were nothing outside the latter;
and yet it could not occur therein unless the act took
place really and independently of the intelligence; and
hence this act likewise is again only the indirect
ground of a presentation in the intelligence. This
indirect reciprocity is what we understand by a preestablished harmony.

But such a harmony is conceivable only between subjects of equal reality, and hence this act must have
proceeded from a subject endowed with just the same
reality as the intelligence itself; that is, it must
have proceeded from another, external intelligence, and
thus by the contradiction noted above we find ourselves
led on to a new principle.

Second Proposition. The act of self-determination,
or the free action of the intelligence upon itself, can
be explained only by the determinate action of an
intelligence external to it.

Proof. This is contained in the deduction just
effected, and rests solely upon the two propositions,
that self-determination must be at once explicable,
and yet not explicable by a producing on the part of
the intelligence. So instead of dwelling any further
on the proof, let us pass on at once to the problems
which we see to emerge from this doctrine and from the
proof adduced for it.

First, then, we see at all events that a determinate action of an extraneous intelligence is the
necessary condition of the act of self-determination,
and thereby of consciousness; but we do not see how,
and in what manner such an external act could be even
the indirect ground of a free self-determination in
ourselves.

Second. We do not perceive how there can be any
external influence at all upon the intelligence, and so
also do not see how the influence of another intelligence upon it may be possible. By now, indeed, this
difficulty has already been met by our deduction, in

that we have deduced an act external to the intelligence
merely as the indirect ground of an action within it.
But now how, then, can we even conceive of this indirect
relationship, or of any such predetermined harmony
between different intelligences?

Third. If this predetermined harmony were to be
accounted for in some such fashion as this, that by a
particular nonacting in myself there would necessarily
be posited for me a particular act on the part of an
intelligence outside me, then presumably the latter,
since it is tied to a contingent condition (my nonacting), is a free action, so that this nonacting of
mine would also be free in nature. But now the latter
is supposed to be the condition of an act whereby
consciousness, and with it freedom, first arise for
me; how can one conceive of a free nonacting prior to
freedom itself?

These three problems must first of all be solved
before we can proceed any further in our enquiry.

Solution of the first problem. By the act of self-
determination I am to arise for myself as a self, that
is, as a subject-object. Moreover, this act is to be a
free one; that I determine myself is to have its ground
wholly and solely in myself. If the act is a free one,
I must have willed what comes about for me through this
act, and it must come about for me only because I have
willed it. But now that which arises for me through
this act is willing itself (for the self is a primordial
willing). I must thus already have willed the willing
before I can act freely, and the concept of willing, like
that of the self, likewise first arises for me only
through this act.

This manifest circle is eliminable only if willing
can become an object for me prior to willing. This is
impossible through my own agency, so it will have to be
simply that concept of willing which would arise for me
through the act of an intelligence.

It is therefore only such an act external to the
intelligence which can become for it an indirect ground
of self-determination, whereby the concept of willing
arises for it; and the problem now changes into this,
namely by what action, then, can the concept of willing
arise for the intelligence?

It cannot be an act whereby the concept of a real
object arises for it, since it would thereby revert to
the point which it is just supposed to have left. It
must therefore be the concept of a possible object,
that is, of something which does not now exist, but
can do so in the moment that follows. But even by that
the concept of willing is not yet engendered. It must
be the concept of an object which can exist only if the
intelligence makes it real. Only through the concept of

such an object can that which is divided in willing be
divided in the self, for the self itself; for insofar
as the concept of an object arises for the self, it is
merely ideal, while insofar as this concept arises for
it as the concept of an object to be realized by its
act, it becomes for the self both ideal and real at once.
Thus by means of this object it at least <u>can</u> become, <u>qua</u>
intelligence, an object to itself. But it only can do
so. For it really to appear so to itself, requires that
it should contrast the present moment (that of ideal
limitation) to that which follows (that of producing),
and should relate the two together. The self can be
obliged to do this only by the fact that this act constitutes a demand for realization of the object. Only
through the concept of obligation does the contrast
arise between the ideal and the producing self. Now
whether the action whereby the required' item is realized
actually ensues, is uncertain, for the condition of the
action that is given (the concept of willing), is a
condition thereof as a <u>free</u> action; but the condition
cannot contradict the conditioned, so that if the former
is posited the action would be necessary. Willing itself
always remains free, and must so remain, if it is not to
cease to be a willing. Only the condition for the
possibility of willing must be generated in the self
without its concurrence. And thus we see forthwith a
complete removal of the contradiction, whereby the same
act of the intelligence had to be both explicable and
inexplicable at once. The concept which mediates this
contradiction is that of a demand, since by means of the
demand the action is <u>explained</u>, <u>if it takes place</u>, without it <u>having</u> to take place on that account. It may
ensue, as soon as the concept of willing arises for the
self, or as soon as it sees itself reflected, catches
sight of itself in the mirror of another intelligence;
but it does not have to ensue.

   We cannot address ourselves at once to the further
conclusions which result from this solution to our
problem, since we must first of all answer the question,
how in fact can this demand of an intelligence outside it
get through to the self; which question, more generally
stated, amounts to this: how then, in general, can
intelligences exert influence upon one another?

   <u>Solution of the second problem</u>. We first investi-
gate this question altogether at large, and without
reference to the special case now before us, to which
the application can easily and automatically be made.

   That an immediate influencing among intelligences
is impossible, according to the principles of transcendental idealism, stands in no need of proof, nor has
any other philosophy rendered such an influence
intelligible. Hence nothing remains but to suppose

an indrect influence between different intelligences,
and here we are concerned merely with the conditions
for the possibility of this.

Among intelligences which are to act upon each
other through freedom, there must, then, in the first
place, be a preestablished harmony in regard to the
common world which they present. For since all determinacy in the intelligence comes about only through the
determinacy of its presentations, intelligences who
intuited utterly different worlds would have absolutely
nothing in common, and no point of contact at which they
could come together. Since I draw the concept of
intelligence solely from myself, an intelligence that
I am to recognize as such must stand under the same
conditions in intuiting the world as I do myself; and
since the difference between it and me is constituted
solely by our respective individualities, that which
remains when I remove the determinacy of this individuality must be common to us both, that is, we must be
alike in regard to the first, the second, and even the
third kind of restrictedness, leaving aside the determinacy of the latter.

But now if the intelligence brings forth everything
objective out of itself, and there is no common archetype
for the presentations that we intuit outside us, the
consilience among the presentations of different intel-
ligences--as regards both the whole of the objective
world and also individual things and events within the
same space and time (which consilience alone compels
us to ascribe objective truth to our presentations)--
is explicable no otherwise than from our common nature,
or from the identity both of our primitive and also of
our derived restrictedness. For just as the original
restrictedness predetermines, for the individual intelligence, everything that may enter into the sphere
of its presentations, so also does the unity of that
restrictedness ensure a thoroughgoing consilience among
the presentations of different intelligences. This
common intuition is the foundation, and, as it were, the
solid earth upon which all interaction between intelligences takes place; a substrate to which, for that
very reason, they constantly revert, so soon as they
find themselves in disharmony about that which is not
directly determined by intuition. --Only here the
explanation should not venture to extend further, to
some absolute principle, which, by operating as the
communal focus of intelligences, or their creator and
agent of uniformity (concepts wholly unintelligible to
us), should contain the common basis of their agreement
in regard to objective presentations. On the contrary,
as surely as there exists a single intelligence, with
all the determinations of its consciousness that we

have derived, so surely are there also other intelligences with the same determinations, for they are conditions of the consciousness of the first, and <u>vice
versa</u>.

But now different intelligences can have in common
only the first and second forms of restriction, and the
third only in a general sense; for the latter is precisely that by virtue of which the intelligence exists
as a specific individual. Hence it seems that, precisely
through this third restrictedness, insofar as it is a
particular one, all community between intelligences is
done away with. However, even through this restriction
of individuality, a preestablished harmony can again be
conditioned, if we do but suppose it to be the opposite
of the previous one. For whereas the latter, which
occurs in regard to their objective presentations,
serves to posit something common among intelligences,
the third restrictedness, by contrast, serves to posit
in every individual something which, precisely for that
reason, is negated by all the others, and which they
cannot therefore intuit as their own action, but only
as other than theirs, that is, as the action of an
intelligence outside them.

The claim, therefore, is that immediately through
the individual restrictedness of every intelligence,
immediately through the negation of a certain activity
therein, this activity is posited for it as the activity
of an intelligence outside it, which thus constitutes a
preestablished harmony of a <u>negative</u> kind.

To demonstrate such a thesis, two propositions must
therefore be proved,

1. That what is not <u>my</u> activity must be intuited
by me, simply because it is not mine, and without the
need of any direct influence upon me from without, as
the activity of an intelligence outside me;

2. That immediately through the positing of my
individuality, without further restriction from outside,
a negation of activity is posited in me.

Now so far as the first proposition is concerned,
we must observe that we are speaking only of conscious
or free acts; now the intelligence is admittedly confined
in its freedom by the objective world, as has already
been shown in general above, but within this restriction it is again unrestricted, so that its activity can,
for example, be directed toward any object it pleases;
now if we suppose that it begins to act, its activity
will necessarily have to be directed toward some particular object, in such a way as to leave all other
objects free and, as it were, undisturbed: but now
there is no seeing how its originally quite indeterminate activity should restrict itself in this fashion,
unless the direction towards these other objects were

somehow made impossible for it, which, so far as we have seen hitherto, is possible only through intelligences outside it. It is thus a condition of self-consciousness that I intuit in general an activity of intelligences outside me (the enquiry as yet being still an entirely general one), because it is a condition of self-consciousness that my activity be directed upon a specific object. But this very direction of my activity is something that is already posited and predetermined by the synthesis of my individuality. By the same synthesis, therefore, other intelligences, whereby I intuit myself as restricted in my free action, and hence also specific actions of these intelligences, are likewise already posited for me, without the need of any further special influence, on their part, upon myself.

We forbear to show the application of this solution to particular cases, or to meet at once the objections that we can anticipate, in order first merely to clarify the solution itself by means of examples.

The following may serve by way of elucidation. -- Among the original drives of the intelligence there is also a drive for knowledge, and knowledge is one of the objects upon which its activity may be directed. Let us suppose this happens, which in fact will be so only if the immediate objects of activity are all already preoccupied, so that the activity of the intelligence is already restricted by that very fact; but in itself this object is again infinite, and so here too it will again have to be confined: if we suppose, therefore, that the intelligence directs its activity upon a specific object of cognition, it will either discover or acquire the knowledge of that object, that is, it will arrive at this kind of cognition through alien influence. Now what serves to posit this alien influence here? Merely a negation in the intelligence itself; for either its individual restrictedness renders it wholly incapable of discovery, or the discovery has already been made, and if so, this too is again posited by the synthesis of its individuality, to which it also appertains that the intelligence has first begun to exist at this particular period of time. Hence it is only through negations of its own activity that the intelligence is exposed, and as it were opened, to alien influence as such.

But now arises a new question, the most important of this enquiry: how then, by pure negation, can anything positive be posited, in such a way that I am obliged to intuit what is not my activity, simply because it is not mine, as the activity of an intelligence outside me? The answer is as follows: to will at all, I must will something determinate, but this I could never do if I could will everything; hence, by

involuntary intuition it must already have been made
impossible for me to will everything; but this is
inconceivable unless already with my individuality, and
hence my self-consciousness, so far as it is a thoroughly
determinate one, limiting points have been set to my
free activity, and such points can now be, not selfless
objects, but only other free activities, that is, actions
of intelligences outside myself.

So if the meaning of the question is this: why then
does that which does not take place through myself have
to take place at all (which in fact is the meaning of
our claim, in that immediately through the negation of
a particular activity in the one intelligence, we have
it affirmatively posited in the other), we answer it
thus: since the realm of possibility is infinite, everything that under given circumstances is possible simply
and solely through freedom must therefore be actual,
unless indeed one single intelligence is to be limited
realiter in its free action, and that actually by
intelligences outside it; so that there remains for it
only the one particular object upon which it directs
its activity.

But if an objection were to be drawn, say, from
totally purposeless acts, we reply by saying that such
acts simply do not belong among free acts, and so are
also excluded from among those which, in respect of
their possibility, are predetermined for the moral world;
on the contrary, they are mere natural consequences,
or phenomena, which like all others are already predetermined by the absolute synthesis.

Or suppose one were to argue in the following
manner: granted that it is already determined through
the synthesis of my individuality that I intuit this
act as the work of another intelligence, it was still
not determined thereby that precisely this individual
should perform it. In reply to this we ask: what, then,
is this individual, if not just the one who acts so and
not otherwise, or what is your conception of him made
up from, if not just from his manner of acting? By
the synthesis of your individuality, it was indeed
only determined for you that some other intelligence
should engage in this particular activity; but by the
very fact that he engages in it, such an other becomes
this particular one that you think him to be. That
you therefore intuit the activity as the work of this
particular individual, was determined, not by your
individuality, but assuredly by his own; though you can
seek the ground thereof only in his free determination
of himself, so that it must also appear to you as
absolutely contingent that it is precisely this individual
who engages in the activity in question.

The harmony derived thus far, and undoubtedly made

intelligible, therefore consists in this, that immediately through the positing of a passivity in myself, which is necessary in the interests of freedom, since it is only through a determinate affection from without that I can attain to freedom, an activity outside me is posited as a necessary correlate, and posited for my own intuition; and this theory is accordingly the reverse of the ordinary one, just as transcendental idealism arises in general through a direct inversion of previous modes of philosophical explanation. According to the ordinary notion, passivity is posited in me through activity outside me, so that the latter is primary and the former a consequence thereof. According to our theory, the passivity posited immediately through my own individuality is the condition for the activity which I intuit outside me. Imagine a quantum of activity, as it were, to be distributed over the whole order of rational beings; every one of them has the same right to the total, but in order simply to be active at all, it has to be active in a particular way; if it could appropriate the whole quantum to itself, then only absolute passivity would be left over for all rational beings outside it. Through negation of activity in itself, therefore, there is posited immediately, that is, not merely in thought, but in intuition also (since everything that is a condition of consciousness must be externally intuited), an activity outside itself, and posited to precisely the extent that such activity is suspended in itself.

We pass on to the second question left unanswered above, namely how far, through the immediate positing of individuality, a negation of activity is also necessarily posited? This question has already been largely answered by what has gone before.

Individuality not only involves being there at a particular time, and whatever other restrictions are posited by existence as an organism; it is also the case that, through action itself, and in the acting, individuality restricts itself anew, to the point where one may say in a certain sense that the more an individual acts, the less free does he become.

But in order merely to be able to start acting, I must already be restricted. That my free activity is originally directed only to a specific object, was explained above by the fact that other intelligences have already made it impossible for me to will everything. Yet a multiplicity of such intelligences cannot have made it impossible for me to will a multiplicity of things; that out of a number of objects, B, C, D, I choose just C, must still have its ultimate ground located in myself alone. But now this ground

cannot lie in my freedom, for it is through this
restriction of free activity to a particular object
that I first become aware of myself, and thus also free;
hence, before I am free, that is, conscious of freedom,
my freedom must already have been restricted, and certain free actions must, even before I am free, have been
made impossible for me. This, for example, is the pro-
vince of what we call talent or genius, and not only
genius in the arts or sciences, but also genius for
action. It is a hard saying, but no less true on that
account, that just as innumerable men are basically
unfitted for the highest functions of the spirit, so an
equal multitude will never be capable of acting with
that freedom and elevation of spirit over even law
itself, which can be granted only to a chosen few.

It is this fact, that _free_ actions have actually
been already made impossible from the start by an unknown
necessity, which compels men to bless or bewail, at
times the grace or disfavor of nature, at times the
decree of fate.

The result of our whole enquiry can now be
summarized most briefly as follows:

To achieve the original self-intuition of my own
free activity, this latter can be posited only quan-
titatively, that is, under restrictions; and since the
activity is free and conscious, these restrictions are
possible only through intelligences outside me, in such
a fashion that, in the operations of these intelligences
upon me, I discern nothing save the original bounds of
my own individuality, and would have to intuit these,
even if in fact there were no other intelligences beyond
myself. That although other intelligences are posited
in me only through negations, I nevertheless must acknowledge them as existing independently of me, will sur-
prise nobody who reflects that this relationship is a
completely reciprocal one, and that no rational being
can substantiate itself as such, save by the recognition of others as such.

But if, now, we apply this general explanation to
the case before us, it leads us to the

Solution of the third problem. For if, indeed, all
influence of rational beings upon me is posited through
a negation of free activity in myself, and yet that first
influence, which is the condition of consciousness, can
come about before I am free (for freedom only arises
with consciousness), the question is, how then can
freedom be restricted in me even before I am conscious
of being free? The answer to this question is already
contained in part in the foregoing, and here we merely
add the remark, that this influence which is the condition of consciousness must be thought of, not just as
an individual act, but as persisting; for the

continuance of consciousness is rendered necessary neither by the objective world alone, nor by the first influence of another rational being; it is a matter, rather, of a continuing influence urging us to become repeatedly orientated anew within the intellectual world; and this comes about in that, through the influence of a rational being, it is not unconscious, but conscious and free activity (which merely glimmers through via the medium of the objective world), that is reflected and becomes an object to us as free. This progressive influence is what we call education, in the widest sense of the world, wherein education is never completed, but persists as a condition of the continuance of consciousness. But now there is no understanding how this influence neces- sarily persists, unless for every individual, even before it is free, a certain quantity of free actions-- as we may be allowed to put it, for the sake of brevity-- is negated. The never-ceasing interaction of rational beings, regardless of their ever-increasing freedom, is thus alone made possible by what we call diversity of talents and characteristics, which, for that very reason, however much it may seem opposed to the drive for freedom, is itself necessary as a condition of consciousness. But as to how this original restricted- ness may be reconciled with freedom itself in regard to moral actions, whereby, for example, it is impossi- ble for a man throughout his whole life to attain to a certain degree of excellence, or to outgrow the tutelage of others--that is a question with which transcendental philosophy does not have to be concerned; for its task is everywhere merely to deduce phenomena, and freedom itself, for it, is nothing else but a necessary phenomenon, whose conditions, for that reason, must have a similar necessity; seeing that the question whether these phenomena are objective and true in themselves has no more meaning than the theoretical question, whether there are things-in-themselves.

The solution of the third problem therefore con- sists simply in this, that there must already be in me from the start a free, though unconscious, nonacting, that is, the negation of an activity which, if it were not originally suspended, would be free, but of which, since it is suspended, I cannot in fact become con- scious as an activity of my own.

With this second principle of ours, the thread of the synthetic enquiry that was cut off earlier is now again tied together. As was observed at the time, it was the third restrictedness which had to contain the ground of the action whereby the self is posited for itself as intuiting. But this third restrictedness was in fact individuality, whereby, indeed, was already determined in advance the existence and influence of

other rational beings upon the intelligence, and therewith freedom, the power of reflecting upon the object,
of becoming conscious of oneself, and the whole sequence
of free and conscious acts. The third restrictedness,
or that of individuality, is thus the synthetic point
or pivot of theoretical and practical philosophy, and
only now have we really arrived in the territory of the
latter, and the synthetic enquiry begins afresh.

Since the restrictedness of individuality, and hence
that of freedom, was originally posited only in that the
intelligence was obliged to intuit itself as an organic
individual, we simultaneously perceive here the reason
why--involuntarily, and through a sort of universal
instinct--the contingent features of the organism, the
particular shape and build of the noblest organs
especially, have been regarded as the visible expression, and at least as affording the presumption, of
talent and of character itself.

Additional Remarks

In the course of the investigation that has just been
going on, we have deliberately left undiscussed a number
of subsidiary questions, which, now that the main
enquiry is concluded, require to be given an answer.

1. We claimed that by the operation of other intelligences upon an object the unconscious direction of
the free activity upon it could be rendered impossible.
It was already presupposed in this claim that, in and for
itself, the object is incapable of raising the activity
directed upon it to the level of consciousness; not,
indeed, as if the object behaves with absolute passivity in response to my acting, a thing that, though
the contrary thereof has not yet been proved, was certainly not presupposed either. It is merely that for
itself and without the prior operation of an intelligence, the object is not capable of reflecting the free
activity as such within itself. What, then, is added
to the object by the operation of an intelligence,
which the object does not possess in and for itself?

In answering this question, the preceding discussion at least supplies us with a datum.

Willing does not depend, as producing does, upon
the simple opposition between ideal and real activity,
but upon a twofold opposition between the ideal on the
one side and the ideal and real on the other. In
willing, the intelligence is both idealizing and
realizing at the same time. If it were merely realizing,
indeed, then since all realization contains an ideal
activity as well as the real, it would give expression
to a concept in the object. Since it is not simply
realizing, however, but besides that and independently

of realization is also ideal, it cannot simply express
a concept in the object, but by free action must express
therein a concept of the concept. Now insofar as production depends only on the simple contrast between
ideal and real activity, the concept must so belong to
the nature of the object itself, that it is absolutely
inseparable therefrom; the concept goes no further than
the object does, and each must be exhaustive of the
other. In a production, on the other hand, which contains an ideal activity of the ideal, the concept would
necessarily have to go beyond the object, or as it were
exceed the latter. But this is possible only if the
concept which exceeds the object can exhaust itself
in another object beyond the first, that is, if the
latter is related to something else as a means to an
end. It is therefore the concept of the concept--
this itself being the concept of an end outside the
object--which is appended to it by the free act of
producing. For no object has an end outside it, in
and for itself, since if there are themselves purposive
objects, they can only be purposive in relation to
themselves, and are thus their own ends. It is only
the artifact, in a broad sense of the term, that has
an end outside itself. As surely, then, as intelligences must mutually restrict one another in acting,
and this is as necessary as consciousness itself, so
surely also must artifacts emerge within the sphere of
our outer intuitions. How artifacts may be possible
is undoubtedly an important question for transcendental
idealism, but it has not yet been answered here.

Through the direction upon it of a free and conscious activity, the object is furnished with the concept of the concept, whereas in the object of blind
production, on the other hand, the concept passes
directly over into the object, and can be distinguished
from it only by means of the concept of the concept,
though this can only arise for the intelligence through
an external influence. If this be the case, the object
of blind intuition will be unable to push reflection any
further, that is, to anything independent of the object,
and so the intelligence will come to a halt at the mere
phenomenon. The artifact, however, though admittedly
it too is at first only my own intuition, by the fact
that it expresses the concept of the concept, will push
reflection immediately to an intelligence outside itself
(for only such a one is capable of thus raising the
concept to a higher power), and hence to something
absolutely independent of itself. So it is through the
artifact alone that the intelligence can be pushed
toward something that is no longer an object, and
thus its own production, but something far higher than

any object, namely an <u>intuition external</u> to it, which,
since it can never become a thing intuited, is for it
the first absolutely objective item entirely independent of itself. Now the object which pushes reflection
toward something beyond any object, posits counter to
free operation an invisible ideal resistance, whereby,
on that very account, it is not the objective, producing
activity that is reflected in ourselves, but an activity
at once ideal and productive. So where it is merely
force, now objective and appearing as physical in
character, which encounters resistance, there can only
be nature present; but where conscious activity, that
is, this ideal activity of the third order, is reflected
in oneself, there is necessarily something invisible
present, additional to the object, which makes a blind
direction of activity upon the object utterly impossible.

Now it cannot, indeed, be suggested, that through
the influence thus exerted by an intelligence upon the
object, my freedom in regard to the latter is absolutely
taken away. All we are saying is that the invisible
resistance which I encounter in such an object compels
me to a decision, that is, to a restriction of myself;
or that the activity of another rational being, insofar
as it is fixated or made manifest in objects, serves to
determine me to self-determination; and this question,
how I am able to will something determinate, was all
that we had to explain.

2. <u>Only by the fact that there are intelligences
outside me, does the world as such become objective to
me</u>.

It has just been shown that only operations of
intelligences upon the world of sense compel me to
accept something as absolutely objective. We are not
now speaking of this, but rather of the fact that the
whole essentiality of objects only becomes real for
me, in that the intelligences are outside me. Nor
are we referring to anything that might first be
evolved through habituation or upbringing, but rather
to the fact that already from the start the notion of
objects outside me simply cannot arise, save through
intelligences external to me. For

a) that the notion of an <u>outside me</u>, as such, could
arise only through the operation of intelligences, either
upon myself, or upon sensory objects whereon they set
their stamp, is already apparent from the fact that
objects in and for themselves are not outside me; for
where objects are, there am I also, and even the space
in which I intuit them is originally only in myself.
The sole original <u>outside me</u> is an <u>intuition</u> outside me,
and this is the point at which the idealism we start
with is first transformed into realism.

b) I am, however, under a special necessity of

envisaging objects as external to and independent of
myself (and that objects appear to me as such must be
deduced as necessary, if it can be deduced at all);
that this necessity is solely due to an intuition
outside me, has now to be proved as follows.

That objects really exist outside me, i.e.,
independently of me, is something of which I can only
be convinced if I am sure that they also exist when I
do not intuit them. That objects existed before the
individual did, is something of which he cannot be
convinced by merely finding himself to be coming in at
a particular point in the succession, since this is
simply a consequence of his second restrictedness.
The sole objectivity which the world can possess for
the individual is the fact of its having been intuited
by intelligences outside the self. (It can also be
deduced from this very fact that there must be states
of nonintuiting, for the individual.) The harmony we
have already predetermined earlier, in regard to the
involuntary presentations of different intelligences,
is thus at the same time to be deduced as the sole
condition under which the world becomes objective to
the individual. For the individual, these other
intelligences are, as it were, the eternal bearers
of the universe, and together they constitute so many
indestructible mirrors of the objective world. The
world, though it is posited solely through the self,
is independent of me, since it resides for me in the
intuition of other intelligences; their common world
is the archetype, whose agreement with my own presentations is the sole criterion of truth. In a transcendental
enquiry we make no appeal to the fact that a discrepancy
in our own presentations with respect to those of others
immediately makes us doubtful as to their objectivity;
nor do we argue that for every unexpected appearance it
is the presentations of others which provide, as it were,
the touchstone; we rely, rather, solely on this, that
intuition, like everything else, can only become
objective to the self through outer objects, which
objects, now, can be nothing else but intelligences
outside us--so many intuitions, that is, of our own
intuiting.

It therefore also follows automatically from the
above, that a rational being in isolation could not only
not arrive at a consciousness of freedom, but would be
equally unable to attain to consciousness of the objective
world as such; and hence that intelligences outside the
individual, and a never-ceasing interaction with them,
alone make complete the whole of consciousness with all
its determinations.

Our task, to discover how the self may recognize
itself as intuitant, is now fully discharged at last.

<u>Willing</u> (with all the determinations which, according to
the foregoing, belong to it) is the action whereby
intuiting itself is fully posited into consciousness.

In accordance with the familiar procedure of our
science there now arises for us the new

E

Problem:

To explain how willing again becomes objective
for the self.

Solution

I

<u>Third Proposition. Willing, at the outset, is necessarily</u>
<u>directed upon an external object.</u>

<u>Proof</u>. By the free act of self-determination, the
self as it were destroys everything material in its
presenting, in that it makes itself wholly free in
regard to the objective; and only by this, in fact,
does willing become willing. But the self could not
become aware of this act as such, if willing did not
once more become an object to it. This however, is
possible only in that an object of intuition becomes the
visible expression of its willing. But every object of
intuition is a particular one, and must therefore be
this particular one only because and insofar as the self
has willed in this particular manner. Only so would the
self become its own cause of the matter of its presenting.

But moreover the action whereby the object becomes
this particular one must not be absolutely identical
with the object itself, for otherwise the action would
be a blind producing, a mere intuiting. The action as
such and the object must therefore remain distinguishable. But now the action conceived as such, is a concept. But that concept and object remain distinguishable is possible only in that the object exists independently of this action, that is, in that the object is
an <u>external</u> one. Conversely, the object, on that very
account, becomes an external one for me only through
willing, for willing is willing only insofar as it is
directed upon something independent of it.

And here already we have light upon what is still
more fully explained in the sequel, namely why the self
can in no way appear to itself as bringing forth an
object as though it were a substance, and why, on the
contrary, all bringing forth in willing appears only as
a forming or shaping of the object.

Our proof has now shown, indeed, that willing as
such can become objective to the self only through being
directed upon an external object; but it is not yet
explained from whence this direction itself can come.

In regard to this question, it is already presupposed that productive intuition persists inasmuch as

I will; or that in willing itself I am compelled to
present determinate objects. No actuality, no willing.
So through willing there straightway arises an opposition, in that by means of it I am aware on the one hand
of freedom, and thus also of infinity, while on the
other I am constantly dragged back into finitude by the
compulsion to present. Hence, in virtue of this contradiction, an activity must arise which wavers in the
middle between finitude and infinity. For the time
being we shall call this activity imagination, merely
for brevity's sake, and without thereby wishing to maintain without proof that what is commonly spoken of as
imagination is in fact such a wavering between finitude
and infinity; or, what comes to the same, an activity
mediating the theoretical and the practical; the proof
of all which will in fact be found in what follows.
This power, therefore, which we refer to meanwhile as
imagination, will in course of this wavering also necessarily produce something, which itself oscillates between
infinity and finitude, and which can therefore also be
regarded only as such. Products of this kind are what
we call Ideas as opposed to concepts, and imagination in
this wavering is on that very account not understanding
but reason; and conversely, what is commonly called
theoretical reason is nothing else but imagination in
the service of freedom. But that Ideas are mere objects
of imagination, having their place only in this wavering between finitude and infinity, is evident from the
fact that, once they are made objects of the understanding, they lead to those insoluble contradictions
which Kant set forth under the name of the antinomies;
contradictions whose existence rests solely on the fact
that either we reflect upon the object, in which case
it is necessarily finite, or else we reflect further
upon our own reflecting, whereby the object again at
once becomes infinite. But now it is obvious that if
the question whether the object of an Idea be finite or
infinite is dependent merely on the free orientation of
reflection, the object as such can itself be neither the
one nor the other; and if so, these Ideas must assuredly
be mere products of imagination, that is, of an activity
such that it produces neither the finite nor the
infinite.

But now how, in willing, the self makes the transition, even in thought, from the Idea to the determinate
object (for how such a transition may be objectively
possible is still not in question at all), is beyond
comprehension, unless there is again some intermediary,
which is for acting precisely what in thinking the
symbol is for ideas, or the schema for concepts. This
mediating factor is the ideal.

Through the opposition between ideal and object

there first arises for the self the opposition between
the object as the idealizing activity demands it, and
the object as it actually is according to constrained
thought; but this opposition at once engenders the drive
to transform the object as it is into the object as it
ought to be. We entitle the activity that arises here
a drive, because on the one hand it is free, and yet on
the other it springs immediately and without any reflection from a feeling, both of which factors together make
up the concept of a drive. For that state of the self
as it wavers between ideal and object is a state of
feeling, since it is a state of being restricted for
itself. But in every feeling a contradiction is felt,
and nothing whatever can be felt save an inner contradiction within ourselves. Now through every contradiction
the condition for activity is immediately given; the
activity springs forth as soon as its condition is but
given, without any further reflection, and if it is at
the same time a free activity, which production, for
example, is not, is for that very reason, and to that
extent only, a drive.

Direction upon an external object therefore finds
expression through a <u>drive</u>, and this drive emerges
directly from the contradiction between the idealizing
and the intuiting self, and is directly bent upon
restoring the lost identity of the self. As necessarily
as self-consciousness is to continue, so this drive
must have causality (for we still go on deducing all the
acts of the self as conditions of self-consciousness,
since through the objective world alone self-consciousness is not completed, but only brought to the point at
which it <u>can</u> begin, though from there onwards it can
be carried forward only through free acts). The
question, then, is merely, <u>how</u> this drive can have
causality?

Here a transition is obviously postulated from the
(purely) ideal into the objective (at once both ideal
and real). We first attempt to establish the negative
conditions for such a transition, and will subsequently
go on to the positive conditions, or those under which
it actually takes place.

A

a) By freedom the ideal self is immediately opened
to infinity, as surely as it is cast into confinement
by the mere objective world; but it cannot make infinity
an object to itself without delimiting it; conversely,
infinity cannot be limited absolutely, but only for
purposes of action, in such a way that if, say, the
ideal is realized, the Idea can be extended further,
and so on indefinitely. Thus the ideal always holds

only for the present moment of action, whereas the
Idea itself, which ever becomes infinite again in
reflecting upon the action, can be realized only in a
progressus ad infinitum. That freedom is at every
moment limited and yet at every moment again becomes
infinite, in respect of its striving, is what alone
makes possible the consciousness of freedom, that is,
the continuance of self-consciousness itself. For it
is freedom which sustains the continuity of self-consciousness. If I reflect upon the producing of time in
my action, it becomes for me, indeed, a magnitude
interrupted and put together out of moments. But in
action itself, time is always continuous for me; and the
more I act, and the less I reflect, the more continuous
it is. The drive in question can therefore have no
causality save in time, which represents the first
determination of our transition. But now since time
can be thought of objectively only as proceeding via
a succession of presentations, in which the later are
conditioned by those that precede, there must equally
be such a succession present in our free producing,
save only that the presentations are related to each
other, not as cause and effect, but as means and end--
seeing that every conscious action contains a concept
of the concept, that is, the concept of an end; and
these two concepts will be related to those of cause
and effect just as a concept of the concept is related
to simple concepts as such. Hence we may perceive it
to be a condition of the consciousness of freedom,
that my realization of any end is not attainable directly, but only through a number of intermediate steps.
      b) It was established that action should not go over
absolutely into the object, for otherwise it would be an
intuition; yet the object has always to remain an external object, separate, that is, from my action; how is
this conceivable?
      According to a), the drive can have causality only
in time. But the object is that which is in opposition
to freedom; yet it now has to be determined through
freedom, and we therefore have a contradiction here.
Let the object contain a determination = a; freedom now
demands the opposite determination = -a. This is no
contradiction for freedom, but it is so for intuition.
For the latter, the contradiction can be removed only
through the common intermediary, time. If I could bring
forth -a in the absence of all time, the transition would
be unthinkable; a and -a would coexist. In the succeeding instant there must therefore be something which
does not now exist, and only so is a consciousness of
freedom possible. But now no succession can be perceived in time without something that persists. The
transition from a to -a in my presentations destroys

the identity of consciousness, and it must thus be
produced once more in the transition. This identity
produced in the transition is substance, and here is the
point at which this concept, like the other categories
of relation, is also posited, by a necessary act of
reflection, in the ordinary consciousness. In acting,
I appear to myself to be entirely free to alter all
the determinations of things; but now the object is
nothing apart from its determinations, and we likewise
think of the object throughout all the changes of its
determinations as the selfsame identical thing, namely
as a substance. Substance is therefore nothing save
that which supports all these determinations, and is
actually a mere expression of our constant reflecting
upon the becoming of the object. Now since, if we
picture ourselves as operating upon objects, we must
necessarily conceive of the object's transition from
a given state into an opposite one, we can similarly
appear to ourselves only as altering the contingent
determinations of things, but not their substantiality.

   c) We have just claimed that in my altering of the
contingent determinations of things, my action must be
accompanied by a constant reflection upon the changing
object. But there is no reflection without resistance.
So these casual determinations must not be alterable
without resistance, if free action with constant reflection is to take place. It is also evident from this
that the contingent determinations of things are the
feature about them which restricts me in acting; and
it is equally apparent from thence, why these secondary
properties of things, such as hardness, softness, etc.
(which are expressions of determinate limitation), have
no existence at all for mere intuition.

   The negative conditions so far derived, for the
transition from the subjective to the objective, still
leave it unexplained, however, as to how in fact this
transition actually occurs, that is, how and under what
conditions I am obliged to envisage any such thing. Such
a transition could not happen at all without a constant
relation between the ideal and the object determined in
accordance therewith, which relation is possible only
through intuition, though it does not itself proceed
from the self, but merely wavers between two opposing
presentations of the self, the freely projected and
the objective. This is self-evident, and we therefore
proceed at once to the main task of the present
enquiry.

B

For purposes of this enquiry we return to the first
requirement. By means of a free action, something is
to be determined in the objective world.

Everything in the objective world is present only insofar as the self intuits it therein. That a thing changes in the objective world is as much as to say that something changes in my intuition, and our requirement amounts to this: by a free action in myself, something in my outer intuition is to be determined.

How anything might be able to pass over from freedom into the objective world would be utterly unintelligible if this world were something subsisting in itself; and unintelligible even by virtue of a preestablished harmony, which again would be possible only by means of a third thing, of which the intelligence and the objective world are common modifications; it would thus be possible only through something whereby all freedom was swallowed up in action. Given that the world itself is merely a modification of the self, the enquiry takes a totally different turn. For then the question is actually this: How can something be determined in me through a free activity, insofar as I am not free, insofar as I am engaged in intuition? --That my free activity has causality means that I look upon it as having causality. The self which <u>acts</u> is distinguished from the self which <u>intuits</u>; and yet both have to be identical in relation to the object; what is posited into the object by the agent must also be posited into the intuitant; the acting self must determine the intuiting self. For that I am that which now acts is assuredly known to me only from the identity of this latter with that which intuits the action and is conscious thereof. The agent (it seems) does not <u>know</u>, it merely acts, it is merely an object; the intuitant alone knows and is for that very reason a mere subject. How then does the identity now come about here, that there is posited in the object precisely what is posited in the subject, and in the subject, precisely what is posited in the object?

We shall first set forth the general tenor of our reply to this question, while leaving the closer treatment of particular points to follow later on.

Something in the objectively intuitant self is to be determined by the freely acting self. Now what, then, is the free-acting self? All free action rests, as we know, on the twofold opposition between the ideal self on the one hand, and the simultaneously ideal and real self on the other. --But what, then, is the intuitant self? --This very self, at once real and ideal, which constitutes the objective in free agency. <u>The free-acting and the intuitant selves are thus different, once we posit that ideal activity which stands opposed to that of production; when we remove it in thought, they are the same</u>. Now this is undoubtedly the point to which we must first direct our attention, and in

which we must look for the ground of that identity we
have postulated, between the freely active and the
objectively intuitant <u>self</u>.

But if we wish to arrive at complete clarity on
this matter, we must repeat the reminder, that everything we have so far deduced has had reference only to
<u>appearance</u>, or was merely a condition under which the
self was to appear to itself, and so did not have the
same reality as the self itself. What we are just now
trying to explain, namely how the self, insofar as it
<u>acts</u>, can determine something in the self, insofar as it
<u>knows</u>--this whole opposition between acting and intuiting
self--undoubtedly also belongs only to the <u>appearance</u>
of the self, and not to the self proper. The self must
appear to itself as though something were determined,
by its action, within its intuition, or, since it is
not conscious of this, within the external world. If
this be presupposed, the following explanation will be
intelligible enough.

We set up an opposition between the free-acting and
the objectively intuitant self. But now this opposition
does not occur objectively, that is, in the self-in-
itself, for the self which acts is itself the intuitant
self, only here become at the same time intuited, objective, and thereby <u>active</u>. If the self which intuits
(with its simultaneously ideal and real activity) were
not here at the same time the intuited, the acting would
still continue to appear as an intuiting; and conversely,
that the intuiting appears as an acting has its ground
merely in this, that the self here is not merely intuitant, but intuited as intuitant. The intuitant intuited
is simply the self which acts. There can thus be no
thought of any mediation between that which acts and
that which outwardly intuits, nor of any, either,
between the free-acting self and the external world.
On the contrary, it would be utterly unintelligible how
an outer intuition could be determined by an action of
the self, if action and intuition were not originally
one. My action, in that I fashion an object, for
example, must at the same time be an intuiting, and
conversely, my intuiting in this case must at the same
time be an action; only the <u>self</u> is unable to perceive
this identity, since the objectively intuiting for the
self here is not the intuitant but the intuited, so that
for the self this identity between the agent and the
intuitant is abolished. The change which comes about,
through free action, in the external world, must take
place entirely according to the laws of productive
intuition, and as though freedom had no part in it at
all. Productive intuition acts, as it were, entirely
in isolation, and produces according to its characteristic laws whatever now results. That this producing

does not appear as an <u>intuiting</u> to the self has its
ground solely in this, that here the concept (the ideal
activity) is opposed to the object (the objective
activity), whereas in intuition subjective and objective activity are both one. But that the concept here
precedes the object is again only due to appearance.
But if the concept precedes the object only for appearance, and not objectively or really so, then free action
as such also belongs only to appearance, and the sole
objective factor is the intuitant. --

Just as one may say, therefore, that in that I
thought I was intuiting, I was in fact acting, so one
may equally say here that in that I think I act upon the
external world, I am in fact intuiting; and everything
that emerges in action, apart from intuiting, properly
belongs only to the appearance of the sole objective
feature, namely intuiting, and conversely, if we separate from acting everything that belongs only to appearance, nothing remains save the intuiting.

The result thus far derived, and, as we think,
sufficiently demonstrated, we now seek to explain and
clarify from still other points of view.

When the transcendental idealist maintains that
there is no transition from the objective into the subjective, and that both are originally one, the objective
being merely a subjective that has become an object,
there is admittedly a major question that he has to
answer: how then, conversely, is it possible to have a
transition from the subjective into the objective, such
as we are obliged to assume when we act? If in every
action a concept freely evolved by ourselves is to pass
over into a nature existing independently of us, although
really this nature enjoys no such independent existence,
how can the transition be conceived of?

Undoubtedly by this alone, that through this very
act we in fact first make the world become objective to
us. We act freely, and the world comes to exist independently of us--these two propositions must be
synthetically united.

Now if the world is nothing else but our own
intuiting, it undoubtedly becomes objective to us when
our intuiting does so. But now we are presently maintaining that our intuiting first becomes objective to
us through action, and that what we call an act is
nothing but the appearance of our intuiting. If this
be accepted, then our proposition: "that which appears
to us as an act upon the external world is, from the
idealist viewpoint, nothing else but a prolonged intuiting," will no longer seem repellent. Thus, for example, if some change in the external world is brought
about by an act, this change, regarded in itself, is
an intuition like any other. Hence the intuiting

itself is here the objective factor which underlies
the appearance; the element thereof which belongs to
appearance is the act upon the supposedly independent
world of sense; so objectively here there is no transition from the subjective into the objective, any more
than there was a transition from the objective into the
subjective. It is only that I cannot appear to myself
as intuitant without intuiting a subjective as passing
over into the objective.

The whole enquiry on this point can be traced back
to the general principle of transcendental idealism,
namely that in my knowing the subjective can never be
determined by the objective. In acting, an object is
necessarily thought of as determined by a causality
exercised by myself in accordance with a concept. Now
how do I arrive at this necessary thought? If I also
assume herein without explanation, that the object is
immediately determined by my act, in such wise that it
is related thereto as effect to agency, how then is this
also determined for my presentation, why am I obliged
also to intuit the object precisely as I had determined
it by my action? My action here is in this case the
object, for acting is the opposite of intuiting or
knowing. But now by means of this acting, this objective, something is to be determined in my knowing, in
my intuiting. According to the principle just enunciated, this is impossible. By action, my knowledge
thereof cannot be determined, for on the contrary, rather,
every action, like everything objective, must originally
be already a knowing, an intuiting. This is so clear
and obvious, that no difficulty can be found anywhere
else, save perhaps in the manner in which we are to think
for purposes of appearance, of this transformation of
what is objectively an intuiting into an act. Reflection here must address itself to three things:

a) to the objective, the intuiting

b) to the subjective, which is also an intuiting,
but an intuiting of the intuiting. --To distinguish it
from the former objective intuiting, we call this latter
the ideal intuiting.

c) to the appearance of the objective. But now it
has already been shown that this objective, the intuiting,
cannot appear unless the concept of an intuition (ideal)
precedes the intuition itself. But if the concept of
intuition precedes the intuition itself, so that the
latter is determined by the former, intuiting is a
producing in accordance with a concept, that is, a free
act. But now admittedly the concept precedes the
intuition itself only to ensure objectification of
the intuition, and thus the action also is merely the
appearance of the intuiting, and that which is objective
therein is the producing as such, in abstraction from
the concept which precedes it.

We shall attempt to make this clearer by means of an example. Some change or other in the external world results from my causality. If we first reflect merely on the occurrence of this change as such, then to say that something happens in the external world undoubtedly means no more than that I produce it, for nothing whatever exists in the external world save by means of my producing. Insofar as this producing of mine is an intuiting, and it is nothing else, the concept of change does not precede the change itself; but insofar as this producing is itself again to become an object, the concept must precede. The object which is to appear here is the producing itself. Thus in producing as such, that is, in the object, the concept does not precede the intuition; it precedes only for the ideal, for the self that intuits itself as intuiting, that is, only for purposes of appearance.

Now here it becomes clear at the same time whence we now first obtain the distinction between objective and subjective, between an in-itself and a mere appearance, which we hitherto had simply not drawn at all. The ground thereof is because here we first have something truly objective, namely that which contains the ground of everything objective, the activity at once ideal and real, which now can never again become subjective, and has separated itself entirely from the merely ideal self. In this activity, insofar as it is objective, ideal and real are simultaneous and identical; while insofar as it appears, and (in contrast to the merely ideal intuiting activity which opposes it) now simply represents the real, the concept precedes it, and only to that extent is it an act.

These explanations having been given, the question might yet arise, as to how the intelligence as such can be intuitant, after we have asserted that producing is concluded for it within the sphere of theoretical philosophy. Our answer is that producing was concluded only insofar as it was subjective; the intelligence, insofar as it is objective, can never be anything other than it is, namely subject and object at once, that is, productive; only now the producing will have to come about within the confines of the ideal activity which stands opposed to the producing activity-- a thing that till now, however, we have not yet derived.

But in order to align ourselves with ordinary consciousness, we continue to ask, how then do we arrive at maintaining this objective which acts to be free, when according to our deduction it is a wholly blind activity? It comes about entirely through the same illusion whereby the objective world also becomes objective for us. For that this act itself belongs only to the objective world (and thus also has the

same reality as the latter), follows from the fact that
it only becomes an act through the process of becoming
objective. From this point, indeed, a new light can in
fact be cast backward upon theoretical idealism. If the
objective world is a mere appearance, so too is the
objective element in our acting, and conversely, only
if the world has reality, does the objective element in
action also possess reality. It is therefore one and the
same reality which we perceive in the objective world,
and in our action upon the world of the senses. This
conjoint status, and indeed mutual conditioning of
objective action and the world's reality, outside and
through each other, is a consequence wholly peculiar
to transcendental idealism, and unattainable through
any other system.

So now how far, in fact, _is_ the self _active_ in the
external world? It acts only in virtue of that identity
of being and appearance which is already expressed in
self-consciousness. --The self exists only in that it
appears to itself; its knowing is a form of being. The
proposition I = I says nothing else but that I, who
know, am the same who _am_, my knowing and my being
mutually exhaust each other, the subject of consciousness
and the subject of activity are one. In consequence of
this identity, therefore, my knowing and free action are
also identical with free action as such; in other words,
the proposition 'I intuit myself as acting objectively'
= the proposition 'I am objectively active'.

II

Now if what appears as an action, as has just been
derived and demonstrated, is in itself an intuition
merely, it follows that all action must be constantly
confined by the laws of intuition, that nothing that
is impossible according to natural laws can be intuited
as coming about through free action. And this is a new
proof of the identity in question. But now a transition
from the subjective into the objective, such as actually
takes place, for appearance at least, is itself a contradiction of natural laws. That which is to be intuited
as operating upon the real, must itself appear as real.
Hence I cannot intuit myself as operating upon the
object immediately, but only as doing so by means of
matter, though in that I act I must intuit this latter
as identical with myself. Matter, as the immediate
organ of free, outwardly directed activity, is the
organic body, which must therefore appear as free
and apparently capable of voluntary movements. That
drive which has causality in my action must appear
objectively as a _natural inclination_, which even without any freedom would operate and bring forth for

itself what it appears to bring forth through freedom.
But in order to be able to intuit this drive as a
natural inclination, I must appear to myself objectively
as driven to all my acts by a compulsion of my organic
constitution (by pain, in its commonest acceptation);
and in order to be objective, all action must be connected, no matter how many the links, with a physical
compulsion, which itself is necessary as a condition
of the appearance of freedom.

Moreover, the intended change in the external world
only comes about in face of the constant resistance of
objects, and hence as a succession. If the change be
termed $\underline{D}$, this will be conditioned by a change $\underline{C}$, which
is its cause, and this in turn by $\underline{B}$, and so on; this
whole series of changes must therefore take place first,
before the final change, $\underline{D}$, can ensue. The complete
result can only make its appearance at the moment in
which all its conditions in the external world are given;
otherwise there is a contradiction of natural laws.
Anything whose conditions simply cannot be given in
nature, must be absolutely impossible. But now if freedom, in order to be objective, must be exactly like
intuition, and wholly subjected to its laws, the very
conditions under which freedom is able to appear again
do away with freedom itself; by the fact that freedom
in its manifestations is a natural phenomenon, it also
becomes explicable through natural laws, and in virtue
of that very fact it is, $\underline{qua}$ freedom, abolished.

The task set forth above, of showing how willing
itself again becomes objective, and becomes so $\underline{as}$
willing, to the self, is therefore not resolved by the
foregoing, for by the very fact that it becomes objective, it ceases to be a willing. There will thus be no
appearance whatever of absolute freedom (in absolute
willing), unless there be some other appearance than
this purely objective one, which is nothing other than
a natural inclination.

The reason for our having become involved in this
contradiction is simply that till now we have reflected
solely on the objective, outward-going element in willing;
and since, as we now know, this latter is originally
only an intuition, and thus objectively no willing at
all, it passes over without any further mediation into
the external world. But now if we proceed to ask how
the whole of willing (not just this objective activity,
at once ideal and real, which is included therein, and
which our foregoing deductions show to be incapable of
freedom, but also the ideal activity opposed thereto),
is able to become an object to the self, we are thereby
required to find an appearance in which both of these
emerge as opposed.

But now since it is itself again an intuitant

activity, the activity that is the objective element in willing is necessarily directed upon something <u>external</u>. The subjective factor in willing, however (the <u>purely ideal</u> activity), has as its immediate object that precise activity, at once ideal and real, which for that very reason is the objective factor in willing itself, and is therefore directed, not upon anything external, but simply upon that objective element incorporated in willing as such.

The <u>ideal</u> activity involved in willing will thus be able to become objective to the self only as the activity directed upon the objective element in willing <u>per se</u>, while this objective element itself will be objectifiable only as an externally directed affair, distinct from willing.

Now the objective activity in willing <u>per se</u>, that is, purely regarded (and only so is it objective to the ideal activity), is nothing else but <u>self-determination in general</u>. The object of the ideal activity in willing is therefore nothing else but <u>pure self-determining itself</u>, or the self itself. The ideal activity involved in willing will thus become objective to the self by being objectified thereto as an activity directed merely upon pure self-determining <u>as such</u>; the objective activity, in contrast, will become an object only by being objectified to the self as an <u>activity directed</u> upon something <u>external, and blindly directed at that</u> (since only to that extent is it an intuitant activity).

So in order to discover that appearance, whereby the whole of willing becomes an object to the self, we must

1. reflect upon that activity solely directed upon pure self-determining as such, and ask how such an activity could become an object to the self.

Pure self-determining as such (abstracted from everything contingent), which first comes about through the direction of that intuitant, and here objective, activity upon something external to it, is, as already stated, nothing else but the pure self itself, and is thus the common foundation upon which all intelligences are as it were supported, the one <u>intrinsic element</u> which they all have in common with each other. In that original and absolute act of will which we have postulated as the condition of all consciousness, pure self-determining thus becomes an immediate object to the self, nor is there anything more contained in this act. But now if this original act of will is itself an absolutely free one, still less by far can there be any theoretical deduction (as necessary) of the act whereby that first act again becomes an object to the self, or by means of which the latter again becomes aware of this activity directed upon pure self-determining. For it, likewise, is a condition of the continuance of consciousness.

Thus this objectifying of the ideal activity can be
accounted for only as the result of a demand. The
ideal activity, directed solely upon pure self-determining, must become an object to the self through a
demand,which demand, indeed, can be no other than this:
the self shall will nothing else put pure self-determining itself, for by this demand the pure activity,
directed solely upon self-determining as such, is held
before it as an object. This demand, however, is itself
nothing other than the categorical imperative, or moral
law, which Kant expresses as follows: thou shalt will
only what all intelligences are able to will. But that
which all intelligences are able to will is simply
pure self-determining itself, pure conformity to law.
Through the moral law, therefore, pure self-determining
(the purely objective element in all willing, insofar
as it is simply objective, i.e., not itself again
intuitant, or directed upon anything external or
empirical) becomes an object to the self. Only to that
extent, too, is the moral law a topic of transcendental
philosophy, for even the moral law is merely deduced
as a condition of self-consciousness. This law originally
applies to me, not insofar as I am this particular intelligence, for indeed it strikes down everything that
belongs to individuality and completely destroys it;
it applies to me, rather, as an intelligence in general,
to that which has as its immediate object the purely
objective, the eternal in me; not, however, to this
objective element itself, insofar as it is directed to
a contingent distinct from and independent of the self,
and on that very account the moral law is also the sole
condition under which the intelligence becomes aware
of its own consciousness.
    2. Reflection must now address itself to the
objective activity, directed upon something external,
lying outside the compass of willing itself, and enquire
how this becomes an object to the self. --
    This question, however, has already been largely
answered in what has preceded, and so here we can merely
attempt to set forth the answer in a new perspective.
    The objective activity, directed upon something
distinct from willing and present outside it, is to be
opposed in consciousness to that ideal activity which
is directed upon that selfsame objective activity, simply as such and insofar as it is a pure self-determining.
    But now this ideal activity could become an object
to the self only by means of a demand. So if the
opposition is to be perfect, the objective activity must
become objective by itself, i.e., without a demand,
and its becoming objective must be presupposed. That
whereby it becomes objective to the self as an activity
directed upon something external, to which it is related

exactly as the ideal activity is related to it, must
therefore be something necessitated, and since this can
still be only an activity, it must be a mere natural
inclination, such as we deduced in the preceding section (I); an inclination which works, like productive
intuition, entirely blindly, and is itself no willing at
all, but only becomes such by contrast with the pure
willing, directed solely upon self-determining as such.
This urge, since through it I become conscious of myself
solely as an individual, is that which is called in
moral theory self-interest; and its object is what we
call happiness in the widest sense.

There is no command, no imperative, of happiness.
It is senseless to suppose one, for that which happens
of itself, i.e., according to a natural law, is in no
need of being commanded. This inclination to happiness
(as we call it for brevity, the further development of
this concept being the concern of moral theory) is
nothing else but the objective activity, directed to
something independent of willing, and again become
objective to the self; an urge which is therefore as
necessary as the consciousness of freedom itself.

Thus the activity, whose immediate object is pure
self-determining itself, cannot come to consciousness
save in contrast to an activity whose object is something
external, to which it is quite blindly directed. As
necessarily, therefore, as there is a consciousness
of willing, a contrast must exist between what is
demanded by the activity which becomes an object through
the moral law, and is directed solely to self-determining as such, and what is demanded by the natural
inclination. This opposition must be real, that is,
both actions--that which is commanded by the pure will
become an object to itself, and that which is called
for by the natural inclination--must present themselves in consciousness as equally possible. By the
laws of nature, therefore, no action could be forth-
coming, for they each cancel out the other. So if an
action results, and it does so as surely as consciousness persists, this action cannot result from natural
law, that is, necessarily, and hence is due solely to
free self-determination; it results, that is, from an
activity of the self which, in that it wavers in the
middle between what we have so far called the subjective
and the objective, and determines the one by the other,
or the other by the one, without itself being again
determined, brings forth the conditions under which,
as soon as they are given, the action, which is always
merely the determined, results entirely blindly and
seemingly of itself.

This opposition of equally possible actions in
consciousness is therefore the condition under which

alone the absolute act of will can again become an object
to the self itself. But now this <u>opposition</u> is precisely
what turns the absolute will into <u>choice</u>, so that <u>choice</u>
is the appearance we were seeking of the absolute <u>will</u>--
not the original willing itself, but the absolute act of
freedom become objectified, with which all consciousness
begins.

That a freedom of the will exists is something the
ordinary consciousness can be persuaded of only through
the act of choice, that is, by the fact that in every
willing we are aware of a choice between opposites. But
now it is argued that choice is not the absolute will
itself, for this, as demonstrated earlier, is directed
only to pure self-determining as such; it is, rather, the
appearance of the absolute will. So if freedom = choice,
then freedom too is not the absolute will itself, but
merely the appearance thereof. Thus of the will absolutely regarded it cannot be said that it is either free
or not free, since the absolute cannot be thought of as
acting from a law that was not already prescribed to it
by the inner necessity of its own nature. Since, in the
absolute act of will, the self has as its object only
self-determining as such, no deviation from this is
possible for the will in its absolute sense; if it can
be called free at all, it is thus <u>absolutely</u> free, since
that which is a command for the will that appears is,
for the absolute will, a law that proceeds from the
necessity of its own nature. But if the absolute is
to appear to itself, it must figure to itself as dependent in its objective upon something else, something
alien to it. This dependence, however, does not belong
to the absolute itself, but merely to its appearance.
This alien factor, on which the absolute will is dependent for purposes of appearance, is the natural inclination, in contrast to which alone the law of the pure
will is transformed into an imperative. In its absolute sense, however, the will has originally no other
object save pure self-determining, that is, itself.
So nor can there be any obligation or law for it,
<u>demanding</u> that it <u>be</u> an object to itself. Hence the
moral law, and freedom, insofar as it consists in
choice, are themselves merely conditions for the
appearance of that absolute will, which is constitutive
of all consciousness, and to that extent also a condition
of the consciousness that becomes an object to itself.

Now by this result, without actually meaning to, we
have simultaneously resolved that notable problem which,
so far from having been settled, has so far scarcely been
properly understood--I mean the problem of transcendental freedom. In this problem it is not a question
whether the self is absolute, but whether, insofar as
it is <u>not absolute</u>, insofar as it is <u>empirical</u>, the

self is free. But now it appears indeed from our solution, that just precisely insofar as the will is
empirical, or appears, so to that extent it can be
called free in the transcendental sense. For insofar
as it is absolute, the will itself transcends freedom,
and so far from being subjected to any law, is in fact
the source of all law. But insofar as the absolute will
appears, it can only do so, in order to appear as
absolute, in the form of choice. This phenomenon of
choice can therefore no longer be explained objectively,
for it is not anything objective, having reality per se,
but is rather the absolute subjective, the intuition of
the absolute will itself, whereby the latter becomes,
ad infinitum, an object to itself. But this very
appearance of the absolute will is in fact true freedom,
or what is commonly understood by the term freedom. Now
since, in free action, the self intuits itself ad infinitum as absolute will and in its highest power is itself
nothing else but this intuition of the absolute will,
the aforementioned appearance of choice is likewise as
certain and indubitable as the self itself. --Conversely,
also, the phenomenon of choice can be thought of only as
an absolute will, though a will that appears under the
confines of finitude, and is thus an ever-recurring
revelation of the absolute will within us. It should
be noted, however, that if we had sought to infer backwards from the phenomenon of choice to that which lies
at the root of it, we should assuredly have had difficulty in ever hitting upon the correct explanation of
it, though Kant, in his Doctrine of Law, has at least
pointed to the contrast between the absolute will and
the faculty of choice, even if he does not yet give
the true relationship of the one to the other. And
this, then, is a new proof of the superiority of a
method which presupposes no phenomenon as given, but
first becomes acquainted with each of them through its
grounds, as though it were totally unknown.
     And now by this we also resolve all the doubts
which could be drawn, say, from the common assumption
that the will is free, concerning the claim put forward
earlier, that the objective self which appears to engage
in action is in itself merely intuitant. For it is not
that merely objective self, operating quite mechanically
in both action and intuition, and in all free action the
determinate, to which the predicate of freedom is
ascribed; it is rather that self which wavers between
subjective and objective factors of willing, determining
one by the other--viz. the self-determinant of the second
order--to which alone freedom is and can be attributed,
in that the objective self, which in regard to freedom
is merely the determined, still continues, in and for
itself or regardless of the determinant, to remain

what it was before, namely a mere intuiting. Thus if
I reflect merely upon the objective activity as such,
the self contains only natural necessity; if I reflect
merely upon the subjective activity, it contains only
an absolute willing which by nature has no other object
save self-determining as such; if I reflect finally
upon the activity determinant at once of both subjective and objective, and transcending them both, the
self contains choice, and therewith freedom of the will.
From these different lines of reflection arise the
various systems concerning freedom, of which the first
absolutely denies freedom; the second posits it simply
in pure reason, i.e., in that ideal activity directed
immediately to self-determining (by which assumption we
are compelled, in all actions determined contrary to
reason, to postulate an utterly groundless quiescence
of the latter, whereby, however, all freedom of the will
is actually done away with); the third view, on the
other hand, deduces an activity, extending beyond both
the ideal and the objective, as that alone to which
freedom can belong.

Nor, indeed, for this absolutely determining self,
is there any predetermination, since this applies only
to the intuiting, objective self. The fact that for the
latter all action, insofar as it passes over into the
external world, is predetermined, can no more prejudice
the absolutely determinant self, superior as it is to
all appearances, than does the fact that everything in
nature is predetermined; for in relation to the free
self the objective self is a mere appearance, having no
reality in itself, and like nature is merely the external basis of its action. For from the fact that an
action is predetermined for appearance, or for the
purely intuitant activity, I cannot infer back to its
also being so for the free activity, since the two are
wholly unequal in dignity; so that while the merely
apparent is certainly quite independent of the determinant which does not appear, the latter is equally
independent of the former, and each acts and proceeds
on its own account, the one from free choice, the other,
having once been so determined, entirely in accordance
with its own peculiar laws; and this mutual independence of each from the other, despite their consilience,
is in fact rendered possible only through a preestablished harmony. Here, therefore, is the point of first
entry of the predetermined harmony we earlier deduced
between the freely determinant and the intuitant, in
that each of them is so separated from the other, that
no reciprocal influence of one on the other would be
possible at all, unless a conformity between them were
set up by something lying outside them both. But what
this third thing may be, we have absolutely no means

of explaining at present, and must be content to have
given merely a preliminary indication and presentation
of this point, the most elevated of our whole enquiry,
and to await its further elucidation by the investigations that are to follow.

We shall merely observe, that if there is even a
predetermination for the freely determinant, such as we
have certainly maintained in the foregoing, insofar as
we have required an original negation of freedom as
necessary for individuality, and indirectly for the
interaction between intelligences, this predetermination
is itself actually thinkable in turn only through an
original act of freedom, which admittedly does not attain
to consciousness, and concerning which we must refer
the reader to Kant's enquiries into original evil.

If we may now review once more the entire course of
the foregoing investigation, we first of all attempted to
explain the prior assumption of ordinary consciousness,
which, standing at the lowest level of abstraction, distinguishes the object acted upon from that which acts
or operates upon it; whereby the question arose, as to
how the object could be determined by that which acts
on it? Our answer was: the object acted upon and the
action itself are one, in that both are merely an
intuiting. This yielded the conclusion that in willing
we have but one determinate, namely the intuitant, which
is simultaneously the agent. This objective agent and
the external world do not therefore exist originally in
independence of each other, and what is posited in the
one is ipso facto also posited in the other. But now
this merely objective stood confronted in consciousness
with a subjective, which becomes objectified to the self
through an absolute requirement, in that this purely
objective was objectified to the self through an outward
tendency wholly independent of the same. There was
thus no action whereby the whole of willing could become
an object to the self, without a self-determinant, which,
elevated above both subjective and objective alike, was
first able to drive us to the question: how, then, by
this absolute determinant extending beyond everything
objective, could the objective or intuitant nevertheless
be determined?

Additional Remarks

But before we can set ourselves to answering this
question, another stands in our path, namely this:
in whatever way the self determines itself, whether
through the subjective determining the objective or
vice versa, the outward-going activity (the inclination)
is in any case the sole vehicle whereby anything can
make its way from the self into the external world;

and thus even by self-determination the inclination cannot be abolished. The question, then, is this: in what relation does the moral law put this outgoing drive vis-à-vis the ideal activity directed solely to pure self-determination?

We can furnish only the main points of our answer to this question, since here in fact it arises merely as a link in the chain of enquiry. --Assuredly the pure will cannot become an object to the self without at the same time having an external object. But now, as we have just demonstrated, this external object actually has no reality _per se_, being simply a medium for the appearance of the pure will, and meant to be nothing else but the expression of that will for the external world. Thus the pure will cannot become an object to itself without identifying the external world with itself. But now when analysed precisely, the concept of happiness contains no other thought than that of just such an identity between what is independent of willing and the willing itself. Thus happiness, the object of natural inclination, must be merely the appearance of the pure will, that is, be one and the same object as the pure will itself. The two must be absolutely one (so that no _synthetic_ relation is possible between them, such as that between conditioning and conditioned), while yet in such a way that they simply cannot exist _independently_ of each other. If happiness is taken to mean something that is possible even independently of the pure will, then there can be absolutely no such thing. If, however, happiness is merely the identity of the external world with the pure will, then they are both one and the same object, only seen from different sides. But just as little as happiness can be anything independent of the pure will, so equally is it unthinkable that a finite being should strive after a purely formal morality, since morality itself, for such a being, can become objective only through the external world. The immediate object of all striving is not the pure will, still less happiness, but rather the external object as expression of the pure will. This absolute identical pure will, which is sovereign in the external world, is the sole and supreme good.

Now although nature does not behave with absolute passivity in regard to action, it still cannot offer any absolute resistance to the execution of the supreme purpose. Nature cannot _act_ in the proper sense of the word. But rational beings can act, and an interaction between such beings through the medium of the objective world is actually the condition of freedom. Now whether or not all rational beings restrict their action by the possibility of free action on the part of all others, is something which depends upon an absolute contingency,

namely choice. This cannot be the case. The holiest
ought not to be entrusted to chance. It must be made
impossible, through the constraint of an unbreakable
law, that in the interaction of all the freedom of the
individual should be abolished. Now this constraint
cannot, to be sure, be directed immediately against
freedom, since no rational being can be constrained,
but only determined to constrain himself; nor can this
constraint be directed against the pure will, which has
no other object save what is common to all rational
beings, namely self-determining as such; it can be
directed only against the self-interested drive emanating from the individual and returning back to him
again. But against this drive there is nothing which
can be used as a sanction or a weapon except itself.
The external world would have, as it were, to be so
organized that it compels this drive, in that it oversteps its boundaries, to act against itself, and opposes
to it something on which the free being can exert his
will, insofar, that is, as he is a rational being, though
not insofar as he is a natural one; whereby the agent
is thrown into contradiction with himself, and at least
made mindful of the fact that he is divided within
himself.

In and for itself, the objective world cannot contain the ground of such a contradiction within itself,
for it behaves with complete indifference toward the
operations of free beings as such; the ground of this
contradiction of the self-interested drive can therefore be lodged in it only by the rational being.

A second and higher nature must, as it were, be
set up over the first, governed by a natural law quite
different, however, from that which prevails in visible
nature, namely a natural law on behalf of freedom. As
inexorably, and with the same iron necessity whereby
effect follows cause in sensible nature, an attack upon
the freedom of another must be succeeded, in this second
nature, by an instantaneous counter to the self-interested drive. A law of nature such as that just depicted is to be found in the rule of law, and the second
nature in which its authority prevails is the legal
system, which is thereby deduced as a condition of the
continuance of consciousness.

It will be evident from this deduction that law is
no branch of morality, nor in any sense a practical
science, but rather a purely theoretical one, which
stands to freedom precisely as mechanics does to motion,
in that it merely sets forth the natural mechanism under
which free beings as such can be thought of as interacting; a mechanism, indeed, which can undoubtedly itself
be set up only through freedom, and to which nature con-
tributes nothing. For nature, as the poet says, is

without feeling, and God, as the gospel tells us, permits
His sun to shine on the just and the unjust alike. From
the very fact, however, that the legal system has to be
considered merely as a supplement to visible nature,
it follows that the legal order is not a moral one, but
a purely natural order, which freedom has no more power
over than it has over sensible nature. It is no wonder,
therefore, that all attempts to transform it into a
moral order present themselves as detestable through
their own perversity, and through that most dreadful
kind of despotism which is their immediate consequence.
For although the legal system performs the same office,
materially speaking, that we expect, in fact, from
Providence, and is altogether the best theodicy that man
is able to contrive, it still does not do this in form,
or does not do it qua Providence, that is, with judgment
and forethought. It has to be viewed as a machine
primed in advance for certain possibilities, and
operating automatically, i.e., entirely blindly, as soon
as these cases are presented; and although this machine
is constructed and primed by the hands of men, it is
obliged, once the hand of the artificer is withdrawn,
to operate like visible nature according to its own
laws, and independently, as though it existed on its
own. Thus, while a legal system becomes the more
deserving of respect to the extent that it approximates
to an order of nature, a regime governed, not by law but
by the will of the judge and by a despotism which
operates the law as a providence looking into the heart
of things, in that it constantly interferes with the
natural course of the legal process, presents the most
unworthy and revolting spectacle that can exist for
anyone imbued with feeling for the holiness of the law.
     But now if the legal system is a necessary condi-
tion for the freedom existing in the external world, it
is undoubtedly an important question, how such a freedom can be thought of even as existing, since the will
of the individual can do absolutely nothing in this
regard, and presupposes as its necessary supplement
something independent of it, namely the will of everyone else.
     It is to be supposed that even the first emergence
of a legal order was not left to chance, but rather to a
natural compulsion which, occasioned by the general
resort to force, drove men to bring such an order into
being without their own knowledge of the fact, and in
such a way that its earliest workings affected them
unawares. But now it is also easy to see that an order
brought about by need could have no inherent stability,
partly because what is fashioned out of need is also
devised only for immediate requirements, and partly
because the mechanism of such a system directs its

sanctions against free beings, who will only allow themselves to be compelled so long as they find advantage
therein. Since in matters of freedom there is no
a priori, the unification of such beings under a common
mechanism is one of those problems which can be solved
only through innumerable attempts; especially since the
mechanism whereby the system itself is again set in
motion, the link between the idea of the system and its
actual execution, is entirely different from the system
itself, and must undergo quite different modifications,
depending upon differences in degree of culture, in
national character, and so forth. It is therefore to be
presumed that at first purely temporary systems arose,
all carrying the seeds of their downfall within them,
and because they were originally set up, not through
reason but through pressure of circumstances, would
sooner or later dissolve. For it is natural that under
force of circumstances a people should give up many
rights which it cannot alienate forever, and which it
sooner or later reclaims; at which point the collapse
of the system is inevitable, and all the more certain,
the more perfect it happens to be in a formal sense,
since if this is so, the powers that be will certainly
not restore these rights of their own free will, since
this would already indicate an internal weakness of the
system itself.

But suppose, now, however it happens, that there
eventually comes into existence a system truly legal,
and not based merely on oppression, as is necessary at
the outset; experience, which indeed will forever be
inadequate not only to prove a universal principle but
even to provide strong evidence, still shows nonetheless
that the very subsistence of such a regime, which for
the individual state is the most perfect possible, is
made to depend on the most palpable chance.

Suppose that, on the model of nature, which
establishes nothing self-subsistent, or any inherently
stable system, which is not based upon three mutually
independent forces, the legality of the regime is founded
upon the separation of the three basic powers of the
state as independent of each other; even so, the very
objections which can legitimately be made to this
separation, though it cannot be denied to be necessary
for a legal system, demonstrate an imperfection in this
arrangement, which cannot, indeed lie within the system
itself, but must be sought outside it. The security of
each individual state against the rest makes absolutely
inevitable a most decided preponderance of the executive
power over the others, and particularly over the legislative, the retarding force of the state machine; and
hence the subsistence of the whole will still ultimately
rest, not on the jealousy of the opposing powers, that

most superficially conceived of safety devices, but
solely on the good will of those who hold supreme power
in their hands. But now nothing appertaining to the
defense and protection of the law should depend on
chance. Yet to render the subsistence of such a regime
independent of good will would again be possible only
through a sanction, whose ground, however, can obviously not lie in the regime itself; for to achieve that,
a fourth power would be necessary, to which either the
sovereignty is entrusted, in which case it is itself
the executive power, or which is otherwise left impotent,
in which case its operation depends on mere chance, and
at very best, namely when the people side with it, there
is no avoiding the insurrection which ought, in a good
constitution, to be no more possible than it is in a
machine.

No assured existence is therefore thinkable even for
a single regime merely, however perfectly conceived,
without an organization extending beyond the individual
state; a federation of all states, who mutually guarantee their respective regimes, though such general reciprocal guarantees are again impossible until firstly, the
principles of a true legal system are generally diffused,
so that individual states have but one interest, namely
to preserve the constitutions of all; and until secondly,
these states have again submitted to a single communal
law, just as was formerly done by individuals in forming
each particular state. By so doing, the individual
states can in turn belong to a state of states, and the
mutual quarrels of peoples be referred to an internation-
al tribunal, composed of members of all civilized nations,
and having at its command against each rebellious state-
individual the power of all the rest.

Now how such a universal constitution, extending
even over individual states, and enabling them to emerge
from the state of nature in which they previously stood
to each other, is to be realized through freedom, which
plays its boldest and least inhibited game in this
mutual relation between states, is a thing entirely
beyond comprehension, unless this play of freedom, whose
entire course is the history of mankind, is again governed
by a blind necessity, which objectively appends to freedom what would never have been possible through the
latter alone.

And thus, in the course of our discussion, we find
ourselves driven back to the question posed above, as to
the ground of identity between freedom, on the one hand,
insofar as it expresses itself in choice, and that which
is objective or law-abiding on the other; a question
which from now on acquires a far higher significance,
and must be answered in its most universal form.

III

The emergence of the universal constitution cannot be
consigned to mere chance, and is accordingly to be
anticipated only from the free play of forces that we
discern in history. The question arises, therefore, as
to whether a series of circumstances without plan or
purpose can deserve the name of history at all, and
whether in the mere concept of history there is not
already contained also the concept of a necessity which
choice itself is compelled to serve.
      Here it is primarily a question of our ascer-
taining the concept of history. --
      Not everything that happens is on that account an
object of history; natural circumstances, for example,
owe their historical character, if they attain it,
merely to the influence which they have had upon human
actions; still less by far, however, do we regard as a
historical object that which takes place according to a
known rule, periodically recurs, or is in general a
consequence that can be calculated a priori. If we
wanted to speak of a history of nature in the true sense
of the word, we should have to picture nature as though,
apparently free in its productions, it had gradually
brought forth the whole multiplicity thereof through
constant departures from a primordial original; which
would then be a history, not of natural objects (which
is properly the description of nature), but of genera-
tive nature itself. Now how would we view nature in a
history of this sort? We would view her, so to speak,
as ordering and managing in various ways with one and
the same sum or proportion of forces, which she could
never exceed; we should thus regard her, to be sure,
as acting freely in this creation, but not on that
account as working in utter lawlessness. Nature would
thus become an object of history, on the one hand,
through the appearance of freedom in her productions,
since in fact we would be unable to determine a priori
the directions of her productive activity, although
there would be no doubt at all that these directions
had their specific law; but she would also be an object,
on the other hand, through the confinement and conformity to law inherent in her, owing to the proportion
of the forces at her command; whence it is therefore
apparent that history comes about neither with absolute
lawfulness nor with absolute freedom either, but exists
only where a single ideal is realized under an infinity
of deviations, in such a way that, not the particular
detail indeed, but assuredly the whole, is in conformity
thereto.
      But now such a successive realizing of an ideal,
where only the progress as a whole, as it might be

seen by an intellectual intuition, does justice to the
ideal, can moreover be thought of as possible only
through such beings as have the character of a species;
for the individual, in fact, precisely because he is so,
is incapable of attaining to the ideal, though the latter,
which is necessarily determinate, has still got to be
realized. We therefore see ourselves led on to a new
feature of history, namely that there can only be a
history of such beings as have an ideal before them,
which can never be carried out by the individual, but
only by the species. And for this it is needful that
every succeeding individual should start in at the very
point where the preceding one left off, and thus that
continuity should be possible between succeeding
individuals, and, if that which is to be realized in
the progress of history is something attainable only
through reason and freedom, that there should also be
the possibility of tradition and transmission.

But now from the foregoing deduction of the concept of history it is self-evident that an absolutely
lawless series of events is no more entitled to the
name of history than an absolutely law-abiding one;
whence it is apparent:

a) that the idea of progress implicit in all history
permits no conformity to law such as would limit free
activity to a determinate and constantly recursive
succession of acts;

b) that nothing whatever can be an object of history
which proceeds according to a determinate mechanism, or
whose theory is a priori. Theory and history are totally
opposed. Man has a history only because what he will do
is incapable of being calculated in advance according
to any theory. Choice is to that extent the goddess of
history. Mythology has history begin with the first
step out of the domain of instinct into the realm of
freedom, with the loss of the Golden Age, or with the
Fall, that is, with the first expression of choice.
In the schemes of the philosophers, history ends with
the reign of reason, that is, with the Golden Age of
law, when all choice shall have vanished from the earth,
and man shall have returned through freedom to the same
point at which nature originally placed him, and which
he forsook when history began;

c) that neither absolute lawlessness, nor a series
of events without aim or purpose, deserve the name of
history, and that its true nature is constituted only
by freedom and lawfulness in conjunction, or by the
gradual realization, on the part of a whole species
of beings, of an ideal that they have never wholly lost.

After this derivation, now completed, of the main
characteristics of history, we must now enquire more
closely into the transcendental possibility thereof;

and this will lead us to a philosophy of <u>history</u>, which
latter is for the practical part of philosophy precisely
what nature is for the theoretical part.

A

The first question which can justifiably be asked of a
philosophy of history is, no doubt, how a history is
conceivable at all, since if everything that exists is
posited for each of us only through his own consciousness, the whole of past history can likewise be posited
for each through his consciousness alone. Now we do in
fact also maintain that no individual consciousness
could be posited, with all the determinations it is
posited with, and which necessarily belong to it, unless
the whole of history had gone before; and if we needed
to do the trick, this could very easily be shown by
means of examples. Thus past history admittedly belongs
merely to appearance, just as does the individuality of
consciousness itself; it is therefore no more, but also
no less real for each of us than his own individuality
is. This particular individuality presupposes this
particular period, of such and such a character, such
and such a degree of culture, etc.; but such a period
is impossible without the whole of past history. His-
toriography, which otherwise has no object save that of
explaining the present state of the world, could thus
equally set out from the current situation and infer to
past history, and it would be no uninteresting endeavor
to see how the whole of the past could be derived from
this in a strictly necessary manner.

Now it might be objected to this account that past
history is not posited with <u>each</u> individual consciousness, nor is the <u>whole</u> of the past posited with any,
but only the main happenings thereof, which are indeed
recognizable as such only through the fact that they
have extended their influence up to the present time,
and so far as the individuality of each single person;
but to this we reply, in the first place, that a history
exists only for those upon whom the past has operated,
and even for these, only to the extent that it has worked
upon them; and secondly, that all that has ever <u>been</u> in
history is also truly connected, or will be, with the
individual consciousness of each, not immediately, maybe,
but certainly by means of innumerable linkages, of such
a kind that if one could point them out it would also
become obvious that the <u>whole</u> of the past was necessary
in order to put this consciousness together. But now
it is admittedly certain that, just as the great
majority of men in every age have never had any existence
in the world wherein history properly belongs, so also
is this true of a multitude of happenings. For just as

it is insufficient, for the remembrance of posterity, to
have perpetuated oneself merely as a physical cause by
means of physical effects, so likewise it is not enough
to deserve even a place in history that one is a mere
intellectual product or mere intermediary, whereby, as
a mere medium, without having oneself been the cause of
a new future, the culture acquired by the past is trans-
mitted to later generations. Thus assuredly, with the
consciousness of each individual, only so much is posited
as has so far continued to exert an effect; but then this
in turn is also the only thing that belongs in history
and has existed therein.

But now so far as the transcendental necessity of
history is concerned, it has already been deduced in
the foregoing from the fact that the universal reign of
law has been set before rational beings as a problem,
realizable only by the species as a whole, that is, only
by way of history. We content ourselves here, therefore, with merely drawing the conclusion, that the sole
true object of the historian can only be the gradual
emergence of a political world order, for this, indeed,
is the sole ground for a history. All other history
which is not universal can only be set forth pragmati-
cally, that is, according to the notion already
vouchsafed to the ancients, as being directed toward
a particular empirical goal. Whereas, conversely, a
pragmatic universal history is a self-contradictory
conception. Everything else, however, which is otherwise commonly included in the writing of history, the
progress of the arts and sciences etc., properly does
not belong in history at all, or else serves therein
merely as a document or a connecting link; because even
discoveries in the arts and sciences, primarily through
the fact that they multiply and enhance the means of
mutual injury, and give rise to a plethora of other
evils previously unknown, serve the purpose of accelerat-
ing man's progress toward the setting up of a universal
legal order.

B

That the concept of history embodies the notion of an
infinite tendency to progress, has been sufficiently
shown above. But it cannot, indeed, be straightway
concluded from this that the human race is infinitely
perfectible. For those who deny it could equally well
maintain that man is no more possessed of a history than
the animal, being confined, on the contrary, to an
eternal circuit of actions, in which, like Ixion upon
his wheel, he revolves unceasingly, and despite continuous oscillations and at times even seeming deviations
from the line of curvature, still constantly finds

himself back at the point from which he started. There
is all the less expectation, moreover, of arriving at a
sensible answer to this question, in that those who pur-
port to resolve it, either for or against, find themselves in the greatest perplexity as to the standard
whereby progress is to be measured. Some address themselves to the moral advances of mankind, of which we
should certainly be glad to possess the yardstick;
others, to progress in the arts and sciences, although,
seen from the historical (practical) standpoint, this
represents a regress, or at best a movement against the
course of history, on which point we could appeal to
history itself, and to the judgment and example of those
nations (such as the Romans), who may be termed classical
in the historical sense. But if the sole object of history is the gradual realization of the rule of law, there
remains to us, even as a historical measure of man's
progress, only the gradual approximation to this goal,
whose final attainment, however, can neither be inferred
from experience, so far as it has hitherto unfolded,
nor be theoretically demonstrated a priori, but will be
only an eternal article of faith to man as he acts and
works.

C

We now pass on, however, to the primary characteristic
of history, namely that it should exhibit a union of
freedom and necessity, and be possible through this
union alone.
    But now it is just this union of freedom and law-
fulness in action which we have already deduced to be
necessary, from an entirely different point of view, as
following simply from the concept of history itself.
    The universal rule of law is a condition of freedom,
since without it there is no guarantee of the latter.
For freedom that is not guaranteed by a universal order
of nature exists only precariously, and--as in the
majority of our contemporary states--is a plant that
flourishes only parasitically, tolerated in general by
way of a necessary inconsistency, but in such wise that
the individual is never certain of his freedom. That is
not how it should be. Freedom should not be a favor
granted, or a good that may be enjoyed only as a for-
bidden fruit. It must be guaranteed by an order that
is as open and unalterable as that of nature.
    But now this order can in fact be realized only
through freedom, and its establishment is entrusted
wholly and solely to freedom. This is a contradiction.
That which is the first condition of outward freedom is,
for that very reason, no less necessary than freedom
itself. And it is likewise to be realized only through

freedom, that is, its emergence is consigned to chance. How can this contradiction be reconciled?

The only way of resolving it is that in freedom itself there should again be necessity; but how, then, can such a resolution be conceived of?

We arrive here at the supreme problem of transcendental philosophy, which has admittedly been set forth above (II), but has not been resolved.

Freedom is to be necessity, and necessity freedom. But now in contrast to freedom, necessity is nothing else but the unconscious. That which exists in me without consciousness is involuntary; that which exists with consciousness is in me through my willing.

To say that necessity is again to be present in freedom, amounts, therefore, to saying that through freedom itself, and in that I believe myself to act freely, something I do not intend is to come about unconsciously, i.e., without my consent; or, to put it otherwise, the conscious, or that freely determining activity which we deduced earlier on, is to be confronted with an unconscious, whereby out of the most uninhibited expression of freedom there arises unawares something wholly involuntary, and perhaps even contrary to the agent's will, which he himself could never have realized through his willing. This statement, however paradoxical it may seem, is yet nothing other than a mere transcendental expression of the generally accepted and assumed relationship between freedom and a hidden necessity, at times called fate and at times providence, though neither of these terms expresses any clear idea; a relationship whereby men through their own free action, and yet against their will, must become cause of something which they never wanted, or by which, conversely, something must go astray or come to naught which they have sought for freely and with the exertion of all their powers.

Such intervention of a hidden necessity into human freedom is presupposed, not only, say, in tragedy, whose whole existence rests on that presumption, but even in normal doing and acting. Without such a presumption one can will nothing aright; without it, the disposition to act quite regardless of consequences, as duty enjoins us, could never inspire a man's mind. For if no sacrifice is possible without the conviction that the species we belong to can never cease to progress, how is this conviction itself possible, if it is wholly and solely based upon freedom? There must be something here that is higher than human freedom, and on which alone we can reckon with assurance in doing and acting; something without which a man could never venture to undertake an act fraught with major consequences, since even the most perfect calculation thereof can be so completely

upset by the incursion of other men's freedom, that an
outcome may result from his action entirely different
from what he intended. Duty itself cannot bid me, once
my decision is made, to be wholly at ease over the consequences of my actions, unless, though my acting surely
depends on me, that is, upon my freedom, the consequences
of those actions, or that which will emerge from them
for all mankind, depend not at all on my freedom, but
rather upon something quite different and of a higher
sort.

It is thus a presumption which itself is necessary
for the sake of freedom, that though man is admittedly
free in regard to the action itself, he is nonetheless
dependent, in regard to the finite result of his actions,
upon a necessity that stands over him, and itself takes
a hand in the play of his freedom. Now this presumption requires a transcendental explanation. To account
for it by providence or fate is not to explain it at all,
for providence or fate are precisely what need to be
explained. We are not in doubt about providence, any
more than we are about what is called fate, for we sense
its incursions into our own doings, in the success and
failure of our own enterprises. But what, then, is this
fate?

If we reduce our problem to transcendental terms,
it amounts to this: how, when we act quite freely, that
is, with consciousness, can something arise for us
unconsciously, which we never intended, and which freedom, left to itself, could never have brought about?

That which arises for me unintended, arises as the
objective world does; but now by means of my free action, something else objective, a second nature, the
moral order, is also to arise for me. But by free
action nothing objective can arise for me, for everything objective arises, as such, without consciousness.
It would thus be unintelligible how this second objective order could arise through free action, did not an
unconscious activity stand in contrast to the conscious
activity.

But an objective arises for me without consciousness only in intuition, so this proposition says, in
effect: the objective in my free acting must in fact
be an intuition; by which we thereupon come back to an
earlier principle, which is in part explained already,
but in part can only here for the first time attain to
its full clarity.

For here in fact the objective element in acting
acquires a significance quite different from what it has
hitherto possessed. All my actions, in fact, proceed, as
to their final goal, toward something that can be realized, not by the individual alone, but only by the entire
species; at least all my actions ought to proceed

towards this. The success of my actions is thus dependent not upon myself, but upon the willing of everyone
else, and I can accomplish nothing toward such a goal
unless everyone wills that goal. But this is assuredly
doubtful and uncertain, indeed impossible, since the
vast majority do not even have this goal in mind. How
then can we extricate ourselves from this uncertainty?
One might here perhaps think oneself driven immediately
toward a moral world-order, and postulate the latter as
a condition of attaining this goal. But how is one to
furnish the proof that this moral world-order can be
thought of as objective, as existing in absolute independence of freedom? The moral world-order, one might
say, exists as soon as we establish it, but where, then,
is it established? It is the communal effect of all
intelligences, so far, that is, as they all, directly or
indirectly, will nothing else but an order of this very
sort. So long as this is not the case, the order itself
has no existence either. Every individual intelligence
can be regarded as a constitutive part of God, or of the
moral world-order. Every rational being can say to
himself: I too am entrusted with the execution of the
law, and the practice of righteousness within my sphere
of influence; I too have assigned to me a portion of the
moral government of the world; but what am I, against so
many? That order exists only insofar as all others
think as I do, and exercise, each of them, his divine
right to see that righteousness prevails.

Thus either I appeal to a _moral_ world-order, but
than cannot conceive it as absolutely objective; or else
I demand something absolutely objective, which shall
assure and as it were guarantee, in a manner wholly independent of _freedom_, the success of actions in contributing
to the highest goal, and then, since the only objective
element in willing is the unconscious element, I find
myself driven toward an _unconscious_ factor, whereby the
external success of all _actions has_ got to be assured.

For only if an unconscious lawfulness again prevails in the arbitrary, that is, wholly lawless actions
of men, can I conceive of a finite unification of all
actions toward a communal goal. But lawfulness is to be
found only in intuition, and so this lawfulness is not
possible unless that which appears to us as a free action
is, objectively or regarded in itself, an intuition.

But now we are here of course talking, not of the
individual's action, but of the act of the entire
species. This second objective element which is to
arise for us can be realized only by the species, that
is, in history. But history, objectively regarded, is
nothing else but a series of data which appears only
subjectively as a series of free actions. The objective
factor in history is thus an intuition indeed, but not

an intuition of the individual, for it is not the
individual who acts in history, but rather the species;
hence the intuitant, or the objective factor in history,
will have to be one for the entire species.

But now although the objective element in all intelligences is the same, yet every distinct individual acts
with absolute freedom, and thus the actions of different
rational beings would not necessarily harmonize; on the
contrary, the freer the individual, the more contradiction there would be in the whole, unless this objective
factor common to all intelligences were an absolute
synthesis, wherein all contradictions were resolved and
eliminated beforehand. --From the wholly lawless play of
freedom, in which every free being indulges on his own
behalf, as though there were no other outside him (which
must always be assumed as a rule), something rational
and harmonious is still to emerge eventually, and this
I am obliged to presuppose in every action. Such a thing
is inconceivable unless the objective factor in all
acting is something communal, whereby all the acts of
men are guided to one harmonious goal; and are so guided,
that however they may set about things, and however
unbridled the exercise of their choice, they yet must
go where they did not want to, without, and even against,
their own will; and this owing to a necessity hidden
from them, whereby it is determined in advance that by
the very lawlessness of their act, and the more lawless
it is, the more surely, they bring about a development
of the drama which they themselves were powerless to
have in view. But this necessity can itself be thought
of only through an absolute synthesis of all actions,
from which there develops everything that happens, and
hence also the whole of history; and in which, because
it is absolute, everything is so far weighed and calculated that everything that may happen, however contradictory and discordant it may seem, still has and
discovers its ground of union therein. But this absolute
synthesis must itself be posited in the absolute, which
in all free action is the intuitant, and the eternally
and universally objective.

But now this whole viewpoint still leads us only to
a natural mechanism, whereby the final outcome of all
actions is assured, and by which, without any contribu-
tion from freedom, they are all directed toward the
highest goal of the entire species. For the eternally
objective factor--and the only one--for all intelligences is simply the lawfulness of nature, or of intuition, which in willing becomes something utterly independent of the intelligence. But now this unity of
the objective for all intelligences serves only to
disclose to me a predetermination of all history for

intuition, by means of an absolute synthesis, whose
mere development in a variety of sequences is what
constitutes history. It does not tell me how this
objective predetermination of all actions accords with
the freedom of action itself. So this unity also explains to us but one of the determinations in the
concept of history, namely conformity to law, which, as
can now be seen, comes about solely in regard to the
objective factor in acting; (for this does in fact
really belong to nature, and thus must obey law just
insofar as it is nature; whence it would also be wholly
useless to wish to derive this objective lawfulness
of acting from freedom, since it generates itself quite
mechanically and by itself, so to speak). But this
unity does not explain for me the other determination,
namely the coexistence of lawlessness, i.e., of freedom,
with conformity to law. In other words, it leaves us
none the wiser as to how that harmony is effected between
this objective element, which brings forth what it
generates through its own lawfulness, in complete independence of freedom, and the freely determining element.
    At the present stage of our reflection there stand
confronted--on the one hand the intelligence in itself
(the absolutely objective element common to all intelligences), and on the other the freely determinant,
absolutely subjective. The intelligence in itself
serves to predetermine once and for all the objective
lawfulness of history, but the objective and the freely
determining factors are wholly independent of each
other, and dependent each on itself alone--so how am I
to be sure that objective predetermination and the
infinite possibilities open to freedom are mutually
exhaustive, and that the objective element is thus really
an absolute synthesis for the whole of all free acts?
And how, in that case, since freedom is absolute and
can in no wise be determined by the objective, is there
assurance nonetheless of a continuing agreement between
the two? If the objective is always the determined,
how then does it come to be precisely so determined
that it accords objectively to freedom, which vents
itself solely in choice, that which cannot itself lie
therein, namely conformity to law? Such a preestablished
harmony of the objective (or law-governed) and the
determinant (or free) is conceivable only through some
higher thing, set over them both, and which is therefore
neither intelligence nor free, but rather is the common
source of the intelligent and likewise of the free.
    Now if this higher thing be nothing else but the
ground of identity between the absolutely subjective
and the absolutely objective, the conscious and the
unconscious, which part company precisely in order to
appear in the free act, then this higher thing itself

can be neither subject nor object, nor both at once,
but only the <u>absolute identity</u>, in which is no duality
at all, and which, precisely because duality is the
condition of all consciousness, can never attain thereto.
This eternal unknown, which, like the everlasting sun
in the realm of spirits, conceals itself behind its own
unclouded light, and though never becoming an object,
impresses its identity upon all free actions, is
simultaneously the same for all intelligences, the
invisible root of which all intelligences are but powers,
and the eternal mediator between the self-determining
subjective within us, and the objective or intuitant;
at once the ground of lawfulness in freedom, and of
freedom in the lawfulness of the object.

But now it is easy to see that this <u>absolutely</u>
<u>identical principle</u>, which is already divided in the
first act of consciousness, and by this separation
generates the entire system of finitude, cannot, in
fact, have any predicates whatever; for it is the
absolutely simple, and thus can have no predicates
drawn either from intelligence or free agency, and
hence, too, can never be an object of knowledge, being
an object only that is eternally presupposed in action,
that is, an object of belief.

But now if this absolute is the true ground of harmony between objective and subjective in the free action,
not only of the individual, but of the entire species,
we shall be likeliest to find traces of this eternal
and unalterable identity in the lawfulness which runs,
like the weaving of an unknown hand, through the free
play of choice in history.

Now if our reflection be directed merely to the
<u>unconscious</u> or <u>objective</u> aspect in all action, we are
obliged to suppose all free acts, and thus the whole of
history, to be absolutely predetermined, not by a conscious foreordaining, but by a wholly blind one, finding
expression in the obscure concept of destiny; and this
is the system of <u>fatalism</u>. If reflection be directed
solely to the <u>subjective</u> in its arbitrary determining,
we arrive at a system of absolute lawlessness, the
true system of <u>irreligion</u> and <u>atheism</u>, namely the claim
that in all doing and acting there is neither law nor
necessity anywhere. But if reflection be elevated to
that absolute which is the common ground of the harmony
between freedom and intelligence, we reach the system
of providence, that is, <u>religion</u> in the only true
sense of the word.

But now if this absolute, which can everywhere only
<u>reveal</u> itself, had actually and fully revealed itself in
history, or were ever to do so, it would at once make an
end of the appearance of freedom. This perfect revelation would come about if free action were to coincide

completely with predetermination. But if there ever
were such a coincidence, if the absolute synthesis,
that is, were ever completely evolved, we should recognize that everything which has come about through freedom in the course of history, was governed in this whole
by law, and that all actions, although they seemed to be
free, were in fact necessary, precisely in order to
bring this whole into being. The opposition between
conscious and unconscious activity is necessarily an
unending one, for were it ever to be done away with,
the appearance of freedom, which rests entirely upon
it, would be done away with too. We can therefore conceive of no point in time at which the absolute syn-
thesis--or to put it in empirical terms, the design of
providence--should have brought its development to
completion.

     If we think of history as a play in which everyone
involved performs his part quite freely and as he pleases,
a rational development of this muddled drama is conceivable only if there be a single spirit who speaks in
everyone, and if the playwright, whose mere fragments
(disjecta membra poetae) are the individual actors, has
already so harmonized beforehand the objective outcome
of the whole with the free play of every participant,
that something rational must indeed emerge at the end
of it. But now if the playwright were to exist independently of his drama, we should be merely the actors
who speak the lines he has written. If he does not
exist independently of us, but reveals and discloses
himself successively only, through the very play of our
own freedom, so that without this freedom even he himself would not be, then we are collaborators of the
whole and have ourselves invented the particular roles
we play. --The ultimate ground of the harmony between
freedom and the objective (or lawful) can therefore
never become wholly objectified, if the appearance of
freedom is to remain. --The absolute acts through each
single intelligence, whose action is thus itself
absolute, and to that extent neither free nor unfree,
but both at once, absolutely free, and for that very
reason also necessary. But if now the intelligence
steps out from the absolute point of view, that is,
out of the universal identity in which nothing can be
distinguished, and becomes conscious of (distinguishes)
itself, which comes about in that its act becomes
objective to it, or passes over into the objective
world, the free and the necessary are then separated
therein. It is free only as an inner appearance, and
that is why we are and believe ourselves to be always
inwardly free, although insofar as it passes into the
objective world the appearance of our freedom, or our
freedom itself, falls just as much under laws of nature

as any other occurrence.

Now it can straightway be inferred from the foregoing, which view of history is the only true one.
History as a whole is a progressive, gradually self-
disclosing revelation of the absolute. Hence one can
never point out in history the particular places where
the mark of providence, or God Himself, is as it were
visible. For God never exists, if the existent is
that which presents itself in the objective world; if
He existed thus, then we should not; but He continually
reveals Himself. Man, through his history, provides a
continuous demonstration of God's presence, a demonstration, however, which only the whole of history can render
complete. Everything depends upon these alternatives
being understood. If God exists, that is, if the objective world constitutes a perfect manifestation of God,
or what comes to the same, of the total congruence of
the free with the unconscious, then nothing can be
otherwise than it is. But the objective world is
assuredly not like this. Or is it, perhaps, really a
complete revelation of God? --Now if the appearance of
freedom is necessarily infinite, the total evolution of
the absolute synthesis is also an infinite process, and
history itself a never wholly completed revelation of
that absolute which, for the sake of consciousness, and
thus merely for the sake of appearance, separates itself into conscious and unconscious, the free and the
intuitant; but which itself, however, in the light
inaccessible wherein it dwells, is eternal identity
and the everlasting ground of harmony between the two.

We can presume three periods of this revelation,
and thus three periods of history. The ground for such
a division is provided by the two opposites, destiny
and providence, between which the middle ground is
occupied by nature, which supplies the transition from
one to the other.

The first period is that wherein the ruling power
still operates as destiny, i.e., as a wholly blind force,
which coldly and unwittingly destroys even what is
greatest and most splendid; to this period of history,
which we may call the tragic period, belongs the downfall
of the glory and the wonder of the ancient world, the
collapse of those great empires of which scarcely the
memory has survived, and whose greatness we deduce only
from their ruins; the downfall of the noblest race of
men that ever flourished upon earth, and whose return
there is simply a perennial wish.

The second period of history is that wherein what
appeared in the first as destiny, or a wholly blind
power, reveals itself as nature, and the dark decree
which formerly prevailed at least appears transformed
into a manifest natural law, compelling freedom and

wholly unbridled choice to subserve a <u>natural plan</u>, and
thus gradually importing into history <u>at least a mechanical conformity to law.</u> This period seems to start
with the expansion of the mighty republic of Rome, from
which point onwards the unruly will, expressing itself
in a general urge to conquer and subdue, is brought under
constraint. In first joining the nations generally
together, and in bringing into mutual contact such
customs and laws, such arts and sciences, as had hitherto been merely conserved in isolation among particular
peoples, it was compelled unconsciously, and even against
its will, to subserve a natural plan which, in its full
development, is destined to lead to a general comity of
nations and the universal state. All events which fall
within this period are thus to be regarded also as mere
natural consequences, so that even the fall of the Roman
Empire has neither a tragic nor a moral aspect, being
a necessary outcome of nature's laws, and indeed a mere
tribute that was paid over to nature.
        The third period of history will be that wherein
the force which appeared in the earlier stages as destiny or nature has evolved itself as <u>providence</u>, and
wherein it will become apparent that even what seemed
to be simply the work of destiny or nature was already
the beginning of a providence imperfectly revealing
itself.
        When this period will begin, we are unable to tell.
But whenever it comes into existence, God also will then
<u>exist</u>.

F

Problem:

To explain how the self itself can become
conscious of the original harmony between
subjective and objective

Solution

I

1. All action can be understood only through an original
unification of freedom and necessity.[1] The proof is that
every action, alike of the <u>individual</u> and of the entire
<u>species</u>,must be conceived of, <u>qua</u> action, as free, but

Henceforward the footnotes and interpolations in
brackets give additions and corrections from a copy
annotated by Schelling himself. (Tr.)

[1]The absolute postulate of all action is an original....

qua objective consequence, as standing under natural laws.
Subjectively, therefore, for inner appearance, we act,
but objectively we never act; it is rather that another
acts through us, as it were.
2. But now this objective agency, which acts through me,
must again be myself.[1] Yet I alone am the conscious,
whereas this other is the unconscious. Hence the unconscious in my act must be identical with the conscious.
This identity, however, cannot be evidenced in free
action itself, since precisely for the sake of free
action (i.e., the objectification of this objective)[2]
it abolishes itself. Hence this identity must be
exhibited subsequently to the objectification in question.[3] But that which in free action becomes the objective factor, independent of us, is, prior to appearance,
intuition; so this identity must allow of being evidenced in intuition.

But now it does not allow of being evidenced in
intuiting itself. For either the intuiting is absolutely
subjective, and so not objective at all, or else it becomes objective [in acting], and then this identity has
been abolished therein, precisely for the sake of the
objectification. Hence the identity will have to be
evidenced only (we may suppose) in the products of the
intuiting.

This identity cannot be exhibited in the objective
of the second order, since the latter only comes about
through an abolition of such identity, and through a
separation that never terminates. This objective can
indeed be explained no otherwise than by the assumption
that it is something originally posited in harmony, which
separates itself in the free act for the sake of appearance. But now this identical element is first to be
evidenced for the self itself, and since it is the ground
for the explanation of history, it cannot, conversely,
be demonstrated from history.

So this identity can be exhibited only in the
objective of the first order.

We attributed the emergence of the objective world
to a wholly blind mechanism of the intelligence. But
now how such a mechanism could be possible in a nature
whose basic feature is consciousness, would be hard to
understand, unless this mechanism were already determined beforehand by the free and conscious activity.
It would be equally hard to understand how a realization

[1] The free [agency]

[2] [Parenthesis canceled in MS].

[3] be exhibited subsequently to the free act, subsequently
to the point at which the unconscious element confronts me as
objective.

of our purposes in the external world could ever be
possible through conscious and free activity, unless a
susceptibility to such action were already established
in the world, even before it becomes the object of a
conscious act, by virtue of that original identity of
the unconscious with the conscious activity.

But now if all conscious activity is purposive,
this coincidence of conscious and unconscious activity
can evidence itself only in a product that _is purposive_,
without _being purposively brought about_. Nature must be
a product of this sort, and this, indeed, is the principle of all teleology, in which alone we may seek for the
solution of the problem posed above.[1]

[1] and nature, insofar as it is this, provides for us the
first answer to the question, how or by what means this absolute
harmony of necessity and freedom, postulated for the sake of making
action possible, can again itself become objective to us.

PART FIVE

Essentials of Teleology according to the
Principles of Transcendental Idealism

As surely as the appearance of freedom is to be comprehended only through a single identical activity, which
has divided itself, purely for the sake of appearing,
into conscious and unconscious forms,[1] so surely must
nature, as that [which lies beyond this separation and]
is brought forth without freedom, appear as a product
that is purposive without being brought forth in accordance with a purpose; as a product, that is, which
although it is the work of unseeing mechanism, yet
looks as though it were consciously brought about.
Nature must [a)] appear as a purposive product.
The transcendental proof[2] is established by reference
to the necessary harmony of the unconscious and conscious activities. The proof from experience has no
place in transcendental philosophy, and we therefore
pass at once to the second principle, namely,
Nature is [b)] not purposive in its production
[bringing-forth], that is, although in itself it bears
all the marks of a purposive product, it is nevertheless not purposive in origin, and the endeavor to
explain it as due to a purposive production does away
with the character of nature, and indeed abolishes that
which makes it such. For the peculiarity of nature
rests upon this, that in its mechanism, and although
itself nothing but a blind mechanism, it is nonetheless purposive. If I take away the mechanism, I take
away nature itself. All the magic which surrounds
organic nature, for example, and which can first be
entirely penetrated only by aid of transcendental
idealism, rests upon the contradiction, that although
this nature is a product of blind natural forces, it
is nevertheless purposive through and through. But
this very contradiction, which can be deduced a priori
on transcendental principles [those of idealism], is
eliminated by teleological modes of explanation.[3]
Nature in its purposive forms speaks figuratively

[1] through a single absolute harmony, which has divided itself,
for the sake of appearing, into conscious and unconscious activity.

[2] the speculative and original proof.

[3] for nature is there presented as purposive in the sense that
the intention to create is insisted on. The point, however, is
that the highest degree of purposiveness appears precisely where
intention and purpose are absent.

to us, says Kant; the interpretation of its cipher yields
us the appearance of freedom in ourselves. In the
natural product we still find side by side what in free
action has been separated for purposes of appearance.
Every plant is entirely what it should be; what is free
therein is necessary, and what is necessary is free.
Man is forever a broken fragment, for either his action
is necessary, and then not free, or free, and then not
necessary and according to law. The complete appearance
of freedom and necessity unified in the external world
therefore yields me organic nature only,[1] and this could
already have been inferred beforehand from the place
that nature occupies, in theoretical philosophy, in the
series of productions; seeing that, according to our
distinctions, nature itself is already a producing
become objective, and to that extent therefore approximates to free action, but is nevertheless an unconscious
intuiting of producing, and hence to that extent is
itself again a blind producing.

Now this contradiction, whereby one and the same
product is at once a blind product, and yet is purposive,
is utterly inexplicable in any system except that of
transcendental idealism, inasmuch as every other denies
either the purposiveness of the products, or the mechanism involved in bringing them about, and so must do
away with this same coexistence. One possibility is to
suppose that matter shapes itself automatically into
purposive products, whereby it at least becomes intelligible how matter and the concept of purpose interfuse
in the products; and then one either ascribes absolute
reality to matter, as happens in hylozoism, a nonsensi-
cal system, inasmuch as it supposes matter _itself_ to be
intelligent; or else not, in which case matter must be
thought of as merely the mode of intuition of an intelligent being, so that the concept of purpose and the
object thereupon merge, in fact, not in matter, but in the
intuition of that intelligence, whereby hylozoism itself then leads back once more to transcendental idealism. The other possibility is to suppose matter to be
absolutely inert, and to have the purposiveness in its
products brought about by an intelligence outside it,
in such a way that the concept of this purposiveness
must have preceded production itself; but then there is
no seeing how concept and object can have been everlastingly interfused, or how--in a word--the product
can be a work, not of artifice, but of nature. For the
difference between artifact and natural product resides
precisely in this, that in the former the concept is
impressed only upon the surface of the object, while in

[1]either in the particular case, or in nature as a whole,
which is an absolutely organic being.

the latter it has gone over into the object itself and
is utterly inseparable therefrom. But now this absolute
identity of the purposive concept with the object itself
is attributable only to a type of production in which
conscious and unconscious activity are united; but this
in turn is possible only within an intelligence. But now
it is readily intelligible how a creative intelligence
should be able to present a world to itself, yet not how
it could do so to others outside itself. So here once
more we find ourselves driven back upon transcendental
idealism.

The purposiveness of nature, alike in the large and
in individual products, can be grasped only through an
intuition in which the concept of the concept and the
object itself are originally and inseparably united; for
then indeed the product will have to appear as purposive,
since the production itself was already determined by
that principle which separates, for the sake of consciousness, into the free and the nonfree; and yet again
the concept of purpose cannot be thought to have preceded
production, since both, in this intuition, were still
inseparable. Now that all teleological modes of explanation, e.g., those which have the purposive concept that
corresponds to the conscious activity taking precedence
over the object that corresponds to the unconscious
activity, in fact do away with all true explanation of
nature, and thereby themselves become pernicious to
knowledge in its fullness, is so palpably self-evident
from what has gone before, that even by way of examples
it requires no further elucidation.

II

Nature, in its blind and mechanical purposiveness, admittedly represents to me an original identity of the
conscious and unconscious activities, but [for all that,]
it does not present this identity to me as one whose ultimate ground resides in the self itself. The transcendental philosopher assuredly recognizes that the principle
of this [harmony] is that ultimate in ourselves[1] which
already undergoes division in the primary act of self-
consciousness, and on which the whole of consciousness,
with all its determinations, is founded; but the self
itself is not aware of this. Now the aim of our whole
science was in fact precisely this, of explaining how
the ultimate ground of the harmony between subjective
and objective becomes an object to the self itself.

An intuition must therefore be exhibitable in the
intelligence itself, whereby in one and the same

[1]the intrinsic nature, the essence of the soul

appearance the self is at once conscious and unconscious
for itself, and it is by means of such an intuition
that we first bring forth the intelligence, as it were,
entirely out of itself; by such an intuition, therefore,
that we also first resolve the entire [the supreme]
problem of transcendental philosophy (that of explaining the congruence between subjective and objective).

By the first specification, namely that conscious
and unconscious activity become objective in one and the
same intuition, this intuition is distinguished from
that which we were able to deduce[1] in practical philosophy, where the intelligence was conscious only for
inner intuition, but for outer remained unconscious.

By the second specification, namely that in one and
the same intuition the self become simultaneously conscious for itself, and unconscious, the intuition here
postulated is distinguished from that which we have in
the case of natural products, where we certainly recognize this identity, but not as an identity whose principle lies in the self itself. Every organism is a mono-
gram[2] of that original identity, but in order to recognize itself in that reflected image, the self must
already have recognized itself directly in the identity
in question.

We have only to analyze the features of this
intuition we have now deduced, in order to discover the
intuition itself; and, to judge beforehand, it can be
no other than the intuition of art.

[1] from the self-intuition involved in the free act

[2] an intricate outline

PART SIX

Deduction of a Universal Organ of Philosophy, or:
Essentials of the Philosophy of Art according
to the Principles of Transcendental Idealism.

§1

Deduction of the Art-Product as Such

The intuition we have postulated is to bring together
that which exists in separation in the appearance of
freedom and in the intuition of the natural product;
namely identity of the conscious and the unconscious in
the self, and consciousness of this identity. The product of this intuition will therefore verge on the one
side upon the product of nature, and on the other upon
the product of freedom, and must unite in itself the
characteristics of both. If we know the product of
the intuition, we are also acquainted with the intuition
itself, and hence we need only derive the product, in
order to derive the intuition.

With the product of freedom, our product will have
this in common, that it is consciously brought about;
and with the product of nature, that it is unconsciously
brought about. In the former respect it will thus be
the reverse of the organic natural product. Whereas
the unconscious (blind) activity is reflected out of
the organic product as a conscious one, the conscious
activity will conversely be reflected out of the product here under consideration as an unconscious (objective) one; whereas the organic product reflects its
unconscious activity to me as determined by conscious
activity, the product here being derived will conversely
reflect conscious activity as determined by unconscious.
To put it more briefly: nature begins as unconscious
and ends as conscious; the process of production is not
purposive, but the product certainly is so. In the
activity at present under discussion, the self must
begin (subjectively) with consciousness, and end without consciousness, or objectively; the self is conscious in respect of production, unconscious in regard
to the product.

But now how are we to explain transcendentally to
ourselves an intuition such as this, in which the unconscious activity operates as it were, through the conscious, to the point of attaining complete identity
therewith? --Let us first give thought to the fact that
the activity is to be a conscious one. But now it is
utterly impossible for anything objective to be brought
forth with consciousness, although that is being demanded
here. The objective is simply that which arises without

consciousness, and hence what is properly objective in
this intuition must likewise be incapable of being
brought forth with consciousness. On this point we
may appeal directly to the arguments already brought forward in regard to free action, namely that the objective
factor therein is supplied by something independent of
freedom. The difference is merely this, [a)] that in the
free act the identity of the two activities must be
abolished, precisely in order that the act may thereby
appear as free, [whereas here, the two are to appear as
one in consciousness itself, without negation thereof].
Moreover, [b)] in the free act the two activities can
never become absolutely identical, whence even the
object of the free act is necessarily an infinite one,
never completely realized, for if it was, the conscious
and the objective activities would merge into one, that
is, the appearance of freedom would cease. Now that
which was utterly impossible through freedom is to
become possible through the act here postulated, though
as the price of this the latter must cease to be a free
act, and becomes one in which freedom and necessity are
absolutely united. But now the production was still
supposed to take place with consciousness, which is
impossible unless the two [activities] are separated.
So here is a manifest contradiction. [I present it
once again.] Conscious and unconscious activities are
to be absolutely one in the product, just as they also
are in the organic product, but they are to be one in
a different manner; the two are to be one for the self
itself. This is impossible, however, unless the self
is conscious of the production. But if it is so, the
two activities must be separated, for this is a necessary condition for being conscious of the production.
So the two activities must be one, since otherwise there
is no identity, and yet must both be separated, since
otherwise there is identity, but not for the self. How
is this contradiction to be resolved?
     The two activities must be separated for purposes
of the appearing, the becoming-objective of the production, just as in the free act they had to be separated
in order that the intuition might become objective. But
they cannot be separated ad infinitum, as in the free
act, since otherwise the objective element would never
be a complete manifestation of this identity.[1] The
identity of the two was to be abolished only for the
sake of consciousness, but the production is to end in
unconsciousness; so there must be a point at which the
two merge into one; and conversely, where the two merge

---

[1]That which lies, for the free act, in an infinite progress,
is to be, in the current engendering, a thing present, is to become
actual, objective, in something finite.

into one, the production must cease to appear as a free one.[1]

If this point in production is reached, the producing must absolutely stop, and it must be impossible for the producer to go on producing; for the condition of all producing is precisely the opposition between conscious and unconscious activity; but here they have absolutely to coincide, and thus within the intelligence all conflict has to be eliminated, all contradiction reconciled.[2]

The intelligence will therefore end with a complete recognition of the identity expressed in the product as an identity whose principle lies in the intelligence itself; it will end, that is, in a complete intuiting of itself.[3] Now since it was the free tendency to self-intuition in that identity which originally divided the intelligence from itself, the feeling accompanying this intuition will be that of an infinite tranquillity. With the completion of the product, all urge to produce is halted, all contradictions are eliminated, all riddles resolved. Since production set out from freedom, that is, from an unceasing opposition of the two activities, the intelligence will be unable to attribute this absolute union of the two, in which production ends, to freedom; so as soon as the product is completed, all appearance of freedom is removed. The intelligence will feel itself astonished and blessed by this union, will regard it, that is, in the light of a bounty freely granted by a higher nature, by whose aid the impossible has been made possible.

This unknown, however, whereby the objective and the conscious activities are here brought into unexpected harmony, is none other than that absolute[4] which contains the common ground of the preestablished harmony between the conscious and the unconscious. Hence, if this absolute is reflected from out of the product, it

---

[1]At that point the free activity has wholly gone over into the objective, the necessary aspect. Hence production is free at the outset, whereas the product appears as an absolute identity of the free activity with the necessary one.

[2][This paragraph canceled in the author's copy. - Tr.]

[3]For it (the intelligence) is itself the producer; but at the same time this identity has wholly broken loose therefrom, and become totally objective to the intelligence, i.e., totally objective to itself.

[4]the primordial self.

will appear to the intelligence as something lying above
the latter, and which, in contrast to freedom, brings
an element of the unintended to that which was begun
with consciousness and intention.

   This unchanging identity, which can never attain to
consciousness, and merely radiates back from the product,
is for the producer precisely what destiny is for the
agent, namely a dark unknown force which supplies the
element of completeness or objectivity to the piecework
of freedom; and as that power is called destiny, which
through our free action realizes, without our knowledge
and even against our will, goals that we did not envisage,
so likewise that incomprehensible agency which supplies
objectivity to the conscious, without the cooperation of
freedom, and to some extent in opposition to freedom
(wherein is eternally dispersed what in this production
is united), is denominated by means of the obscure concept of genius.

   The product we postulate is none other than the
product of genius, or, since genius is possible only
in the arts, the product of art.

   The deduction is concluded, and our next task is
simply to show by thoroughgoing analysis that all the
features of the production we have postulated come
together in the aesthetic.

   The fact that all aesthetic production rests upon
a conflict of activities can be justifiably inferred
already from the testimony of all artists, that they
are involuntarily driven to create their works, and that
in producing them they merely satisfy an irresistible
urge of their own nature; for if every urge proceeds
from a contradiction in such wise that, given the contradiction, free activity becomes involuntary, the
artistic urge also must proceed from such a feeling
of inner contradiction. But since this contradiction
sets in motion the whole man with all his forces, it is
undoubtedly one which strikes at the ultimate in him,
the root of his whole being.[1] It is as if, in the excep-
tional man (which artists above all are, in the highest
sense of the word), that unalterable identity, on which
all existence is founded, had laid aside the veil wherewith it shrouds itself in others, and, just as it is
directly affected by things, so also works directly
back upon everything. Thus it can only be the contradiction between conscious and unconscious in the
free act which sets the artistic urge in motion; just
as, conversely, it can be given to art alone to pacify
our endless striving, and likewise to resolve the final
and uttermost contradiction within us. Just as aesthetic

[1]the true in-itself.

production proceeds from the feeling of a seemingly
irresoluble contradiction, so it ends likewise, by the
testimony of all artists, and of all who share their
inspiration, in the feeling of an infinite harmony; and
that this feeling which accompanies completion is at the
same time a deep emotion, is itself enough to show that
the artist attributes that total resolution of his conflict which he finds achieved in his work of art, not to
himself [alone], but to a bounty freely granted by his
own nature, which, however unrelentingly it set him in
conflict with himself, is no less gracious in relieving
him of the pain of this contradiction.[1] For just as the
artist is driven into production involuntarily and even
in spite of himself (whence the ancient expressions pati
deum, etc., and above all the idea of being inspired by
an afflatus from without), so likewise is his production
endowed with objectivity as if by no help of his own,
that is, itself in a purely objective manner. Just as
the man of destiny does not execute what he wishes or
intends, but rather what he is obliged to execute by an
inscrutable fate which governs him, so the artist, however deliberate he may be, seems nonetheless to be
governed, in regard to what is truly objective in his
creation, by a power which separates him from all other
men, and compels him to say or depict things which he
does not fully understand himself, and whose meaning
is infinite. Now every absolute concurrence of the
two antithetical activities is utterly unaccountable,
being simply a phenomenon which although incomprehensible,[2] yet cannot be denied; and art, therefore, is the
one everlasting revelation which yields that concurrence,
and the marvel which, had it existed but once only,
would necessarily have convinced us of the absolute
reality of that supreme event.
     Now again if art comes about through two activities
totally distinct from one another, genius is neither one
the other, but that which presides over both. If we are
to seek in one of the two activities, namely the conscious, for what is ordinarily called art, though it is
only one part thereof, namely that aspect of it which is
exercised with consciousness, thought and reflection,
and can be taught and learnt and achieved through
tradition and practice, we shall have, on the other hand,
to seek in the unconscious factor which enters into art
for that about it which cannot be learned, nor attained
by practice, nor in any other way, but can only be

[1]attributes...to a bounty freely granted by his own nature,
and thus to a coincidence of the unconscious with the conscious
activity [Author's copy].

[2]from the standpoint of mere reflection.

inborn through the free bounty of nature; and this is
what we may call, in a word, the element of poetry
in art.

It is self-evident from this, however, that it would
be utterly futile to ask which of the two constituents
should have preference over the other, since each of
them, in fact, is valueless without the other, and it is
only in conjunction that they bring forth the highest.
For although what is not attained by practice, but is
born in us, is commonly regarded as the nobler, the gods
have in fact tied the very exercise of that innate power
so closely to a man's serious application, his industry
and thought, that even where it is inborn, poetry without
art engenders, as it were, only dead products, which can
give no pleasure to any man's mind, and repel all judgment and even intuition, owing to the wholly blind force
which operates therein. It is, on the contrary, far
more to be expected that art without poetry should be
able to achieve something, than poetry without art;
partly because it is not easy for a man to be by nature
wholly without poetry, though many are wholly without
art; and partly because a persistent study of the
thoughts of great masters is able in some degree to make
up for the initial want of objective power. All that
can ever arise from this, however, is merely a semblance
of poetry, which, by its superficiality and by many
other indications, e.g., the high value it attaches to
the mere mechanics of art, the poverty of form in which
it operates, etc., is easily distinguishable in contrast
to the unfathomable depth which the true artist, though
he labors with the greatest diligence, involuntarily
imparts to his work, and which neither he nor anyone
else is wholly able to penetrate.

But now it is also self-evident that just as
poetry and art are each individually incapable of engendering perfection, so a divided existence of both is
equally inadequate to the task.[1] It is therefore clear
that, since the identity of the two can only be innate,
and is utterly impossible and unattainable through
freedom, perfection is possible only through genius,
which, for that very reason, is for the aesthetic what
the self is for philosophy, namely the supreme absolute
reality, which never itself becomes objective, but is
the cause of everything that is so.

[1]Neither has priority over the other. It is, indeed, simply
the equipoise of the two (art and poetry) which is reflected in the
work of art.

§2

Character of the Art-Product

a) The work of art reflects to us the identity of the conscious and unconscious activities. But the opposition between them is an infinite one, and its removal is effected without any assistance from freedom. Hence the basic character of the work of art is that of an <u>unconscious infinity</u> [synthesis of nature and freedom]. Besides what he has put into his work with manifest intention, the artist seems instinctively, as it were, to have depicted therein an infinity, which no finite understanding is capable of developing to the full. To explain what we mean by a single example: the mythology of the Greeks, which undeniably contains an infinite meaning and a symbolism for all ideas, arose among a people, and in a fashion, which both make it impossible to suppose any comprehensive forethought in devising it, or in the harmony whereby everything is united into one great whole. So it is with every true work of art, in that every one of them is capable of being expounded <u>ad infinitum</u>, as though it contained an infinity of purposes, while yet one is never able to say whether this infinity has lain within the artist himself, or resides only in the work of art. By contrast, in the product which merely apes the character of a work of art, purpose and rule lie on the surface, and seem so restricted and circumscribed, that the product is no more than a faithful replica of the artist's conscious activity, and is in every respect an object for reflection only, not for intuition, which loves to sink itself in what it contemplates, and finds no resting place short of the infinite.
b) Every aesthetic production proceeds from the feeling of an infinite contradiction, and hence also the feeling which accompanies completion of the art-product must be one of an infinite tranquillity; and this latter, in turn, must also pass over into the work of art itself. Hence the outward expression of the work of art is one of calm, and silent grandeur, even where the aim is to give expression to the utmost intensity of pain or joy.
c) Every aesthetic production proceeds from an intrinsically infinite separation of the two activities, which in every free act of producing are divided. But now since these two activities are to be depicted in the product as united, what this latter presents is an infinite finitely displayed. But the infinite finitely displayed is beauty. The basic feature of every work of art, in which both the preceding are comprehended, is therefore <u>beauty</u>, and without beauty there is no work

of art. There are, admittedly, sublime works of art,
and beauty and sublimity in a certain respect are opposed
to each other, in that a landscape, for example, can be
beautiful without therefore being sublime, and vice
versa. However, the opposition between beauty and
sublimity is one which occurs only in regard to the
object, not in regard to the subject of intuition. For
the difference between the beautiful and the sublime
work of art consists simply in this, that where beauty
is present, the infinite contradiction is eliminated in
the object itself; whereas when sublimity is present,
the conflict is not reconciled in the object itself, but
merely uplifted to a point at which it is involuntarily
eliminated in the intuition; and this, then, is much as
if it were to be eliminated in the object.[1] It can also
be shown very easily that sublimity rests upon the same
contradiction as that on which beauty rests. For whenever an object is spoken of as sublime, a magnitude is
admitted by the unconscious activity which it is impossible to accept into the conscious one; whereupon the
self is thrown into a conflict with itself which can
end only in an aesthetic intuition, whereby both activities are brought into unexpected harmony; save only
that the intuition, which here lies not in the artist,
but in the intuiting subject himself, is a wholly involuntary one, in that the sublime (quite unlike the merely
strange, which similarly confronts the imagination with
a contradiction, though one that is not worth the trouble
of resolving) sets all the forces of the mind in motion,
in order to resolve a contradiction which threatens our
whole intellectual existence.

Now that the characteristics of the work of art
have been derived, its difference from all other products has simultaneously been brought to light.

For the art-product differs from the organic product of nature primarily in these respects: [a] that
the organic being still exhibits unseparated what the
aesthetic production displays after separation, though
united; b)] that the organic production does not proceed
from consciousness, or therefore from the infinite
contradiction, which is the condition of aesthetic
production. Hence [if beauty is essentially the resolution of an infinite conflict] the organic product of
nature will likewise not necessarily be beautiful, and
if it is so, its beauty will appear as altogether

[1]This passage replaced in the author's copy by the following:
For although there are sublime works of art, and sublimity is cus-
tomarily contrasted with beauty, there is actually no true objective
opposition between beauty and sublimity; the truly and absolutely
beautiful is invariably also sublime, and the sublime (if it truly
is so) is beautiful as well.

contingent, since the condition thereof cannot be
thought of as existing in nature. From this we may
explain the quite peculiar interest in natural beauty,
not insofar as it is beauty as such, but insofar as it
is specifically natural beauty. Whence it is self-
evident what we are to think of the imitation of nature
as a principle of art; for so far from the merely contingent beauty of nature providing the rule to art, the
fact is, rather, that what art creates in its perfection
is the principle and norm for the judgment of natural
beauty.

It is easy to conceive how the aesthetic product is
to be distinguished from the common artifact, since all
aesthetic creation is absolutely free in regard to its
principle, in that the artist can be driven to create by
a contradiction, indeed, but only by one which lies in
the highest regions of his own nature; whereas every
other sort of creation is occasioned by a contradiction
which lies outside the actual producer, and thus has in
every case a goal outside itself.[1] This independence of
external goals is the source of that holiness and purity
of art, which goes so far that it not only rules out
relationship with all mere sensory pleasure, to demand
which of art is the true nature of barbarism; or with the
useful, to require which of art is possible only in an
age which supposes the highest efforts of the human
spirit to consist in economic discoveries.[2] It actually
excludes relation with everything pertaining to morality,
and even leaves far beneath it the sciences (which in
point of disinterestedness stand closest to art), simply
because they are always directed to a goal outside themselves, and must ultimately themselves serve merely as
a means for the highest (namely art).

So far as particularly concerns the relation of art
to science, the two are so utterly opposed in tendency,
that if science were ever to have discharged its whole
task, as art has always discharged it, they would both
have to coincide and merge into one--which is proof of
directions that they are radically opposed. For though
science at its highest level has one and the same business as art, this business, owing to the manner of
effecting it, is an endless one for science, so that one
may say that art constitutes the ideal of science, and
where art is, science has yet to attain to. From this,
too, it is apparent why and to what extent there is no
genius in science; not indeed that it would be impossible for a scientific problem to be solved by means

[1](absolute transition into the objective).

[2]Beetroots.

of genius, but because this same problem whose solution
can be found by genius, is also soluble mechanically.
Such, for example, is the Newtonian system of gravitation, which could have been a discovery of genius, and
in its first discoverer, Kepler, really was so, but
could equally also have been a wholly scientific discovery, which it actually became in the hands of Newton.
Only what art brings forth is simply and solely possible
through genius, since in every task that art has discharged, an infinite contradiction is reconciled. What
science brings forth, can be brought forth through
genius, but it is not necessarily engendered through
this. It therefore is and remains problematic in
science, i.e., one can, indeed, always say definitely
where it is not present, but never where it is. There
are but few indications which allow us to infer genius
in the sciences; (that one has to infer it is already
evidence of the peculiarity of the matter). It is, for
example, assuredly not present, where a whole, such as
a system, arises piecemeal and as though by putting
together. One would thus have to suppose, conversely,
that genius is present, where the idea of the whole has
manifestly preceded the individual parts. For since the
idea of the whole cannot in fact become clear save
through its development in the individual parts, while
those parts, on the other hand, are possible only through
the idea of the whole, there seems to be a contradiction
here which is possible only through an act of genius,
i.e., an unexpected concurrence of the unconscious with
the conscious activity. Another ground for the presumption of genius in the sciences would be if someone were
to say and maintain things whose meaning he could not
possibly have understood entirely, either owing to the
period at which he lived, or by reason of his other
utterances; so that he has thus asserted something
apparently with consciousness, which he could in fact
only have asserted unconsciously. It could, however
be readily shown in a number of ways, that even these
grounds for the presumption may be delusive in the
extreme.

    Genius is thus marked off from everything that con-
sists in mere talent or skill by the fact that through
it a contradiction is resolved, which is soluble absolutely and otherwise by nothing else. In all producing, even of the most ordinary and commonplace sort,
an unconscious activity operates along with the conscious one; but only a producing whose condition was
an infinite opposition of the two activities is an
aesthetic producing, and one that is only possible
through genius.

Corollaries

Relation of Art to Philosophy

Now that we have deduced the nature and character of the
art-product as completely as was necessary for purposes
of the present enquiry, there is nothing more we need do
except to set forth the relation which the philosophy of
art bears to the whole system of philosophy.

1. The whole of philosophy starts, and must start,
from a principle which, <u>qua</u> absolutely identical, is
utterly nonobjective. But now how is this absolutely
nonobjective to be called up to consciousness and under-
stood--a thing needful, if it is the condition for understanding the whole of philosophy? That it can no more
be apprehended through concepts than it is capable of
being set forth by means of them, stands in no need of
proof. Nothing remains, therefore, but for it to be
set forth in an immediate intuition, though this is
itself in turn inconceivable, and, since its object is
to be something utterly nonobjective, seems, indeed, to
be self-contradictory. But now were such an intuition
in fact to exist, having as its object the absolutely
identical, in itself neither subjective nor objective,
and were we, in respect of this intuition, which can
only be an intellectual one, to appeal to immediate
experience, then how, in that case, could even this
intuition be in turn posited objectively? How, that is,
can it be established beyond doubt, that such an intuition
does not rest upon a purely subjective deception, if it
possesses no objectivity that is universal and acknowledged by all men? This universally acknowledged and
altogether incontestable objectivity of intellectual
intuition is art itself. For the aesthetic intuition
simply is the intellectual intuition become objective.[1]

[1]The preceding is replaced in the author's copy by:
The whole of philosophy starts, and must start, from a
principle which, as the absolute principle, is also at
the same time the absolutely identical. An absolutely
simple and identical cannot be grasped or communicated
through description, nor through concepts at all. It
can only be intuited. Such an intuition is the organ
of all philosophy. --But this intuition, which is an
intellectual rather than a sensory one, and has as its
object neither the objective nor the subjective, but the
absolutely identical, in itself neither subjective nor
objective, is itself merely an internal one, which cannot
in turn become objective for itself: it can become
objective only through a second intuition. This second
intuition is the aesthetic.

The work of art merely reflects to me what is otherwise
not reflected by anything, namely that absolutely identical which has already divided itself even in the self.
Hence, that which the philosopher allows to be divided
even in the primary act of consciousness, and which would
otherwise be inaccessible to any intuition, comes, through
the miracle of art, to be radiated back from the products
thereof.

It is not, however, the first principle of philosophy, merely, and the first intuition that philosophy
proceeds from, which initially become objective through
aesthetic production; the same is true of the entire
mechanism which philosophy deduces, and on which in turn
it rests.

Philosophy sets out from an infinite dichotomy of
opposed activities;[1] but the same dichotomy is also the
basis of every aesthetic production, and by each individual manifestation of art it is wholly resolved.[2] Now
what is this wonderful power whereby, in productive
intuition (so the philosopher claims), an infinite
opposition is removed? So far we have not been able to
render this mechanism entirely intelligible, since it
is only the power of art which can unveil it completely.
This productive power is the same whereby art also
achieves the impossible, namely to resolve an infinite
opposition in a finite product. It is the poetic gift,
which in its primary potentiality constitutes the primordial intuition, and conversely,[3] what we speak of as
the poetic gift is merely productive intuition, reiter-
ated to its highest power. It is one and the same
capacity that is active in both, the only one whereby
we are able to think and to couple together even what
is contradictory--and its name is imagination. Hence,
that which appears to us outside the sphere of consciousness, as real, and that which appears within it,
as ideal, or as the world of art, are also products of

[1]Philosophy makes all production of intuition proceed from a
separation of activities that were previously not opposed.

[2]The final words, "and . . . resolved," struck out in the
author's copy.

[3]Replaced in the author's copy by: That productive power
whereby the object arises is likewise the source from which an object
also springs forth to art, save only that in the first case the
activity is dull and limited, while in the latter it is clear and
boundless. The poetic gift, regarded in its primary potentiality,
is the soul's most primitive capacity for production, insofar as
the latter declares itself in finite and actual things, and
conversely. . . .

one and the same activity. But this very fact, that
where the conditions of emergence are otherwise
entirely similar, the one takes its origin from outside
consciousness, the other from within it, constitutes
the eternal difference between them which can never be
removed.

To be sure, then, the real world evolves entirely
from the same original opposition as must also give rise
to the world of art, which has equally to be viewed as
one great whole, and which in all its individual products depicts only the one infinite. But outside consciousness this opposition is only infinite inasmuch
as an infinity is exhibited by the objective world as
a whole, and never by any individual object; whereas
for art this opposition is an infinite one in regard to
every single object, and infinity is exhibited in every
one of its products. For if aesthetic production proceeds from freedom, and if it is precisely for freedom
that this opposition of conscious and unconscious
activities is an absolute one, there is properly speaking but one absolute work of art, which may indeed
exist in altogether different versions, yet is still
only one, even though it should not yet exist in its
most ultimate form. It can be no objection to this view,
that if so, the very liberal use now made of the predicate 'work of art' will no longer do. Nothing is a work
of art which does not exhibit an infinite, either
directly, or at least by reflection. Are we to call
works of art, for example, even such compositions as
by nature depict only the individual and subjective?
In that case we shall have to bestow this title also
upon every epigram, which preserves merely a momentary
sensation or current impression; though indeed the
great masters who have practiced in such genres were
seeking to bring forth objectivity itself only through
the totality of their creations, and used them simply
as a means to depict a whole infinite life, and to
project it back from a many-faceted mirror.

2. If aesthetic intuition is merely transcendental[1] intuition become objective, it is self-evident
that art is at once the only true and eternal organ and
document of philosophy, which ever and again continues
to speak to us of what philosophy cannot depict in
external form, namely the unconscious element in acting
and producing, and its original identity with the conscious. Art is paramount to the philosopher, precisely
because it opens to him, as it were, the holy of holies,
where burns in eternal and original unity, as if in a
single flame, that which in nature and history is rent
asunder, and in life and action, no less than in thought,
must forever fly apart. The view of nature, which the
philosopher frames artificially, is for art the original

[1]intellectual (author's correction).

and natural one. What we speak of as nature is a poem
lying pent in a mysterious and wonderful script. Yet
the riddle could reveal itself, were we to recognize
in it the odyssey of the spirit, which, marvelously
deluded, seeks itself, and in seeking flies from itself;
for through the world of sense there glimmers, as if
through words the meaning, as if through dissolving
mists the land of fantasy, of which we are in search.
Each splendid painting owes, as it were, its genesis
to a removal of the invisible barrier dividing the real
from the ideal world, and is no more than the gateway,
through which come forth completely the shapes and
scenes of that world of fantasy which gleams but imperfectly through the real. Nature, to the artist, is
nothing more than it is to the philosopher, being simply
the ideal world appearing under permanent restrictions,
or merely the imperfect reflection of a world existing,
not outside him, but within.
     But now what may be the source of this kinship of
philosophy and art, despite the opposition between
them, is a question already sufficiently answered in
what has gone before.
     We therefore close with the following observa-
tion. --A system is completed when it is led back to
its starting point. But this is precisely the case
with our own. The ultimate ground of all harmony
between subjective and objective could be exhibited in
its original identity only through intellectual intuition; and it is precisely this ground which, by means
of the work of art, has been brought forth entirely
from the subjective, and rendered wholly objective, in
such wise, that we have gradually led our object, the
self itself, up to the very point where we ourselves
were standing when we began to philosophize.
     But now if it is art alone which can succeed in
objectifying with universal validity what the philosopher is able to present in a merely subjective
fashion, there is one more conclusion yet to be drawn.
Philosophy was born and nourished by poetry in the
infancy of knowledge, and with it all those sciences
it has guided toward perfection; we may thus expect
them, on completion, to flow back like so many individual streams into the universal ocean of poetry
from which they took their source. Nor is it in
general difficult to say what the medium for this
return of science to poetry will be; for in mythology
such a medium existed, before the occurrence of a
breach now seemingly beyond repair.[1] But how a new

---

[1]The further development of this idea is contained in a
treatise On Mythology, already sketched out a number of years
ago.

mythology is itself to arise, which shall be the creation, not of some individual author, but of a new race,
personifying, as it were, one single poet--that is a
problem whose solution can be looked for only in the
future destinies of the world, and in the course of
history to come.

GENERAL OBSERVATION ON THE WHOLE SYSTEM

If the reader, who has followed our discussion attentively up to this point, now considers once more the
interconnection of the whole, he will doubtless remark
as follows:

That the whole system falls between two extremes,
of which one is characterized by intellectual, the other
by aesthetic intuition. What intellectual intuition is
for the philosopher, aesthetic intuition is for his object. The former, since it is necessary purely for
purposes of that special direction of the mind which it
takes in philosophizing, makes no appearance at all in
ordinary consciousness; the latter, since it.is nothing
else but intellectual intuition given universal currency,
or become objective, can at least figure in every consciousness. But from this very fact it may also be
understood that, and why, philosophy as philosophy can
never become generally current. The one field to which
absolute objectivity is granted, is art. Take away
objectivity from art, one might say, and it ceases to
be what it is, and becomes philosophy; grant objectivity
to philosophy, and it ceases to be philosophy, and
becomes art. --Philosophy attains, indeed, to the highest,
but it brings to this summit only, so to say, the frac-
tion of a man. Art brings the whole man, as he is, to
that point, namely to a knowledge of the highest, and
this is what underlies the eternal difference and the
marvel of art.

That moreover the whole sequence of the transcendental philosophy is based merely upon a continual raising
of self-intuition to increasingly higher powers, from
the first and simplest exercise of self-consciousness,
to the highest, namely the aesthetic.

The following are the powers through which the
object of philosophy takes its course, in order to bring
forth the entire edifice of self-consciousness.

The act of self-consciousness in which that
absolute identical first divides itself, is nothing else
but an act of self-intuition as such. By this act,
therefore, nothing determinate can as yet be posited
in the self, since it is only first through it that any
determinacy is posited at all. In this primary act
the identical first becomes at once both subject and
object, i.e., becomes a self at all--not for itself,

though certainly for philosophical reflection.

(What the identical may be, abstracted from and, as it were, prior to this act, simply cannot be asked. For it is that which can only reveal itself through self-consciousness, and cannot anywhere part company from this act.)

The second self-intuition is that whereby the self intuits that determinacy posited in the objective of its activity; and this takes place in sensation. In this intuition the self is an object for itself, whereas in the preceding one it was object and subject only for the philosopher.

In the third self-intuition the self also becomes an object to itself qua sensing, that is, even what has hitherto been subjective in the self is carried over to the objective; thus everything in the self is now objective, or the self is wholly objective, and qua objective is subject and object at once.

Of this stage of consciousness, nothing else will be able to remain behind, therefore, save what will be found, after consciousness has arisen, as the absolute objective (the external world). --This intuition, which is already raised to a higher power, and is for that very reason productive, contains, apart from the objective and subjective activities, which are both objective in the present case, yet a third, the truly intuitant or ideal activity; this it is which afterwards comes to light as the conscious activity, but which, since it is merely the third derived from these two, can neither be separated from them nor opposed to them. --Thus in this intuition a conscious activity is already implicit, or the unconscious objective is determined by a conscious activity, save only that the latter is not distinguished as such.

The intuition that follows will be that whereby the self intuits itself as productive. But now since the self is at present purely objective, this intuition too will be purely objective, i.e., once more without consciousness. There is indeed present in this intuition an ideal activity, having as its object that intuitant, equally ideal activity involved in the preceding intuition; here, therefore, the intuitant activity is an ideal activity of the second order, i.e., a purposive, albeit an unconsciously purposive one. That which remains of this intuition in consciousness will thus indeed appear as purposive, but not as a product purposively brought forth. Such a product is organization, in its whole extent.

By means of these four stages, the self as an intelligence is completed. It is evident that up to this point nature keeps wholly in step with the self, and hence that nature undoubtedly lacks only the final

phase, whereby all these intuitions acquire for it the
same meaning as they have for the self. But what this
final phase may be, will appear from what follows.

If the self were to continue to be purely objective, self-intuition could go on rising to higher powers
ad infinitum, but the process would merely lengthen
the series of products in nature without ever giving
rise to consciousness. The latter is possible only if
that purely objective element in the self becomes
objective to the self itself. But the ground of this
cannot lie in the self itself. For the self is
absolutely identical with this purely objective element.
The ground can therefore lie only outside a self which,
by progressive limitation, has gradually been restricted
into an intelligence, and even to the point of individuality. But outside the individual, i.e., independent
of him, there is only the intelligence itself. But
[according to the mechanism deduced] the intelligence
itself, where it exists, must restrict itself into
individuality. Hence the ground we are looking for
outside the individual can only lie in another individual.

The absolutely objective can only become an object
to the self itself through the influence of other rational beings. But the intention of such influence must
already have been present in these beings. Hence, freedom is always presupposed in nature (nature does not
engender it), and where it is not already there from
the first, it cannot arise. It therefore becomes evident here, that although up to this point nature is
entirely similar to the intelligence, and traverses
with it the same sequence of powers, freedom, if it
exists (though that it does so, cannot be theoretically
demonstrated), must be superior (natura prior) to nature.

From this point onwards, therefore, we begin a new
sequence of acts, which are not possible through nature,
and in fact leave it behind.

The absolutely objective, or the law-governed
nature of intuiting, becomes an object to the self
itself. But intuiting becomes an object to the intuitant only through willing. The objective factor in
willing is intuiting as such, or the pure lawfulness
of nature; the subjective factor, an ideal activity
directed upon this lawfulness as such. The act in
which this occurs is the absolute act of will.

The absolute act of will itself in turn becomes an
object to the self, in that the objective element in
willing, directed to something external, becomes an
object to the self in the form of a natural urge, while
the subjective, directed to lawfulness as such, is
objectified in the form of absolute will, i.e., as a
categorical imperative. But this, too, is impossible
without an activity superior to them both. This

activity is <u>choice</u>, or free activity accompanied by consciousness.

But now if this consciously free activity, which in acting is opposed to the objective, although required to be one with it, is intuited in its original identity with the objective--a thing utterly impossible through freedom--we finally obtain by this the highest power of self-intuition; and this, since it already lies out beyond the <u>conditions</u> of consciousness, and is indeed itself the consciousness that creates itself <u>ab initio</u>, must appear, where it exists, as absolutely contingent; and this absolute contingency in the highest power of self-intuition is what we designate by means of the idea of <u>genius</u>.

These are the phases, unalterable and fixed for all knowledge, in the history of self-consciousness; they are characterized in experience by a continuous step-wise sequence; and they can be exhibited and extended from simple stuff to organization (whereby unconsciously productive nature reverts into itself), and from thence by reason and choice up to the supreme union of freedom and necessity in art (whereby consciously productive nature encloses and completes itself).

Index

Index

Absolute, xi, xix, xxiii-vi, xxviii, xxxi-v, 17, 115-19,
155, 190-1, 207, 209-11, 221, 230. see also Identity,
Synthesis

Abstraction, 134-44, 147-52, 155, 193

Acts, Actions, Activities (of the Self), xiii, xvii,
xxvii-viii, xxx, 9, 24, 32, 35-49, 52-6, 60-85, 90-1,
94-103, 113-16, 122, 124, 129-36, 139, 142, 148-89,
192-4, 199, 205-6, 212-25, 228-36

Animal (and Vegetable), 123-4

Antinomies, 176

A priori (and A posteriori), xxvi, 93, 148, 150-4

Aristotelianism, 153

Arithmetic, 145

Art, xi, xxiv, xxviii-ix, 12, 223-4, 227-33, 236
Philosophy of, xv, xxii, xxiv, 4, 12, 14, 219, 229
Work of, 137-8, 219, 222-32

Artifact, 107, 137, 172, 216, 227

Atheism, 209

Atomism, 92-3

Attraction, 85

Autonomy, 18, 157

Beauty, 225-7

Being, 16-19, 32, 35, 40, 57-8, 153, 185

Berkeley, G., 153

Breadth, 88

Categorical Imperative, 188, 190, 235

Categories, 24, 87, 95, 107, 112, 126, 133, 140-7, 150-1,
179

Causality, 17, 57, 74, 107, 110-14, 122-3, 126, 129, 133, 146, 154, 177-80, 183-5, 195, 202

Change, 186

Chemical process, 89, 126

Check, 73-4

Choice, xxvi, xxxi, 49, 107, 190-4, 198-200, 207-9, 212, 236

Coexistence, 111, 143, 150

Coleridge, S.T., xi

Concept, 9, 23, 25, 73, 135-45, 147-55, 158, 161-3, 171-2, 175-8, 182-4, 216-17, 229

Consciousness, xvii, xxiii-vii, xxxii, 25, 32, 44, 47-8, 60, 65, 74-7, 95, 99, 101, 103, 112-18, 124-7, 130, 133-6, 144, 148-51, 154-8, 161, 164-5, 168-75, 179, 184, 187-90, 193-5, 201-4, 209-13, 217, 220-2, 226-36 see also Self-consciousness, Unconscious

Constitution, 198-9

Death, 128

Demand, 163, 188, 190

Descartes, R., xv, 72

Despotism, 196

Destiny, see Fate

Determination, 10-11, 36, 59-60, 63-4, 70-1, 83, 96, 100, 108-10, 117-18, 139-40, 145-6, 150, 164-7, 179, 183, 189, 208   see also Predetermination, Self-determination

Determinism, xix, xxxi-ii

Dialectic, xiii-v

Dimensions, 86, 126

Dogmatism, 17-18, 35, 37, 43, 54, 58, 68, 70, 74

Drive, 166, 170, 177-8, 185-6, 194-5

Duty, 204-5

Education, 170

Electricity, 87-8, 91, 126

Empiricism, 61, 65, 70, 99, 122, 127

Ethics, xxxi, 189

Experience, xiv, xxv, 10, 92-3, 108, 136, 197

Extensity (and Intensity), 103-5, 111, 145, 147

Facticity, xxv, 34

Fatalism, xxx, 209

Fate, 116, 169, 204-5, 211-12, 222-3

Fichte, J.G., xi-xvii, xix-xxiii, xxv, xxvii-viii, xxxii,
    xxxiv, 28

Force, 79-81, 83-92, 105, 114, 173, 197, 199

Form (and Content), 20-1, 49-50, 122

Freedom, xi-xiii, xvii-xx, xxx, xxxii, 3, 24, 26-8, 30, 33,
    35, 42, 47, 49, 65, 75, 102, 112, 116-19, 128-32, 140,
    150, 152, 156-9, 162-200, 203-25, 231, 235-6

Freud, S., xxxiii

Galvanism, 89, 126

Genius, 169, 222-4, 227-8, 236

Geometry, 28-9, 140, 143, 145

God, xxi, xxvii, 47, 74, 153, 196, 206, 211-12

Gravitation, 6, 80-1, 85, 114, 119, 228

Happiness, 189, 194

Harmony, Pre-established, xv, xviii, xxxi, 4, 11-12, 35,
    129, 154, 161-5, 168, 174, 180, 192, 207-15, 217, 221,
    223-6

Hearing, 123-4

Hegel, G.W.F., xv, xvii, xxxiv

Heidegger, M., xix, xxii, xxxiii

Hemsterhuis, F., 92

History, xv, xix-xx, xxiii, xxvi, xxx-i, xxxv, 4, 34,
    198-203, 206-13, 231
    Philosophy of, xiv, xvii, xix, 201

Hylozoism, 216

'I am', xi, 8-9, 14, 26, 31, 34

'I think', 26

Idea, 138, 154, 176-8

Idealism, xviii, xxvi, xxix, 14, 34, 37, 41, 58, 70, 73-4,
    92, 107, 116, 118, 173, 185
    Transcendental, xi, xvii, xxii-iv, 1-4, 7, 10, 16-19,
        27-9, 34-6, 41, 47, 57-8, 90-4, 107, 116, 120,
        122, 129, 140, 151, 155-8, 163, 168, 170, 172,
        182-5, 188, 204, 215-18, 233
Ideal-Realism, xii, xxii, 41

Identity, xi, xv-vi, xxii, xxiv, xxviii, xxx-iii, 4-5, 10,
    12, 22-6, 29-31, 40, 45-6, 53, 72, 75, 78, 98, 113,
    120, 126-8, 135-6, 144, 153-4, 159, 164, 177-81,
    185, 194, 198, 208-14, 217-25, 229-35
    System of, xviii-ix, xxii-iii, xxv, xxxv

Illness (and Health), 128-9

Image, 136-7

Imagination, xviii, 13-14, 51, 72, 76, 153, 176, 226, 230

Inclination, Natural, 185-6, 189-90, 193-4, 235

Individuality, xx, xxvi, 31, 59-60, 116-17, 125, 128, 135,
    142, 164-71, 174, 188-9, 193-6, 200-9, 212, 235

Infinite, 82-3, 121, 144, 147, 176-7

Inner Sense, 13, 29, 98-100, 103-6, 112, 132, 141-7

Intelligence, xxvi, xxix, 3, 5, 7, 57, 59, 73-8, 90-4, 99,
     105-31, 134, 138, 142, 144, 148-67, 171-3, 180, 184,
     187-8, 193, 206-10, 213, 216-18, 221-2, 234
     External, 161-74, 235

Intuition, xxiii, 3, 9, 13, 58, 60, 70-82, 85, 94-8, 104-5,
     122, 125-8, 132-53, 156-60, 164-70, 173-5, 178-87,
     191-3, 205-8, 213, 216-18, 224-6, 229-30, 235
     Aesthetic, xv, xxiv, xxvii, xxxv, 12-13, 218-20,
          226, 229, 231, 233
     Inner (and Outer), 97-9, 103, 120, 127, 143, 147, 156,
          172, 218
     Intellectual, xxiii-iv, xxvii, xxxv, 14, 27-9, 33,
          98, 200, 229, 231-3
     Productive, xiv, xxix, 70-9, 85, 99-100, 106, 113, 126,
          132, 136, 142-9, 156, 175, 181, 189, 230, 234
     of Self, 24, 27, 37-8, 40, 43, 52-6, 60-1, 67-70, 77-8,
          90, 94-8, 121-4, 128, 134, 169, 191, 221, 233-6
     Sensory, 73-4, 79, 143

Irritability, 126

Judgment, 136-8, 140, 142, 148, 227

Kant, I., xi, xv-viii, xxi-iv, xxvii, xxxiv, 31, 85, 95,
     99, 112, 176, 188, 191, 193, 216

Kepler, J., 228

Kielmeyer, 124

Knowledge, xxiii, xxx, xxxiv, 1-2, 5-7, 9-10. 15-23, 26-7,
     30, 57, 73-4, 93, 113, 133, 151-4, 166, 183-5
     Science of, xi, xiii, xviii, xix, xxi, xxiii, xxv,
          xxviii, xxxiv, 2, 16, 19, 21, 31, 34

Language, 137-8

Law, xii, xxxi, 6, 14, 128, 157, 169, 185-6, 189-92, 195,
     198-203, 207-13, 216
     Moral, 188-90, 194   see also System

Leibniz, G.W. von, 35, 92, 120, 124, 129, 154

Length, 86-9

Life, 124-7

Light, 75, 124-5, 127, 153

Limitation (of Activity), xxvi, xxix, 16, 35-44, 47-73,
     76-87, 90, 94, 97-102, 106, 115-18, 121, 123, 125,
     130-3, 140-2, 149-50, 163-74, 177-9, 232, 235

Locke, J., 154

Logic, 20-1, 24, 140

Magnetism, 6, 86-8, 126

Malebranche, N., 153

Materialism, 57

Mathematics, 13, 80, 119, 143

Matter, 3, 26-7, 51-2, 57, 72, 74, 82-92, 113, 125-6, 153,
     185, 216
     Mind and, 82, 90-2, 128

Means (and End), 172, 178

Mechanism, 3-4, 6, 12, 35, 73-5, 126, 144, 195-7, 200, 207,
     215-16

Mind-Body Relation, 82, 128-9

Modality, 141-2

Monad, 35, 37, 92

Morality, 194-5, 227   see also Law

Motion, 120, 124-9, 144-5, 195

Methology, xx, xxxvi, 138, 200, 225, 232-3

Nature, 2-7, 12, 17, 30, 52, 72, 91-2, 107, 112, 114, 124-7,
     138, 159, 169, 173, 182, 186, 192-201, 207, 211-12,
     215-19, 225-7, 231-6
     Organic, 122-7, 215-16
     Philosophy of, xiv, xix, xxii, 2-3, 6-7
     State of, 198

Necessity (and Contingency), 97, 105, 117, 150-1, 192, 195,
     198-9, 202-7, 210-12, 216, 220-1, 236

Newton, Sir I., 228

Nietzsche, F., xxv, xxxiii, xxxv

Not-Self, xxviii, 37, 54-6, 62

Nothing, 111

Number, 146-7, 150

Objective (and Subjective), xii, xxix, 3, 5-11, 15, 17,
    21-6, 30, 36, 42-5, 49, 51, 53, 57, 73, 85, 90, 107,
    131, 136, 173-4, 179-93, 207-9, 212-13, 217-19, 229,
    232, 234

Obligation, 163, 190

Opposition (Negation), 36-7, 44-55, 60-1, 68, 70, 72, 77-83,
    89, 97, 100, 105-6, 109-10, 113-14, 120, 130-4, 136,
    141, 144, 157, 171, 176-7, 181, 189-90, 210, 221, 225,
    230-1

Optics, 6

Organism, xxii, 3, 73, 107, 112, 122-30, 135, 153, 168,
    171, 185, 218-19, 226

Organization, 122-7, 133, 156, 198, 234, 236

Orsini, G., xi

Outer Sense, 98, 100, 103-6, 112, 132, 141-6

Pain, 186

Passivity, 37, 60-1, 64-7, 70-1, 78-9, 100-1, 131-2, 168,
    171, 194

Past, 117-19, 132, 201

Phenomenology (Hegel), xiv, xxiv, xxxiv

Philosophy, 7, 14, 18-19, 28, 49-50, 75, 80, 224, 229-33
    Moral, 155
    Practical, xv, xxiii, xxvi, 4, 11, 129, 149, 155, 157,
        218
    Theoretical, 50, 63, 134, 216
    Theoretical and Practical, xii-iv, xvii-xx, 6, 11, 33-5,
        41, 50, 149, 151, 157-8, 171, 201
    Transcendental, see Idealism

Physics, 80, 87, 91-3, 120, 126

Plotinus, xxxiii

Poetry, 14, 224, 230, 232

Possibility (and Actuality), 142, 150-1, 167

Powers, Separation of, 197-8

Predetermination, 192-3, 207-10

Prejudice, 2, 8-10

Present, 103, 107, 110, 115, 118-19, 121, 132, 163, 178, 201

Presentation, xiv, xvi, xviii, xxviii, 10-11, 23-5, 35, 48,
    54-60, 73-4, 107-14, 118-29, 133, 137, 143, 147, 154,
    160, 164-5, 174-5, 178-9, 183

Production, xxiii, 12-14, 27-32, 36, 38, 44, 46, 57-8, 64-9,
    74-85, 94-101, 104, 106-7, 111-15, 118-39, 152, 156-63,
    171-84, 199, 215-22, 228, 231
    Aesthetic, 222-31

Progress, 199-204, 211

Providence, 196, 204-5, 209-12

Purposiveness, 4, 12, 172, 214-19, 225, 234

Quality (and Quantity), 146-7, 150

Real and Ideal (Activity), 40-3, 46, 49-52, 62-3, 67, 70-2,
    98, 102, 131-2, 149-50, 157-8, 163, 171-2, 177, 180-7,
    232

Realism, xxvi, 14, 41, 58, 73, 116, 173   see also Dogmatism

Reason, xvi-vii, xx-xxi, xxv, xxxv, 6, 8, 117-18, 176, 192,
    197, 200, 236
    Practical, xvii

Reciprocity, 110-14, 121, 126, 133, 142, 146, 150

Reflection, xiv, 6, 13, 24, 48, 83, 95, 130-1, 134-5, 140-6,
    150-1, 157, 171-3, 176-9, 183, 188, 192, 209, 234

Reinhold, K.L., 28

Religion, xx, 209

Reproduction, 102

Restrictedness, see Limitation

Rights, 197, 206

Scepticism, 8, 15, 21

Schematism, xvi, 99, 136-8, 140-50, 176

Schiller, F., xxxvi

Schopenhauer, A., xxxiii, xxxv

Science, Natural, 3, 5-6, 14, 17, 30, 52, 81, 91, 227-8

Secondary Qualities, 179

Self, xii, xvii-viii, xxvii, xxx, xxxiv, 3, 5, 7, 25-57,
    61-85, 90-119, 127, 131-5, 138, 146-9, 152-8, 162-3,
    174-81, 184-94, 212-13, 217-20, 224, 230-5   see also
    Intelligence, Intuition

Self-Consciousness, xiv, xxvii-xxx, xxxiii-v, 2, 14-18, 25,
    30-2, 36-51, 56-61, 68-9, 73, 90, 94-5, 115, 122, 131,
    148, 157-9, 167, 171, 177-8, 185, 188, 217, 233-4
    History of, xxxiv, 2, 50, 90-2, 116, 236

Self-Determination, 155-62, 167, 173, 175, 187-95

Self-in-itself, 69-70, 75, 181

Self-Interest, 189, 195

Sensation, 54-76, 91, 100, 103, 123-6, 132, 135, 149-50,
    156, 234

Sense-object, 100, 173

Sensibility, 126

Sight, 25, 123-4

Simultaneity, 111, 114

Sleep, 135

Soul, 153-4

Space, 28, 32, 58, 84, 103-8, 111, 120, 132, 135-7, 140-7,
    150, 164, 173

Species, 200, 202, 205-9, 212

Spinoza, B., xix, xxxiii, 17

Spirit, xxxiv-v, 74, 128, 169, 210, 232

State, 197-8, 212

Sublimity, 226

Substance (and Accident), 105-14, 121, 126, 141-6, 175, 179

Succession, 107-27, 133, 143, 146-7, 174, 178, 186, 200

Symbol, 136, 138, 176

Synthesis, 22-3, 30, 42-51, 59-60, 72, 79, 82, 85, 104-6,
     112-25, 134, 141-2, 145, 148-50, 166-7, 170-1, 207-11,
     225

System, xii-iv, xviii-xxiii, xxvii, xxx, 1-2, 4, 15, 18-19,
     34, 73, 118-19, 197, 228, 232-3
     Legal, 195-8, 202-3

Talent, 169-71, 228

Teleology, xv, xxiv, 3-4, 12, 214-17

Thickness, 88

Thing-in-itself, xviii, xxix, 9-10, 32, 54-5, 58, 61, 65,
     68-72, 75-81, 91, 97, 99, 101, 119, 131, 170

Time, xvi, xxvi, xxxv, 32, 48, 84, 103-11, 115-20, 132,
     143-51, 156, 159, 164, 166, 168, 178

Touch, 124

Truth, 5, 8, 14-15, 23, 164

Unconscious, xxvi, xxvii-xxxii, 58, 75, 77, 79, 90, 94, 100-
     107, 129, 151, 159, 170-1, 204-28, 231, 234, 236

Understanding, 73, 107, 137, 145, 176

Unity (and Plurality), 146-7

Universe, 114-25, 142, 174   see also World

Will, xv, xix, xxvi, xxix-xxxi, 12, 156, 162-3, 166-8,
     171-6, 186-96, 204-7, 212, 235

World, External or Objective, xxvi, xxx, 3, 8-11, 14, 34-5,
     48, 74, 95, 98, 118, 121, 123, 129, 135, 149, 151-4,
     158, 164-5, 170, 173-86, 192-6, 205, 210-16, 231-4
     Intellectual, 170
     Moral, 167, 196, 205-6
     Political Order, xxxi, xxxv, 202-3